Winning and Keeping
Industrial Customers

Winning and Keeping Industrial Customers

The Dynamics of Customer Relationships

Barbara Bund Jackson
Index Systems

Lexington Books
D.C. Heath and Company/Lexington, Massachusetts/Toronto

Library of Congress Cataloging in Publication Data

Jackson, Barbara B.
    Winning and keeping industrial customers.

    Bibliography: p.
    Includes index.
    1. Industrial marketing. 2. Customer relations. I. Title.
HF5415.J28   1985   658.8'12   84-48376
ISBN 0-669-09341-6 (alk. paper)

Published simultaneously in Canada
Printed in the United States of America on acid-free paper
Casebound International Standard Book Number: 0-669-09341-6
Paperbound International Standard Book Number: 0-669-11146-5
Library of Congress Catalog Card Number: 84-48376

Contents

8. Relationship Marketing: Making the Concepts Work 165

Figures

Preface and Acknowledgments

Customers are the basis of successful marketing. Industrial marketing practitioners, especially, have long known the value of being close to their customers. And recently the influential book *In Search of Excellence* has stressed and documented the attraction of being close to the customer. Relationships between industrial vendors and individual customer accounts are frequently close, long lasting, and important to both parties. But not all customer relationships last. Some customers in some situations take a short-term view of their commitments to suppliers. They make purchase decisions on the basis of immediate inducements to buy, and they expect to be able to change their commitments relatively easily.

Relationship marketing, or marketing oriented toward strong, lasting relationships with individual accounts, can be extremely successful where it is appropriate—but it can also be costly and ineffective if it is not. Conversely, transaction marketing, or marketing that emphasizes the individual sale, can be profitable and successful where it is appropriate but a serious mistake where it is not.

Perhaps surprisingly, marketing practice shows confusion and mistakes between relationship marketing and transaction marketing. Managers in one marketing firm may want so badly to be close to the customer that they attempt costly relationship marketing with customers who are unwilling or unable to make lasting commitments to the vendor; the marketers may feel almost betrayed when the customers do not respond as desired. On the other hand, under pressure for short-term profits and performance, managers in another firm may focus on immediate individual sales despite their customers' desires for longer-term, strongly supportive relationships with the vendor; the managers would thereby fail to build a foundation for continued success in the market.

The marketing and general business literatures do not appear to pay adequate attention to the dynamics of customer relationships over extended periods—to the in-depth understanding of customer behavior over time that provides the foundation for successful relationship marketing. They do not distinguish clearly between situations in which relationship marketing is appropriate and those in which transaction marketing would be the more sensible choice.

This book addresses the needs of marketing practitioners and the gap in the literature. It explores the importance of the time dimension of industrial marketing relationships. It argues that the effects on the individual account should be a central concern in all marketing decisions, with marketing broadly construed to include such things as product policy and research and development. It also argues that the individual account has for too long been the province of the sales force rather than of sales, marketing, and, indeed, the full vendor organization. It especially emphasizes longer-lasting relationships between vendors and individual customer accounts, showing how to distinguish them (in advance) from shorter-lasting relationships, how to win customer accounts that are likely to remain committed, and how to maintain or increase the strength of relationships with existing customers.

The introduction in chapter 1 discusses the importance of individual account relationships. By example, it shows the strong differences between long-term customer commitments or relationships and short-term ones. It illustrates the danger of attempting relationship marketing when transaction marketing would be the more appropriate choice, and vice-versa.

Because actual account relationships are so complex and varied, the following chapters describe at some length concepts and tools for understanding them and, especially, for understanding their characteristics over time. Chapter 2 introduces the lost-for-good and always-a-share abstractions (or models) of the behavior of accounts over time. It explores the extremely different implications of the two models and shows that the models provide the endpoints of a spectrum of behavior that is useful for understanding the behavior of real customers. Chapter 3 discusses switching costs, the key determinants of customers' locations along the behavior spectrum between lost-for-good and always-a-share. It considers more tangible switching costs (the customer's investments in terms of dollars, people, lasting assets, and procedures) and less tangible costs (exposure or risk). Chapter 4 further contrasts long-term and short-term commitments by industrial customers, providing additional ways to distinguish the two.

Armed with a sound understanding of customers' likely behavior over time, vendors can use that understanding to achieve marketing success. Chapter 5 introduces the concept of the time dimension of marketing tools. It discusses the need to fit marketing tools to customers' commitments in regard to time and considers tools for relationship marketing and for transaction marketing.

As useful and appropriate as it can be to fit marketing approaches to customers' behavior, it can sometimes be even more useful and profitable to use marketing approaches that substantially alter customers' positions along the behavior spectrum. Chapter 6 shows that marketing approaches (especially but not exclusively approaches based on information technology) can change customers' positions.

Finally, chapter 7 explicitly addresses the additional complications of what this book calls cascaded demand—situations in which a customer purchases an item of equipment and then makes follow-on purchases of supplies, parts, and/or service for that equipment. Chapter 8 summarizes the major points of the book and suggests ways in which they can be applied successfully. As illustrations, it explores two examples. First, it uses the concepts to consider the question of why customers may insist on using more than one vendor for the same or related products. It describes two different motivations for multisourcing, with important different implications for the vendor. Second, it uses this book's concepts to analyze the dynamics of the computer marketplace during three decades.

Winning and Keeping Industrial Customers is based on a project of intensive field research, on a large number of additional discussions with business practitioners and business academics, and on the business press and academic literature. The fieldwork emphasized industrial marketing relationships that extended over sequences of different individual products. Its core consisted of extensive interviews with managers about their organizations' histories of purchases and usages of communications equipment (private branch exchanges, or PBXs, and related products) and of computers. The sample included eleven organizations as customers of communications equipment and sixteen as computer purchasers. Additional customer interviews explored purchases of office automation and LANs (local area networks), offset platemakers and supplies, and other products. In addition, the basic fieldwork contained discussions with approximately thirty-five industry experts and/or vendors' representatives. (Vendor representatives were not included, however, if it appeared that legal and regulatory concerns would make them especially reluctant to talk about how their organizations built and maintained strong ties to customers.)

The list of references at the end of the book cites key sources that helped provide background and foundation for this work. In addition, each chapter cites the references most germane to that chapter's discussion.

The bulk of the work on which this book is based took place while I was on the faculty of Harvard Business School. I appreciate the financial support for the work and am especially grateful for the interested, helpful, and constructive comments of several of my colleagues there: Robert Eccles, James Heskett, Warren McFarlan, and Howard Stevenson of Harvard and Richard Cardozo of the University of Minnesota. I completed the work after joining Index Systems, a consulting firm headquartered in Cambridge, Massachusetts, that helps clients use information and information technology for competitive advantage. My colleagues at Index have helped me understand in considerably more depth the potential importance of information, computers, and communications in relationship marketing. Discussions with a large number of other practitioners and industry experts were extremely important to the work. Because many of those discussions were confidential, I cannot acknowledge the participants by name, but I would like to thank them very much as a group. Finally, I owe special thanks to Fran Charon, whose excellent and conscientious secretarial work made the writing process considerably less painful than it would normally be.

Reference

Peters, Thomas J., and Waterman, Jr., Robert H. *In Search of Excellence.* New York: Harper & Row, 1982.

Winning and Keeping
Industrial Customers

1
Introduction

Marketing begins with the customer. Indeed, it can be defined as the identification and satisfaction of customers' needs. Marketers recognize customers as a business's most important asset. Especially in industrial marketplaces, relationships between vendors and individual customer accounts are frequently close, long lasting, and important to both parties. Yet, surprisingly, there are gaping holes in the coverage of individual customer relationships by marketing academics and by marketing practitioners. Extremely few marketing practitioners can provide meaningful estimates of the profitability of their individual customer accounts. Surprisingly few practitioners even keep clear and accessible records of the histories of sales from specific customer accounts. Literature on marketing clearly acknowledges the importance of the customer, but it pays surprisingly scant attention to the dynamics of customer relationships over extended periods: to patterns of account relationships over time and to strategies and tactics for winning and keeping customers for the long term.

For several reasons, this is an especially appropriate time to consider in depth the topic of winning and keeping industrial customers. Businesspeople in different marketplaces face heightened competitive pressures, an increased pace of change, and considerably greater willingness of buyers and sellers to use sharp pencils in making business decisions. It often seems as though old rules of thumb for doing business do not work any more. Therefore it seems necessary to reexamine the basics by understanding the assumptions underlying the old, convenient rules and determining how to adapt them for today's changed business environment. Certainly if customers are basic to a business's strategy, then the reexamination should consider customer relationships.

In addition, changes in technology make it feasible to understand and track customer relationships in considerably more detail than was possible in the past. Information technology allows us to capture, maintain, and use data about individual customers in ways that would have been impractical or even impossible in the past.

Thus, we have both the need and the ability to understand and track individual account relationships over time. This book provides some basic concepts to facilitate such understanding. Solid understanding can then provide the basis for profitable *relationship marketing,* defined as marketing oriented toward strong, lasting relationships with individual accounts. This book provides principles and suggestions for successful relationship marketing.

Individual Accounts and Groups of Accounts

This book focuses on individual accounts rather than on groups of accounts (market segments, for example), as is more usual in marketing discussions. In practice, of course, marketers must also consider more aggregate issues—whether, for example, there are enough accounts of a particular type to warrant tailoring a marketing strategy for them. In addition, marketers face legal restrictions on the extent to which they may treat different accounts differently.

The premise behind this book's approach, however, is that the industrial marketer will often benefit by considering individual account relationships, over time, in detail. In that process, the individual account is the focus for considering all the tools of the marketing mix—product policy as well as sales, for example. With this focus, marketers can find and analyze promising marketing actions that might not be found with existing approaches.

Marketers can then think of segments or other groups of accounts as aggregations or summations of individual accounts. Once they have identified and analyzed marketing actions that have promising impacts on individual customers, marketers can consider whether the potential actions apply to enough individual customers to be worth while.

Importance of the Individual Industrial Account

This book focuses on relationships between individual industrial firms (which, for the sake of variety, it calls marketing firms, marketers, vendors, or sellers) and individual customer firms (which it calls customers, buyers, or accounts). It emphasizes industrial marketing, where relationships between buyers and sellers are frequently close, long lasting, and important to both parties.

In part, relationships with individual customers are important to industrial marketers simply because individual accounts often buy a lot. Practitioners acknowledge the special importance of high-volume accounts with the 80/20 rule (or its cousins, 90/10 and 70/30). According to the 80/20 rule, 80 percent of a seller's sales dollars come from approximately 20 percent of its customers. And even accounts that are not in the top 20 percent can provide large absolute sales volumes.

Individual customer accounts provide sellers with considerably more than immediate sales dollars. They may contribute ideas for product development, serve as test sites for new products, educate vendor salespeople, serve as demonstration or showcase accounts, and provide other market information.

Customers are important for still other reasons. Practitioners today are giving new emphasis to marketing productivity; the high and still increasing costs of marketing resources make practitioners anxious to spend dollars as wisely as possible. In part as a result, many firms have rediscovered their existing customer bases as attractive sources of additional business. Relationship marketing often appears economically attractive. In some cases, a vendor can convince existing accounts to increase purchases of the products or services they already buy more easily than it can convince potential new customers to begin to use those products or services. In other cases, the customer base is the preferred target for a seller's new products and services; existing customers may be considerably easier sales targets because they already know and have confidence in the marketing firm.

Thus individual accounts are critically important to the industrial marketer's current business, its development of products and capabilities, and its future business. Deeper understanding of individual accounts and of how the vendor can affect the behavior of those accounts will contribute to more successful marketing.

Length of Account Relationships

Some relationships between industrial sellers and individual accounts can last for decades; others are short, perhaps as short as a single sale. Longer-lasting relationships usually change substantially over time, and the marketer can benefit from understanding, anticipating, and, if possible, affecting the nature of the change. This book emphasizes the longer-lasting relationships; it explores how to distinguish them (in advance) from shorter-lasting ones, how to win customers likely to remain committed, and how to maintain or increase the strength of relationships with existing customers.

In some product areas, individual accounts make series of purchases from the general product category. For example, a metal fabricating firm might, over some period, make a series of purchases of machine tools. It might originally have purchased only manually controlled tools. Then it might have purchased some numerically-controlled and computer-numerically-controlled machines for general use, together with additional less automated tools for special purposes. Or an appliance manufacturer might make regular purchases of pigments for use on the bodies of its products.

Often a customer's successive purchases from a general product category are of successively larger, more complex, or technically advanced products. Some such changes in buying occur simply because an account grows in size. For example, an expanding firm may hire so many new managers that its existing switchboard cannot handle the needed number of lines for individual telephone users; therefore the firm may procure a new switch for its telephone system. In other situations, an account may change the way it uses a particular type of product and may require larger or technically more powerful or versatile products. For example, a manufacturer that begins to use its computers for monitoring and storing information about individual production lots may need new equipment with considerably more on-line capability than it required in the past.

An account's buying pattern need not involve successively more complex products. An account may purchase the same basic product again and again; it may purchase a mix of more and less technologically advanced products over its sales history; or it may reduce or end its purchases from a particular category.

A variety of forces and players influence changes in customers' usage. Vendor representatives (such as salespeople, service people, and applications engineers) suggest some changes in usage to their customers. Some changes are developed jointly by the vendor and the customer. Some changes are driven by the customer. Actions by the vendor's competitors can also have substantial effects.

Partly as a cause and partly as an effect of changes in customers' usage, product categories also change. Sometimes technological changes make new uses possible; conversely, attractive potential uses may spur new technological developments. Thus a wide and dynamic variety of forces shape any particular customer's history of purchases from a general product category over time.

Even customers that buy similar series of products can differ importantly in their motivations and procedures in making their choices. For example, one electrical utility may become a highly knowledgeable buyer, understanding and exploring the available options for all of the generation, transmission, and distribution equipment it purchases. Another utility may purchase similar products but may rely on others (vendors or engineering consultants) for much of the work in product selection.

The behavior of a particular customer account can also change substantially in terms of motivation and procedures. For example, a manufacturer may use specialty organic chemicals in increasingly sophisticated ways. Initially the customer might have relied on the vendor of those chemicals for considerable engineering assistance. As it gains sophistication and knowledge, however, this same customer might rely less on the vendor, despite the increasingly complex ways in which it uses the chemicals; the customer firm might instead build and rely on its own technical resources. Consequently the buyer might increasingly emphasize price and delivery flexibility rather than technical support from the vendor.

Characterizing individual account relationships that last is not easy. It requires considering usage patterns, motivations, and buying procedures, all of which may be dynamic and hard to predict. Moreover, although lasting relationships can be attractive to the vendor, relationship marketing also poses risks—risks that the vendor's investments in those relationships will not pay off or risks that the vendor will mistakenly invest in an account relationship that will not last. The following chapters suggest ways in which vendors can profitably analyze and affect the complexity of individual account relationships.

Individual Account as an Investment

Marketers may think of the individual account as an uncertain investment. The marketer spends resources to buy an account. These resources may be sales-force attention, a special price deal or payment terms, or any of a wide assortment of other marketing tools. Sometimes the marketer expects the resources to produce a sale quickly; in other cases, sellers make longer-term investments that will not begin to pay soon.

Once the marketer has won a customer, the account may generate additional business over time—but it may not. Even if the account does continue to buy, usually neither the timing nor the specific choice of next product is known for sure in advance. Marketing actions such as product introductions, pricing moves, and sales-force efforts can help influence the decision to buy, the timing of the purchase, and the product choice. In general, however, such actions will be influences only, not determining factors.

The selling firm can also lose its account investment. The seller's product line may not meet the account's new needs, or the seller's sales representatives may not service the account adequately, or a competitor may offer a superior product-price-service bundle, and so on.

Thus, we can think of the marketer as applying resources to obtain a collection (or portfolio) of accounts, applying additional resources to try to maintain or increase business with those accounts, and sometimes (deliberately or not) relinquishing accounts. Vendors investing in account relationships face many of the types of questions considered in analyses of more conventional financial investing: Which investments are attractive? What criteria should be used in assessing attractiveness? What time frame is appropriate for analyzing investments? What risks do possible investments involve? Can those risks be managed or reduced?

The Challenge of Understanding Accounts' Behavior: An Example

The complexity and variety of behavior of individual accounts make understanding customers' behavior a tall challenge. Inadequate understanding can lead to poor marketing decisions. Successful relationship marketing is difficult. The following example begins to illustrate the point; it is hypothetical but is built around elements of several actual examples. (The individuals in it are, however, purely fictitious.)

Superior Shipping Services provided trucking services to large customers. It had always emphasized reliable scheduling and careful handling, and its reputation for both was excellent. In planning for continued success in an environment of decreasing regulation, Superior's managers decided that they needed more marketing orientation. They wanted to build and maintain strong, lasting, and profitable relationships with their customers.

The managers decided to recruit a new marketing-sales manager. At the strong urging of the company president, they sought an experienced marketer from a leading computer vendor. The president had argued that the computer vendor was a renowned marketer and that it trained its people well; in addition, one of its managers would have attitudes and values that would fit well with Superior's reputation and strategy of high-quality service.

Superior hired Dale Spencer, a senior computer salesperson with an impressive record. In his previous job, Spencer was a patient and successful builder of customer relationships, often investing substantial time over long periods to win new accounts. Spencer and the other managers at Superior wanted to establish the same pattern in Superior's customer relationships. They would invest time and effort to study customers' shipping needs and would help customers plan for those needs. As a result, they planned to strengthen their relationships with existing customers and to win commitments from new customers too.

Two years later, Dale Spencer and Superior's other managers were severely disappointed with the results of the new marketing program at Superior. In fact, Spencer was considering leaving the firm. All of the Superior executives were trying to understand what had happened and why.

The customers seemed to love Dale Spencer and the new marketing approach in general. Superior's salespeople had learned better ways to analyze customers' long-term shipping requirements and to identify opportunities for improving them. The Superior executives had heard many compliments about their sales organization and especially about Dale Spencer, who had proven a professional and respected manager and salesperson.

The problem was that sales dollars were down. Few existing customers had left Superior, but many of them had experimented with other shippers. Superior had won commitments from a substantial number of new accounts, but those accounts had frequently not given Superior the most desirable (larger load and more repetitive) parts of their patronage.

Efficiency Truckers was a competitor that had been especially irksome to Superior. Efficiency had used price to convince many of Superior's customers to award it their most regular large shipments, just the business that Superior most wanted. In some cases, it was assistance from Superior salespeople that had helped customers to plan and consolidate their shipping—and thus to create the large, regular shipments in the first place.

Almost all the customers had continued to do business with Superior, but they had been giving Superior the most difficult, less predictable, and smaller shipments. Consequently Superior's sales dollars had slipped at the same time that sales expenses had increased. The firm was having increasing difficulty maintaining its high service levels; the predominance of small, difficult shipments had created severe problems.

What happened? In essence, Superior's managers did not understand the substantial differences between customers' views of computers and customers' views of shipping services. Customers in the two product-marketplaces make different types of commitments to their suppliers and have different time horizons in mind when they do so. Superior's managers sensibly wanted to be close to the customer, but "close to the customer" means different things in the two marketplaces. Vendors' actions should be based on an understanding of the differences.

Customers' Commitments for Computers

In many cases because of sad personal experience, customers for medium and large computer systems understand the costs and difficulties of changing suppliers for the key (hardware and especially operating software) components of their computer systems. Transferring programs from one computer (or one computer operating system) to another entails expense and dislocation.

In the past, there was little compatibility among computer components from different suppliers. Leading computer vendors worked to provide relatively easy conversions of programs from one to another of their own computers or even operating systems. Thus, the vendors made it substantially easier for customers to remain with their established suppliers than to switch.

More recently, customers have been considerably more able to mix and match components that come from different vendors in a computer system. Many peripherals (such as terminals) and software application packages, for example, can work with mainframe computers from different vendors. However, customers still face substantial dislocation in changing the key parts of their installations—the mainframes and the operating systems that define the basic parameters of those installations. Customers still find it much harder to switch than to remain committed to what might be called their lead computer vendor, the firm that provides the key elements of the installation. Because they understand the costs of change, computer customers generally commit strongly to their lead vendors. When they choose such a supplier, customers generally expect to remain committed for an extended period.

To be sure, there are differences in the strengths of the commitments of different computer customers to their lead vendors. Some accounts expressly design their installations to allow use of equipment from more than one vendor (and the number of accounts establishing such designs has been increasing). Some managers and organizations are more willing and able to undergo conversions than are others. Despite this variety, however, the computer marketplace has a large proportion of strong, lasting relationships between customers and vendors.

Relationship marketing can be extremely successful in the computer marketplace. Because their customers generally make commitments that last, leading computer vendors have also been able to take a long view in their investments in customers. They have sensibly invested resources to win commitments, have helped customers with long-range planning for computer usage, and generally have acted as though their customer relationships would last.

Customers' Commitments for Shipping Services

By contrast, a customer for shipping services can usually share its business rather easily among a group of suppliers. A customer can award a small initial order to a new supplier with relatively little risk and can evaluate the supplier's performance. If the initial order is handled well, the customer can award more business to the supplier; if it is not, the damage from using the new vendor will have been relatively contained. A successful new supplier in turn may find that still another competitor has won away some of its business through a similar experimental initial order.

To be sure, some individual customers and some vendors of shipping services have stronger relationships than those suggested by this picture. For example, an information system that allows precise scheduling and monitoring of the customer's shipments may tie the customer and vendor organizations closely together.

Overall, however, customers can switch their commitments for shipping services much more easily than they can switch their commitments for computers. Consequently the customers can view shipping decisions with much shorter time horizons than they use for computer decisions. If today's shipping decision does not work out, the customer can change tomorrow. Even if the decision does work out, the customer can still change next month if another marketing firm offers a lower price, a special service arrangement, or some other immediate inducement to switch.

Relationship marketing, aimed at strong, lasting commitments, will likely be ineffective or harmful in the shipping market. Instead vendors are likely to profit through transaction marketing, marketing that emphasizes the individual sale. Because their customers will have relatively short time horizons and low switching costs, sellers of shipping services should generally not assume that commitments will last. Substantial initial investments to win new accounts will often not be sensible. A vendor that helps its customers plan for their long-term shipping needs cannot assume that it will play a key role in executing the long-term plan. Customers may gratefully accept the planning help today, but if switching costs are low they may also gratefully accept lower prices or other immediate concessions from another source in the future.

A Spectrum of Behavior

Clearly Superior's managers would have benefited from better understanding of the nature of their relationships with customers—from the customers' viewpoint. In many other situations, marketing firms will also benefit from an explicit examination of the commitments they enjoy from customers—consideration of the closeness of the ties between vendor and customer and the time horizon used by the customer in its commitment. Some sellers will identify close ties that are expected to last, like those in the computer example. Others will find weaker, more transient ties, like those in shipping. Others will identify intermediate or even more extreme patterns.

As the Superior Shipping example suggests, understanding of customers' behavior can be important and useful for vendors that are designing marketing programs. It is obviously sensible to fit a marketing program to the customers' patterns of commitment and behavior. In addition, however, understanding of customers' behavior over time can be even more useful when the vendor is able to select marketing actions to affect or change commitments—strengthening an account's links to the vendor or weakening its ties to a competitor.

This book pursues the understanding of customers' behavior for both reasons: so the vendor can select marketing programs that fit customers' behavior and also so the vendor can act to affect that behavior and alter the customers' commitments.

Commitments by Two Parties over Time

The suggestion that marketers view individual accounts as investments is a helpful first step for analysis and understanding, but alone it is not adequate. It tends to suggest that industrial marketing relationships between a vendor and an individual account have one rather than two active participants. Instead the industrial marketing relationship is really an evolving pair of commitments by two parties over time. The paired commitments change as the products change, as the ways the products are used change, and as the methods of selling the products and supporting the relationship change.

Both parties to the relationship invest in it over time. Customers invest in their relationships with vendors in a variety of ways. They spend money on the vendor's products or services; they may hire or train people to use the vendor's offerings; they may invest in plant and equipment or other lasting assets to work with or use the vendor's offerings; they may change or create operating procedures to allow them to work with a vendor and its products and services; they may invest in training the vendor's representatives so that the seller will be able to serve the customer better; and so on. Similarly vendors invest in their relationships with individual accounts in a variety of ways. They spend sales time and attention on the customer; they may tailor products or services to fit the buyer's specific needs; they may provide applications engineering, maintenance, or other forms of service; and so on.

In addition, each party can act to try to influence the actions of the other. Vendors work to get customers to buy; they also work to influence how their products are used by the buyer. Customers act to try to obtain needed service and support; they may also, for example, act to try to influence the vendor's product policy or other decisions for the future. Often the vendor is more aware of and more active in shaping the individual account relationship, and certainly marketing emphasizes attempts by vendors to influence customers. Nevertheless, actions by the customer can also shape commitments, and so can joint actions by the two parties.

Because marketing begins with the customer, this book treats the customer's commitment as fundamental. It views vendors' commitments as actions affecting relationships with and commitments made by customers. In addition, it recognizes that other parties and other influences affect relationships between vendors and individual accounts; actions by the vendors' competitors, legal and regulatory considerations, and major technological developments are examples. In this presentation, the customers' commitments remain the focus; other factors are considered primarily in relation to those commitments.

Summary

Individual account relationships are important in marketing, especially in industrial marketing. Successful relationship marketing can be extremely profitable. Many marketers will benefit from a more thorough and explicit consideration of individual account relationships than is the rule either in marketing practice or in the marketing literature.

Individual industrial marketing relationships can, but need not, last for extended periods. Understanding individual account relationships therefore includes considering time: the time horizon with which a customer makes a commitment to a vendor and also the actual pattern the relationship follows over time. Marketers can view their individual account relationships as uncertain investments, some of them long-term investments. More accurately, they can consider those relationships as pairs of commitments that evolve.

Marketers can benefit from understanding accounts' behavior over time in two major ways: they can select marketing actions that fit their customers' patterns of commitment and behavior, and they can identify and use actions to influence those patterns.

Actual account relationships are complex and varied. Insufficient understanding can lead marketers into trouble—as, for example, in transferring a marketing approach from one industry to another in which it is not appropriate. It can lead vendors to attempt relationship marketing when transaction marketing would be more appropriate, and vice-versa. Therefore sound understanding of likely customer behavior over time is the proper foundation for winning and keeping industrial customers.

References

Arndt, Johan. "Toward a Concept of Domesticated Markets." *Journal of Marketing* (Fall 1979):69–75.

Bursk, Edward C. "View Your Customers as Investments." *Harvard Business Review* (May–June 1966):91–94.

Cardozo, Richard N. *Product Policy: Cases and Concepts.* Reading, Mass.: Addison-Wesley, 1979.

Corey, E. Raymond. *Industrial Marketing: Cases and Concepts.* 2d ed. Englewood Cliffs, N.J.: Prentice-Hall, 1976.

——— . *Procurement Management: Strategy, Organization, and Decision-Making.* Boston: CBI Publishing, 1978.

——— . "Should Companies Centralize Procurement?" *Harvard Business Review* (November–December 1978):102–110.

Eccles, Robert G. "The Quasifirm in the Construction Industry." *Journal of Economic Behavior and Organization* 2 (1981):335–357.

Levitt, Theodore. *Innovation in Marketing.* New York: McGraw-Hill, 1962.

Shapiro, Benson P., and Moriarty, Rowland T. *National Account Management.* Cambridge, Mass., Marketing Science Institute Report 82-100. March 1982.

von Hippel, Eric. "Get New Products from Customers." *Harvard Business Review* (March–April 1982):117–122.

——— . "Successful Industrial Products from Customer Ideas." *Journal of Marketing* (January 1978):39–49.

Webster, Frederick E., Jr. *Industrial Marketing Strategy.* New York: Wiley, 1979.

2
Models for Understanding Accounts' Behavior

Models of Behavior

Two simplified but suggestive pictures of accounts' behavior can help in understanding customers' commitments and likely customer behavior. These pictures, or models, of behavior can be considered the end points of a spectrum of possible behavior by real customers; they are essentially extreme examples that define a wide range of possible behaviors. Actual accounts in real situations will occupy less extreme positions along the spectrum.

In the first model (called *lost-for-good*), an account is either totally committed to the vendor or totally lost and committed to some other vendor. In the second model (called *always-a-share*), the account has a lasting but less intensive tie to the vendor.

The two models imply strikingly different patterns of attractiveness and importance of the individual account relationship to the vendor. They also help highlight the situations for which the concepts of this book are most important. Existing practices and concepts are better suited for behavior more like the always-a-share model—where the account views its commitment to the vendor as less crucial and more changeable. This book emphasizes instead the important customer commitments made with long time horizons that are more typical of lost-for-good behavior, where it is especially important and useful for marketers to consider all marketing decisions, product policy as well as sales force, in the light of the behavior of the individual account over time.

Lost-for-Good Model

The lost-for-good model assumes that a customer repeatedly makes purchases from some product category over time. At any one time, the account is committed to only one vendor. The account faces very high costs of switching vendors, and consequently it changes suppliers only very reluctantly. The account is likely, though not certain, to remain committed to its current supplier.

The lost-for-good model assumes that if a customer does decide to leave a supplier, the account is lost forever—or, alternatively, that it is at least as difficult and costly for the vendor to win back such an account as it was to win the customer in the first place. The model's name emphasizes the pain of losing a lost-for-good customer. The flip side is considerably more cheerful; once won, such a customer is likely to be won for a long time, though not necessarily forever.

Although extreme, the lost-for-good assumption is not an unreasonable simplification for actual situations in which switching vendors involves considerable cost and disruption. It is a useful simplification for the behavior of some but not all purchasers of computer mainframes, communications equipment, office automation systems, heavy construction equipment, and aircraft engines, for example.

Always-a-Share Model

The second model also assumes that the customer purchases repeatedly from some product category. It assumes, however, that buyers can maintain less intense commitments than they do in the lost-for-good model and that they can have commitments to more than one vendor at the same time. The account can easily switch part or all of its purchases from one vendor to another, and therefore it can share its patronage, perhaps over time, among multiple vendors.

With the always-a-share assumption, an individual seller's share of the account's business may fluctuate, but a decline in share does not mean a complete loss of the account. Because the customer faces low switching costs, a vendor can always sensibly assume that it has a chance of winning business from the account—provided that the seller offers an immediately attractive combination of product, price, support, and other benefits. The seller is not locked into an account from which it currently enjoys patronage, nor is it necessarily locked out of one to which it does not now sell.

The model's picture of customers' behavior is extreme; nevertheless, it is a useful simplification for some real purchasers. Examples are some purchasers of commodity chemicals, carbon steel, computer terminals, and shipping services.

In considering behavior of actual customers in relation to the always-a-share model, it is helpful to consider two slightly different versions of the model. In some situations suggesting always-a-share behavior, a customer makes a series of discrete individual purchases over time. The account would select a single vendor for any individual purchase, but over time it could share its patronage among multiple vendors. We can call this model version *always-a-share-over-time*. The vendor wins some individual orders and loses others; it gains its share of the account's total patronage over time. A purchaser of simple machine tools might provide an example of this model version. In other situations suggesting always-a-share, the product under consideration is more divisible. The customer can share its business among multiple vendors during a single time period. We can call this model version *always-a-share-at-one-time;* the vendor obtains a share of the business during every time period. A purchaser of carbon steel might illustrate this model version.

Regardless of whether the sharing is over time or at one time, the essence of this always-a-share model is that the account can easily switch its patronage. It need not view its commitment to a supplier as permanent.

Customer Attitudes

Lost-for-Good Customers

The essence of the lost-for-good model is that customers find changes of vendor traumatic. Commitments made by such customers tend to last. The customer will view its commitment to a vendor as relatively permanent; it is likely to have a long time horizon in its relationship with the vendor.

To be sure, relationships between suppliers and customers suggesting the lost-for-good model can end. The customer may decide that the vendor's performance has been unsatisfactory or perhaps that the vendor's past performance has been adequate but that it appears unlikely that the seller will be able to continue to meet the buyer's needs. The customer may conclude that it must undergo the pain of conversion. For example, discussions with advanced computer users found that a number were changing strong links to their lead computer vendors; their behavior suggested the lost-for-good model, but they were changing suppliers. The customers felt that their previous vendors had run out of steam technically. They were undergoing the pain of conversion to make new commitments to vendors they felt would provide continued technical development for the future.

Nevertheless, lost-for-good customers do not change vendors often, easily, or lightly. Switches are infrequent, serious decisions made with considerable reluctance.

Always-a-Share Customers

By comparison with the lost-for-good model, changes of supplier are considerably more routine for the always-a-share purchaser. Such a customer can easily experiment with new vendors. It can reward a vendor that offers immediately attractive benefits such as lower prices or more convenient delivery by giving that seller a larger share of its patronage. Similarly it can reduce the share of a vendor that performs unsatisfactorily or that simply offers a bit less benefit today than does a competitor.

The always-a-share buyer can choose suppliers on the basis of the immediate benefits they offer; it need not worry about the vendors' abilities to continue to provide adequate benefits in the future. Such a customer is likely to use a short time horizon in its relationships with sellers.

A particular selling firm may in fact enjoy a long relationship with a specific customer even if the account's behavior suggests the always-a-share model. The long relationship generally would not, however, be an intentional long-term commitment from the customer. Instead a vendor that remained successful with the customer for a long period would have had to be immediately attractive along the way, giving the account good immediate reasons for continuing the relationship at each purchase.

Consequently even a long-lasting relationship with an always-a-share buyer should be viewed as the result of a series of shorter-term purchasing decisions or transactions. The established vendor may in fact enjoy advantages on those individual shorter-term decisions. For example, in doing business with the account, the vendor's representatives may learn details of the account's specific needs; they may therefore be able to identify and offer the immediately attractive package of product, terms, and service that fits the customer's current needs better than their competitors can. In other words, the relationship may give the vendor information to select useful immediate inducements to buy, but the relationship does not itself substitute for those immediate inducements.

Marketing and the Behavior Spectrum

The lost-for-good and always-a-share models provide the end points of a spectrum of behavior of industrial customers. The models are simplified and extreme abstractions; actual accounts in real situations are likely to occupy intermediate points on the spectrum.

The behavior spectrum is a useful concept in marketing because different marketing approaches are appropriate for actual accounts whose behavior approximates different parts of the range. Relationship marketing is sensible for customers that suggest the lost-for-good model. Transaction marketing is appropriate for customers like always-a-share.

Accounts' commitments to their lead computer vendors are serious ones that are generally expected to last; they are not made or changed lightly or easily. The behavior of such customers suggests the lost-for-good model. Relationship marketing can be extremely effective with such accounts.

By contrast, customers for shipping services can far more easily shift part or all of their patronage from one supplier to another. Their time horizons in committing to vendors can be short, and they need not feel tied to any one vendor. The behavior of such customers suggests the always-a-share model. Transaction marketing is generally appropriate to such accounts.

The discussion in chapter 1 noted the problems of trying to transfer marketing approaches too mechanically from the computer marketplace to the market for shipping services. There would be similarly serious problems with trying to transfer a marketing approach in the opposite direction. And in general, different marketing strategies and tactics fit customers at different points on the behavior spectrum. Thus understanding what determines position on the spectrum can help the marketer to select and implement successful strategies based on relationship marketing, transaction marketing, or something in between.

In addition, some actions by marketers create changes in customers' positions on the behavior spectrum. Some actions strengthen customers' commitments to the supplier, moving the account closer to the lost-for-good model and away from always-a-share. Other actions allow or encourage the customer to behave more like the always-a-share pattern and less like lost-for-good.

The following chapters examine in more detail the determinants of accounts' positions on the behavior spectrum as the basis for evaluating marketing approaches and for selecting actions to affect accounts' positions. Then the book considers relationship marketing and transaction marketing in more depth. First, however, this chapter probes the differences between the two models by investigating the financial differences in results for the vendor of doing business with customers behaving like each of the two models.

Financial Explorations with the Models

Assumptions

To explore the quantitative implications of the models, this discussion first makes some extremely simple assumptions about how the accounts buy. Those initial assumptions allow relatively clear demonstration of basic differences between the models. Explorations with somewhat more complex and more realistic assumptions turn out to show the same basic principles, though they are not as clear as illustrations. The following discussion refers to the more complicated explorations but does not present them in detail.

To isolate the effects of the lost-for-good and always-a-share assumptions, this illustration considers an extremely simple pattern of purchases by the account. It assumes the customer generates precisely the same contribution, in constant or real dollars, at each purchase after it has begun to buy from the product category. It also assumes that purchases occur at precisely regular intervals—once a year, perhaps.

If the account were to continue to make all of its purchases from a single vendor and to buy indefinitely, that vendor's pattern of contribution from the account would look like figure 2–1 but would extend indefinitely along the time axis to the right. In the lost-for-good model, however, the pattern need

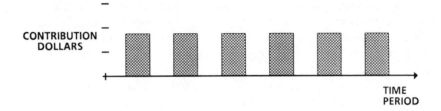

Figure 2–1. Cashflow Pattern

not extend forever; the account may be lost for good after any of the purchases. In the always-a-share-at-one-time model, the vendor receives only a fraction of the contribution from the account at each purchase; with always-a-share-over-time, the vendor receives only a fraction of the discrete individual purchases.

Results of the Lost-for-Good Model

In the lost-for-good model, it is not completely certain that the account will remain with its current supplier at each purchase. The following discussion assumes that the account is characterized by a number between 0 and 1 (or 0 percent and 100 percent),which it calls the *retention probability*. The retention probability is the chance that the account will remain with the vendor for the next purchase, provided that the customer has bought from that vendor on each previous purchase. The discussion labels the retention probability by p.

According to the lost-for-good assumption, if the account does not buy from the vendor on one purchase, it will not buy from that vendor on the next purchase unless the vendor mounts a successful (and likely expensive) campaign to rewin the customer. For now, these explorations do not consider such efforts to win back lost customers; once gone, the account is assumed gone for good.

For the time being, this discussion assumes that the rentention probability p for an account does not change from purchase to purchase; instead, p is a continuing characteristic of the account. Other more complicated explorations instead assume changes over time in the account's retention probability (the chance that it remains with its current supplier).

Figure 2–2 shows possible purchase patterns over time for these assumptions and the lost-for-good model. In part a, the account buys once and then is lost for good. In part b, the customer buys twice before it is lost, and so on.

Most of the remainder of this section discusses the results of the financial explorations, as summarized in figures 2–3 and 2–4. First, however, the next two paragraphs provide interested readers with a bit more detail about where the figures came from.

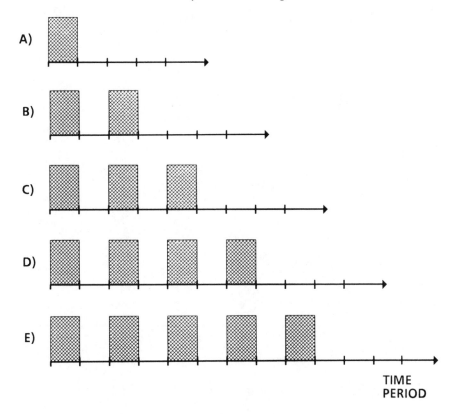

Figure 2–2. Possible Cashflow Patterns

For any specific retention probability p, we can use some rather straightforward calculations to find the probability that the purchase profile for the account looks like part a of figure 2–2, the probability that it looks like part b of the figure, and so on. Other straightforward calculations with any of the patterns in figure 2–2 and with a discount factor can convert the pattern of cash contributions into a single net present value (NPV). Finally, combining the probabilities with the NPV numbers allows us to summarize the entire sequence of possible purchase patterns for some particular retention probability p by a single number—the probability weighted (or expected) value of the NPV of future cash flows. There will be a different summary value of this type for each different value of p (between 0 and 1) or each probability that the account remains with the vendor on any individual purchase.

Figure 2–3 presents in graphical form the summary values for all possible values of p if we use a discount rate of 20 percent. Figure 2–4 provides the summary values if instead the discount rate is 10 percent. For example, suppose

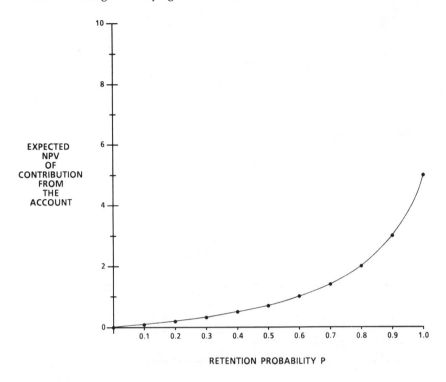

Figure 2–3. Results of the Lost-for-Good Model (20%)

that the account's yearly purchases provide the vendor with a contribution of $1 million. Then the NPV values in the figure would be in millions of dollars.

In figure 2–3, an account with a retention probability of 0.3 (or a 30 percent chance of remaining loyal) would have an expected NPV of $1/3 million; an account with a p level of 0.6 (60 percent chance) would have a $1 million expected NPV; an account with a p level of 0.9 would have an expected NPV of $3 million. In each case, if the account continues to buy, the timing and amounts of the contribution cash flows are the same. With higher ps the account is more likely to remain with the vendor for a longer time; the commitment is more likely to be a longer one.

The most striking feature of figures 2–3 and 2–4 is the steepness of the curves for relatively high values of p. High-p accounts (those with high probabilities of remaining with the same vendor) are much more attractive to the vendor than are lower-p accounts. For example, in figure 2–3, the expected NPV of a 0.6 account is $1 million, that of a 0.7 account is $1.4 million, that of a 0.8 is $2 million, and that of a 0.9 is $3 million. The differences in NPV as p increases show the steepness of the curve: the difference in expected NPV between a p level of 0.7 and one of 0.8 is $600,000; the difference in NPV between p levels of 0.8 and 0.9 is $1 million.

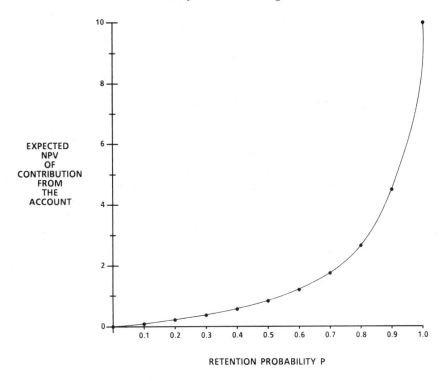

EXPECTED
NPV
OF
CONTRIBUTION
FROM
THE
ACCOUNT

RETENTION PROBABILITY P

Figure 2–4. Results of the Lost-for-Good Model (10%)

One would of course expect accounts with high retention probabilities to be more valuable than accounts with low *p* values; all else being equal, vendors would certainly value higher levels of customer loyalty. Nevertheless, figures 2–3 and 2–4 are even more extreme than most people would expect on the basis of intuition. They show, for example, that increasing the retention probability of an already high-*p* account is worth considerably more than is increasing the *p* of a lower-*p* account by the same amount. High-*p* accounts are valuable and important in a lost-for-good world. Unless it is extraordinarily expensive to do so, increasing the retention probability even more for a high-*p* account appears to be an attractive way to invest marketing resources. Marketers may achieve best results if they strongly focus their attention on high-*p* accounts and potentially high-*p* accounts.

Results of the Always-a-Share Model

To explore the always-a-share-at-one-time model with a similar set of simple calculations, we can assume that on each purchase occasion, the vendor receives a particular fraction, *f*, of the account's purchases. The account would be characterized by that fraction *f*, which, for simplicity in the initial explorations, we would assume did not change with time. The picture of the vendor's sales to the account over time would be just like figure 2–1, but the bars would be only a fraction f of their height in that figure.

To explore the always-a-share-over-time version of the model, we can assume that the account is characterized by a probability p between 0 and 1 (0 percent and 100 percent). The vendor has a chance p of obtaining each individual sale from the account; over time, the vendor can expect to receive a share p of the total individual purchases. For simplicity, we assume that p does not change over time so that the account is characterized by a single p value. The picture of purchases for this model version would be figure 2–1 with some of the bars (those sales that the seller did not win) removed.

For either version of the always-a-share model, we can summarize the expected NPV of the account to the vendor by a single number. There will be a different summary value for each f value in the at-one-time version and a different summary value for each p value in the over-time one. It turns out that the two always-a-share versions give the same mathematical results in terms of expected NPV. Figures 2–5 and 2–6 present the results, with the horizontal

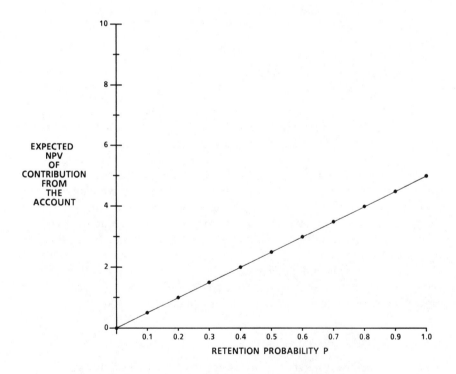

Figure 2–5. Results of the Always-a-Share Model (20%)

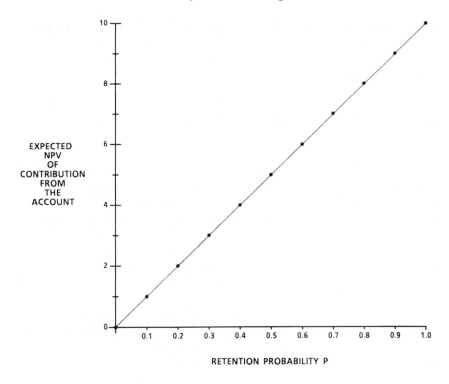

Figure 2–6. Results of the Always-a-Share Model (10%)

axis labeled probability *p*, corresponding to the over-time version. If the axis were instead labeled fraction *f*, it would correspond to the at-one-time version. Figure 2–5 gives results for a discount rate of 20 percent, and figure 2–6 gives the results for 10 percent.

NPV increases linearly with *p* (or *f*) in figures 2–5 and 2–6. Higher *p* levels are more attractive with always-a-share, but the differences in NPV between high-*p* and low-*p* accounts are not nearly as great as they were in figures 2–3 and 2–4. The always-a-share model does not produce the same extreme relative attractiveness of high-*p* accounts as does lost-for-good. In figure 2–5 or figure 2–6, a 0.4 account is worth exactly twice as much as a 0.2 account, a 0.8 account is worth twice as much as a 0.4 account, and so on. Thus, a vendor in an always-a-share world would be just as happy with two 0.4 accounts as it would with a single 0.8 account. In the lost-for-good world, the vendor would strongly prefer the single 0.8 account.

The argument that the vendor facing lost-for-good behavior often should concentrate on high-*p* accounts thus does not carry over to the always-a-share world. In figures 2–5 and 2–6, a change in p from 0.1 to 0.2 is exactly as attractive as a change from 0.8 to 0.9. In an always-a-share world, the vendor need not worry nearly as much about the retention probabilities of its individual customers; it can instead focus on aggregate sales levels.

Further Comparison of the Models

Time Horizons and Durations of Commitments

The essence of the lost-for-good model is that changes of vendor are traumatic for customers. High switching costs make customers reluctant to change. Consequently, in such situations one would usually expect high p levels, indicating that customers were likely to remain with their current vendors. Customers that were aware that their commitments were likely to last would naturally take long time horizons in making those commitments. Lost-for-good commitments tend to be long-term, high-p ones.

By contrast, in an always-a-share world, customers are far more able to switch vendors; changes are less important and less difficult. Such customers can emphasize more immediate issues and can use shorter time horizons than would lost-for-good accounts. Always-a-share commitments tend to be short-term ones.

Competition within an Always-a-Share Account

Looking at the graphs that summarize the financial results of the simple models, we might be tempted to conclude that high p level always-a-share accounts are very attractive—in fact, more attractive than are lost-for-good accounts with the same p levels. In fact, however, marketplace realities suggest that real customers whose behavior is like the always-a-share model would not usually have high p levels. By contrast, the nature of lost-for-good behavior would often engender high p levels.

Why would a customer like the always-a-share model be less loyal—or, in other words, not award a high fraction of its business to a particular vendor? In essence, because it would not have to deal with a single vendor and because many customers see clear benefits in using multiple suppliers. Often they believe that they can play off one vendor against the other, negotiating for concessions in price, delivery terms, or other benefits. Moreover, buyers often believe that using multiple sources protects the buyer, at least in part, from problems encountered by any one vendor—for example, that they would be protected from the full brunt of a strike or a fire suffered by one supplier. Further, buyers may value access to more than one supplier because they want to hear ideas and receive support from the sales and service representatives of more than one marketing organization. Thus, one would often find only medium and low p levels in always-a-share accounts.

In addition, the presence of multiple suppliers in such accounts is likely to lead to increased price competition for the account's business and, in turn, to lower contribution levels to the vendor for any given sales level. Competitors can create pressures on prices and margins by competing through price for large shares of the account's patronage. Moreover, the customer organization can foster competition. The always-a-share customer will be much more able to threaten, cajole, or punish a vendor on an ongoing basis than would a lost-for-good customer. The always-a-share account can make small adjustments in its patronage—small changes in p. It has more easily deployable threats to use in negotiating with a vendor than does the lost-for-good customer, which must either move massively (withdrawing its patronage entirely) or remain committed to the supplier.

Which Type of Behavior Should the Vendor Want?

To a substantial degree, the behavior of a customer—its location along the spectrum between lost-for-good and always-a-share—is beyond the control of the vendor. On the other hand, vendors do have some ability to affect the positions of their customers, and they also can select as targets accounts likely to behave more like one or the other of the two extreme models. We should therefore consider the question of which type of behavior is attractive to the vendor, assuming the vendor can choose or at least influence behavior.

The preceding discussion argued that always-a-share customers are likely to have only low or medium p levels and that competition within the always-a-share account is likely to reduce the contribution margin on whatever share of the business a vendor succeeds in winning. That argument suggests that vendors would prefer lost-for-good customers, which are likely to have high p levels and to make long-lasting commitments to vendors. Today's strong interests (especially by practicing marketers) in the value of strong, lasting customer relationships would support the same conclusion.

In emphasizing long-term relationships between industrial marketers and individual customer accounts, this book also supports a preference for lasting relationships, suggestive of the lost-for-good model; however, the discussion will raise some caveats about such a preference. Lost-for-good customers can be very attractive, but they are also often very difficult to serve satisfactorily. They generally are concerned with both short-term issues (such as immediate price) and long-term issues (such as a vendor's ability to continue to offer adequate products and services for the long run); to be successful, the vendor must address both types of issues. In addition, many customers suggestive of the lost-for-good model are aware of their dependence on their suppliers. They are therefore sensitive to and rather intolerant of any sign of inadequacy of the vendor on which they depend. To serve such an account, the vendor must do a variety of different things well, consistently over time.

Thus, this book argues that long-term customer relationships can be extremely attractive to a marketer but that they can also be difficult to win and to maintain. Close to the customer is generally considered a good place to be—and the vendor in a lasting lost-for-good relationship is often very close to the customer. Getting close—and staying there—is, however, a considerable challenge, requiring in-depth understanding of the customer's needs, concerns, and behavior. The following chapters delve into behavior of customers in long-term relationships, presenting concepts and explanations that can provide some of the needed understanding.

Lessons of the Models and the Real World

Results with More Realistic Assumptions

The preceding explorations of implications of the two behavior models used very simple assumptions. Those simplifications allowed a clear demonstration of the basic lessons of the behavior models: in a lost-for-good world, high-p and potentially-high-p accounts are extremely important. Raising the p level even more for a high-p customer is often an attractive way to use marketing resources. Often vendors serving lost-for-good customers would benefit from concentrating on highly loyal customers. However, high-p accounts are less likely in an always-a-share world, and they are also less overwhelmingly attractive to the vendor. In serving such customers, a marketer can be more concerned with total sales levels across accounts and less concerned with developing individual high-loyalty accounts for the long term.

These lessons are strong ones, drawing a sharp contrast between lost-for-good and always-a-share customers. The reader may reasonably ask whether the lessons are basic to the core behavioral assumptions in the models or whether they are instead an artifact of the strong simplifications used for the financial explorations described.

In fact, the lessons are not an artifact but derive from the basic behavioral assumptions of lost-for-good and always-a-share. The point can be demonstrated by additional financial explorations with the models, explorations that keep the basic behavior assumptions but use other more complicated and more realistic assumptions about such factors as the levels and timing of cash flows to the vendor from the customer. This discussion does not reproduce the more realistic but more difficult explorations; it merely summarizes the types of more complex and realistic assumptions that were explored without changing the lessons in the results.

First, the explorations assumed that the account bought in an entirely regular pattern, generating the same level of contribution on each purchase and purchasing at precisely regular time intervals. More realistic explorations considered patterns of contribution that changed over time, and they also considered less regular time intervals between successive purchases.

The initial model explorations also assumed that the account was characterized by a single p level that did not change. In fact, most real accounts display changing levels of loyalty to their established vendors. In many situtations, the customer's costs of changing vendors would grow as the buyer used more of the seller's products and/or used those products in increasingly important ways and/or worked out comfortable, familiar procedures for dealing with the vendor's sales, service, and other representatives. In other cases, the strength of the customer's commitment to the vendor would decrease with time. For example, the buying organization might become more familiar with the products and less dependent on the vendor's representatives for technical support; as a result, the buyer might become more willing to shop for lower prices, even if those prices implied less support and service.

The financial explorations with the models therefore considered cases in which p levels change with time. They included increasing, decreasing, and other more complex patterns. Although the detailed results are (understandably) more difficult to present simply, the message was clear: the basic lessons about always-a-share and lost-for-good behavior remain true. In a lost-for-good world, high-p and potentially high-p accounts are extremely attractive to the vendor. In an always-a-share world, they are less overwhelmingly attractive.

Finally, the explorations considered whether there might be an important difference in the costs of winning and serving high-p and low-p accounts. In reality, one might find some cases in which more established, loyal customers were more expensive to serve because they used the vendor's products in complex and important ways and because they knew how to find and use support from the vendor's organization. In other cases, the vendor and the highly loyal customer might already have worked out the bugs in their relationship and in the uses of the vendor's products by the customer. As a result, the vendor might find it less rather than more costly to serve the loyal, high-p account, especially when costs were considered in relation to the high sales levels from the account.

The financial explorations with the models considered a variety of assumptions about the marketing and other costs of selling to and servicing customers. They emphasized the lost-for-good model and asked essentially whether marketing and related costs could destroy the relative attractiveness of high-p accounts in the lost-for-good world. The explorations considered two types of costs: initial (one-time) costs of winning the account and ongoing costs of maintaining the account. They emphasized situations in which costs were higher for high-p accounts than for low-p ones. The reverse assumption—that it was less costly to win and serve more loyal customers than it was to serve less loyal ones—was not explored. If that reverse assumption in fact held, high-*p* accounts would become more rather than less relatively attractive.

The explorations considered a variety of patterns of marketing costs; the patterns involved initial and/or ongoing costs of different levels. The explorations produced a strong, clear result: in a lost-for-good world, unless the ongoing costs of maintaining high-retention-probability accounts are essentially punitively high, those accounts remain relatively very attractive.

The table below shows one example of a pattern of ongoing marketing costs:

Retention Probability *p*	Ongoing Marketing Costs
.2	$150,000
.4	250,000
.6	350,000
.8	450,000

It assumes that each $1 million of premarketing contribution is reduced by marketing costs substantially more for high-*p* accounts than for low-*p* ones—for example, that the costs for a 0.8 account are three times those for a 0.2 account. The exploration using the table assumed that the marketing costs reduced contribution on every individual purchase. The effects of these marketing costs on cash contributions would be large. For example, suppose that $1 million in cash contribution before marketing costs was generated by $2 million in sales, thus giving a 50 percent contribution before the marketing costs. In that case, the percentages of cash contribution after the marketing costs are as follows:

Retention Probability *p*	Percentage Cash Contribution
.2	42.5%
.4	37.5
.6	32.5
.8	27.5

The margins are much lower for the high-*p* accounts.

Even with these assumptions about ongoing marketing costs, however, the high-*p* accounts remained relatively very attractive because they were more likely to be retained. Figure 2–7 summarizes the results (in expected net

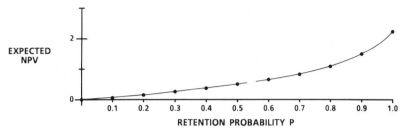

Figure 2–7. Results with Ongoing Marketing Costs

present value) for a 20 percent discount rate; it corresponds to figure 2–3. The expected values of NPV in figure 2–7 are considerably lower than those in figure 2–3; the marketing costs certainly lower the attractiveness of the account, regardless of p level. Nevertheless, the high-p accounts still give appreciably higher expected NPVs in figure 2–7 than do the low-p accounts. The ongoing marketing costs had to be considerably more extreme than those in table 2–1 before high-p accounts lost their relative attractiveness.

Thus, the lesson read from the simple explorations with the lost-for-good model remains true when the lost-for-good assumption is explored in more complex and realistic ways. High-p accounts—loyal customers making long-term commitments—are economically extremely attractive in a lost-for-good world.

Real Accounts and the Behavior Spectrum

The model explorations highlight the strong differences between lost-for-good and always-a-share customers. The example in chapter 1 about Superior Shipping showed two product-marketplaces whose typical customers were at very different points of the behavior spectrum between lost-for-good and always-a-share. Those real customers required substantially different marketing approaches. Hence marketers can benefit from understanding the approximate positions of real accounts on the behavior spectrum—or, because it will generally not be possible to locate customers precisely along the spectrum, at least from locating the general range of the spectrum characteristic of a customer's behavior.

The remainder of the book pursues the question of how to understand and affect the behavior of the individual customer over time, especially how to understand and affect the strength of the customer's commitment to its vendor and its location on the behavior spectrum. First, however, this chapter closes with a few additional examples of product-marketplaces and some suggestions of how customers in those marketplaces might be located on the spectrum.

Customers for carbon steel might seem to be prototypical always-a-share accounts. They would easily be able to share their patronage among multiple vendors for a product that seems essentially to be a commodity. Many real customers for carbon steel would, in fact, display behavior suggestive of the always-a-share model. Others, however, would not. Consider an account that was operating under a policy of just-in-time inventories (or as close to that ideal as possible). The account could conceivably work with more than one supplier of carbon steel, but it might be simpler for the buyer to set up close information links to a single supplier instead, keeping the supplier completely up-to-date about manufacturing levels and inventory levels at the account and making the seller responsible for delivering steel just when it was needed.

The behavior of this just-in-time carbon-steel buyer would not be typical of always-a-share. The account would face appreciable switching costs of changing vendors, for it would have to establish new information links and smooth delivery procedures with the new supplier. Those switching costs would move the account toward the middle of the behavior spectrum.

This example demonstrates two important points about the behavior spectrum, both of which will be explored at length in subsequent discussions. First, product category alone is not enough to determine the position of a buyer on the spectrum. Within the same general product-marketplace, different accounts—even different accounts purchasing precisely the same products—can occupy significantly different points along the spectrum. The second point is that information flows and, especially, links based on information technology can affect the strength of the tie between a vendor and a customer; it can increase the buyer's switching costs and therefore move the account closer to the lost-for-good end of the spectrum. Astute marketers have begun to use information and information technology to win substantial competitive advantage. Chapter 6 discusses the topic and describes examples, such as the by now classic case of American Hospital Supply's ASAP systems.

As another example of behavior suggesting always-a-share, consider the market for copier machines. Most often, a copier is a stand-alone piece of equipment, either in the central reproduction department of an organization or in a satellite location for easy access by many employees. For many customers, the stand-alone usage of the machines would create behavior close to the always-a-share model. Some customers would have stronger ties to one vendor. For example, a customer might want to use a single supplier in order to save money on a maintenance contract for its machines. Or it might decide to use a single vendor so that its own employees would not have to become familiar with the products of more than one seller. Such considerations could move an account a bit away from always-a-share behavior, but they do not produce very high switching costs and would still leave the customer toward the always-a-share end of the spectrum.

In the arena of expert advise and consulting services, some vendors would have considerably stronger ties to individual customers than would others.

Suppose that one consultant is an established expert on heavy industry who is hired by many firms to present talks about trends in manufacturing. Suppose that the expert updates his talk regularly on the basis of his continuing expertise but that he does not study the individual client firms in depth to tailor talks for each. As valuable as the expert's talks might be, they would not necessarily create high switching costs. If a new expert appeared and seemed to have more useful insight than the first, customer firms could easily switch to the new expert for the next time they wanted advice.

By contrast, consider a consultant who works in depth with individual customer firms. Suppose that in the process she learns a great deal about the customers' businesses and that her successive projects with a customer firm draw on the knowledge she gained in the preceding engagements. Obviously it is considerably more difficult for the buyer to change to a new in-depth consultant than it was to change heavy-industry-manufacturing experts. The buyer can change, but doing so will require educating a new consultant about the firm.

Thus, the customers of the heavy-industry expert would display behavior toward the always-a-share end of the spectrum. Those of the in-depth consultant would behave more like an intermediate point on the spectrum, or, if the amount of in-depth knowledge were very high, even like the lost-for-good model.

As a final example, consider the product-marketplace for PBXs (private branch exchanges), the main communications switches used by almost all but the smallest organizations in their telephone systems. Communications have become increasingly important and widespread in businesses over time, and changing an organization's telephone system requires considerable dislocation and expense. Many organizations have in fact changed from products of the Bell system to offerings from other vendors (such as Rolm or Northern Telecom) since increasing deregulation made it possible for them to do so. Changes of PBX vendor have, however, been serious ones, carefully and conservatively made and frequently brought before the buying organization's board of directors for approval.

Changes of PBX vendor are sufficiently disruptive that the behavior of many PBX customers would lie toward the lost-for-good end of the behavior spectrum. At the same time, changes of PBX vendor are generally less traumatic than are changes of lead computer vendor. Hence, the typical PBX vendor would not lie as close to the lost-for-good model as would the typical computer purchaser.

Summary

The lost-for-good and always-a-share models are simplified pictures of accounts' behavior over time. The models are the end points of a spectrum of accounts' behavior.

In the lost-for-good model, the account faces high costs of changing vendors. At any one time, the customer is committed to only one seller. Although the account is likely to remain with that seller for subsequent purchases, the vendor can lose the customer, and, once gone, the account is lost-for-good (or at least as costly to win back as it was to win in the first place). Lost-for-good commitments tend to remain won-for-a-long-time, though not necessarily forever.

In the always-a-share model, the buyer can maintain less intense ties to multiple vendors. Divisibility of the product may allow the customer to share its patronage among vendors in a single time period. In other cases with less divisible products, low switching costs allow the buyer to make successive purchases from different suppliers.

Because of the high switching costs, lost-for-good commitments tend to last. Such buyers are generally relatively aware of the extent of their dependence on their suppliers, and they tend to use long time horizons in making commitments.

By contrast, the low switching costs of the always-a-share buyer mean that such customers can easily experiment with new vendors and can easily change the extent of their commitments to particular vendors. They can make their purchase decisions on the basis of immediate inducements to buy and generally use shorter time horizons in their commitments.

Financial explorations highlight the differences between the two types of customer behavior. In a lost-for-good world, accounts with high retention probabilities are relatively extremely attractive to the seller. Vendors serving such accounts would often benefit from focusing their sales and marketing efforts on high-p and potentially high-p accounts. While high-p accounts are attractive in an always-a-share world, they are not nearly so overwhelmingly attractive as in lost-for-good. The vendor serving always-a-share customers can sensibly consider aggregate sales levels without needing to emphasize the loyalty and behavior of individual accounts.

Vendors that can find lost-for-good customers or that can convince customers to act more like the lost-for-good model will often want to do so. The strong, lasting commitments of such customers are often attractive. In addition, always-a-share accounts by their nature tend not to display high p levels. There is often considerable competition within the always-a-share account, and the competition tends to reduce margins.

At the same time that lost-for-good accounts can be attractive, however, they can also be challenging to serve satisfactorily. Relationship marketing is hard to do well. Such customers are especially sensitive to any failings on the part of their vendors; they expect sellers to do a variety of things well consistently over time.

The behavior of most real customers will correspond to intermediate points on the behavior spectrum between lost-for-good and always-a-share.

Understanding at least the general locations of its customers on the behavior spectrum can be valuable for the marketer for two reasons. Accounts at different parts of the spectrum are best served by different marketing approaches; understanding the positions of customers can therefore help the marketer to select sound marketing approaches. In addition, the spectrum can help marketers identify and explore actions that can change the positions of customers, making them behave more like the lost-for-good model or alternately more like always-a-share.

References

Bass, Frank M. "A New Product Growth Model for Customer Durables." *Management Science* 15 (1969):215–227.

———. "The Relationship between Diffusion Rates, Experience Curves and Demand Elasticities for Consumer Durable Technological Innovations." *Journal of Business* 53 (1980):551–567.

Morrison, Donald G., et al. "Modeling Retail Customer Behavior at Merrill Lynch." *Marketing Science* 1 (1982):123–141.

3
Keys to Understanding: Switching Costs and Exposure

Influences on Location along the Behavior Spectrum

Product Category and the Product

The descriptions in chapter 2 of the lost-for-good and always-a-share models emphasized switching costs. Always-a-share customers face relatively low switching costs and can share their patronage and change vendors rather easily. Lost-for-good customers face high switching costs and cannot easily change vendors. Switching costs are the key to understanding the differences between the two models and to determining approximate locations of real customers along the behavior spectrum.

The preceding discussion used straightforward examples to relate the behavior of real accounts to ranges of the behavior spectrum. Those examples showed that the category of product being bought and sold is one key determinant of position along the spectrum. Purchasers of shipping services tend to behave like the always-a-share model. Purchasers of computers tend to behave like lost-for-good.

Within a general product category, however, even the same purchaser may display behavior characteristics of very different parts of the spectrum in buying different products. Purchasers of computers display behavior suggestive of the lost-for-good model in their commitments to lead computer vendors, the firms from which they obtain their mainframes and operating systems. By contrast, in buying computer terminals or other peripherals, the same purchasers often display behavior much closer to the always-a-share model. Their computer installations may include terminals and other peripherals from several or many vendors.

The administrative vice-president of a large discount retailer provides another example. He discussed several purchases of communications equipment: procurements of telephones for individual discount outlets and the purchase of a large PBX for the corporation's headquarters. The manager explained that telephones in the stores were not especially important for discounters. Customers shopped at such a store primarily for low prices, and they did not expect much service. Indeed, the manager reported that one of the firm's founders had argued that telephones should be entirely removed from the stores, at least for calls from customers, so that customers could not call up to comparison-price shop but would have to come into the stores. The administrative vice-president was experimenting with several different vendors for telephones for the individual stores. He described these experiments as relatively low risk and easy to make. His behavior in purchasing store telephones lay toward the always-a-share end of the behavior spectrum.

The same buyer considered the purchase of a PBX for headquarters to be a considerably higher-risk, more important purchase. The cost of the purchase (over $1.5 million) was substantially higher, and the physical disruption of the change was also substantial. The new headquarters system required new cabling and new handsets for the users in the building. Most important in the eyes of the administrative vice-president, changing to a new telephone system and especially to a new vendor would require teaching users how the new telephones worked. He noted that it was especially difficult to get executives to devote the time and attention needed to master the new system. He believed that most users noticed telephones only when they did not work, not when they worked as expected. He felt that his constituents might prefer the existing system, which, though inadequate, was familiar, to a new system, which, though more powerful and versatile, required getting used to.

Not surprisingly, the buyer used a careful procedure in evaluating the choice of a headquarters PBX. He did consider changing vendors; in fact, he explained that since deregulation had begun in the communications-equipment market, it had become fashionable and a sign of progressive, competent management at least to consider alternative vendors. At the same time, he described his buying behavior as extremely conservative and said that he was extremely reluctant, and unlikely, to switch. In purchasing the headquarters PBX, the buyer's behavior suggested the lost-for-good end of the behavior spectrum. He viewed his firm's commitment as a serious and substantial one and thought it was likely to last for a long time.

Customer's Business Strategy

Another key determinant of an account's location along the behavior spectrum is the way it uses a product or product category—its usage system. One aspect of the usage system is the importance of the category to the buyer's own basic business strategy. For example, consider the preceding discount retailer, whose administrative vice-president suggested that calls from customers might even be undesirable. Service, such as answering customers' telephone inquiries about prices or availability, was not important to the discounter's basic business strategy. The firm competed on price.

A chain of full-service department stores provides a contrast to the discounter. The individual department stores in the chain all had telephones in each major department. Customers frequently called the stores; central operators answered the calls and then switched them to the department requested by the customer. Customers might ask store personnel in the department about whether they had particular brands, products, colors, or sizes in stock, for example.

Service was important to the business strategy of the department store. In fact, service, range and availability of merchandise and merchandising were key dimensions on which the department store was competing against discounters. One of the many aspects of service to the customer was prompt, courteous response to telephone inquiries.

The communications manager of the department-store organization described himself as conservative in his purchasing decisions about telephones. He felt it critical to provide a reliable telephone system with capacity adequate to the needs of the stores. It was not acceptable, for example, for customers to have substantial difficulty in reaching the store or a specific department because of frequent busy signals. This manager also described himself as cost conscious. He gave specific examples of concern with cost; for example, he had the telephones beep after three minutes on outgoing long-distance calls from the executive offices to remind the store's merchandise buyers (and others) of the time and cost. For telephone equipment that would directly affect customer service, however, he considered maintenance, service, and reliability far more important than price. Further, he said that he would be conservative about considering a change of vendor for the telephone equipment. He felt that he could not risk the possibly unsatisfactory service and maintenance of a relatively unknown vendor.

Thus, telephones for the stores were relatively unimportant to the business strategy of the discounter. That customer's behavior lay toward the always-a-share end of the spectrum. Store telephones were considerably more important strategically to the department-store chain. Its behavior lay closer to the lost-for-good end.

Other Aspects of the Usage System

Additional specifics of how an organization uses a product category also influence the location of its behavior on the spectrum. In fact, the large distance on the behavior spectrum between the discounter and department store was caused by more than the difference in the strategic roles of telephones to the customers; it was also caused by other aspects of the department store's usage system.

The department-store chain used a Bell telephone system, called a central attendant system, in which all calls to suburban stores went to one main switch (or PBX) at the main store. The operator answered with the suburban store name, as indicated by the specific line on which the call came in. Callers who asked for specific departments were switched to the appropriate departments in the appropriate stores.

This system of pooling the individual stores' lines saved on operator costs and also allowed more central supervision of the service provided by those operators. The system also reduced the chance that a customer would get a busy signal, an important consideration for the communications manager and the stores. At the same time, however, the centralized system meant that an equipment change would be massive. Any change in PBX vendor would change the entire integrated system. The communications manager reported that he was not willing to consider such action.

A third retailing organization was also a chain of full-service department stores. It was located in the same city as the preceding department-store organization, had a similar market position, and used telephones very similarly in providing service to customers as part of its basic business strategy. The organization did not have a single central attendant system, however; it had a mix of systems. Some of the individual stores were joined in a central attendant system, but others had their own individual PBXs.

The communications manager for the second department-store organization considered telephones important. He was not as comfortable as the discounter about experimenting with new telephones and new vendors to save money. At the same time, however, he was not nearly as conservative as was the manager for the first department-store organization. His organization's less integrated usage system allowed him to try out a new vendor in a relatively contained experiment, perhaps in a single store. He reported that the importance of telephones to his organization meant that he could only experiment cautiously and that he would consider only the few most credible vendors, but he had begun to try equipment from a new vendor. He was monitoring the performance of the equipment and the maintenance and other service provided by the vendor. If his experience turned out to be satisfactory, he would consider additional procurements from the new supplier.

Thus, even for organizations with the same strategy and making purchase decisions for the same product category, differences in what can be called the modularity of the usage system strongly affect accounts' behavior. The first department-store chain's integrated usage system created behavior toward the lost-for-good end of the spectrum. The second organization, with a more modular usage system, was not as close to always-a-share as was the discounter, but its behavior appears to lie between those of the two other retailers.

Modularity in Usage Systems

We can think of customers' usage systems for products as highly modular at one extreme, as fully integrated at the other extreme, or as something in between. The degree of modularity in a customer's usage system is frequently a key influence on the account's purchasing behavior.

A modular usage system is one in which the customer can combine pieces or parts from different vendors, mixing and matching them rather freely. Modularity may occur because a customer uses individual products from some category separately, without trying to join them together. For example, a firm may use word processing equipment for individual secretaries but may not try to link the processors to one another or to any central computer. Except for the possible confusion of having to train different users on different equipment, there may be little reason for the firm not to use products from different vendors in different offices.

Modularity can also occur when products are more tightly linked for use in a system but when the products are designed so that specific items from different vendors can work together. For example, because communication devices must link to the basic telephone network in the United States, there is substantial basic modularity in much of the communications-equipment field. Similarly television broadcast equipment, television sets (receivers), and video recorders have been designed so that items from a variety of vendors fit together into a usage system.

This discussion uses the term *modularity* broadly to mean divisibility— the ability to mix and match parts in a usage system. (The term is thus not restricted to systems of components, such as electronic devices, where readers may be more accustomed to its use.) The broad definition makes the term useful in a wide variety of product categories. For example, suppose that a manufacturer of coated abrasives uses abrasive grain, adhesive, and backing in a batched manufacturing process. The manufacturing equipment must be thoroughly cleaned after each batch. The batched nature of production can create modularity. The firm may be able to use more than one source for a particular input such as adhesive, even if materials from different suppliers are not entirely interchangeable. The plant could simply use a single supplier for adhesive on any one batch but use different suppliers on different batches.

Similarly other usage situations may (or may not) allow substantial divisibility or mixing and matching of inputs from different suppliers. The precise degree of modularity in a particular application depends in part on the individual customer's choice of usage system; the contrasting patterns of the two department-store organizations in the preceding section provides an illustration.

The degree of modularity in usage patterns also depends in part on the nature of the products involved, on the past actions of competitors in the product-marketplace, and on legal, regulatory, and other influences. For example, early in the history of telephones in the United States, the country had numerous competing vendors with separate and often incompatible systems. Then legislation created a monopoly in much of the United States, and AT&T built an integrated telephone network. Apparently in order to promote efficiency, Bell built considerable standardization and modularity into the network. When more recent regulatory rulings opened the market to increased competition, the telephone system had considerable modularity; interconnect (or competitive) vendors could relatively easily link their devices to it.

On the other hand, true compatibility is rare in the computer marketplace—in hardware and especially in software. Until rather recently, there has been little true modularity in complex computer systems.

Product-policy choices by individual vendors also strongly influence the degree of modularity in usage. A vendor can deliberately choose to make its products work more or less easily with products from competing vendors— or, for that matter, with other products from its own lines. Thus, product-policy choices regarding modularity are one way vendors influence customers' behavior along the spectrum between lost-for-good and always-a-share. Chapter 6 will return to the discussion of using modularity or nonmodularity in product policy as a marketing tool.

The opposite of a modular usage system is a fully integrated one: a design in which it is difficult or impossible to mix and match pieces from different vendors. Suppose that a vendor sells electronic components that employ interfaces incompatible with those of other vendors. Customers of that vendor must buy entire systems from a single source; changing vendors requires changing the entire system. Another example of a systems usage pattern occurs when the customer buys equipment and completely proprietary materials to use with that equipment. By contrast, a customer with equipment that could use the materials of several different suppliers has a more modular usage pattern.

As was true with regard to modularity, the precise degree of systems orientation in a usage system depends in part on choices made by the customer. One of the department-store organizations chose an integrated telephone system, and the other chose considerably more modularity. The extent of systems orientation also depends in part on the product category and in part on the choices of a vendor and of its competitors.

It can be helpful to think of a spectrum describing usage systems that runs from full modularity to fully integrated systems. Because complete nonmodularity and complete modularity are rare, most actual situations correspond to intermediate points on the spectrum. The same concepts of modularity and systems define a spectrum of product-policy choices by vendors. Chapter 6 will discuss choices by vendors along this product-policy spectrum and the implications of those choices for customers' behavior over time.

Influence of the Buyer's Characteristics

Even after considering the product category, the customer firm's basic business strategy, and other aspects of the customer's usage system, we still do not have the full set of determinants of the account's location along the behavior spectrum. Characteristics of key individuals within the buying organization are also important influences on location. To illustrate the point, this section continues to consider purchasers of communications equipment.

The communications-equipment marketplace in the early and mid-1980s was a market in transition. Two major forces dominated concerns of the purchasers: buying organizations were using communications in increasingly important and sophisticated ways, and deregulation and restructure were transforming the market. Buyers faced much more choice than they had in the 1970s and 1960s, and they worried about choosing wisely. Moreover, customers believed that the technological pace of the market had increased substantially; they would, they believed, continue to face streams of new products with increasing varieties of uses.

Many organizations had communications managers who had grown up professionally before the turmoil of the late 1970s and 1980s, in the more placid regulated market of the 1960s. In that regulated market, the dominant vendor, AT&T, had enjoyed essentially a legislated monopoly position in much of the United States. Customers had had no choice of vendor. In addition, communications equipment was not considered strategically important to most customer organizations in the 1960s and early 1970s. Individual users in the customer organizations assumed the telephones would work. They were not likely to notice (or compliment the communications manager) when the telephones did work, but they were extremely likely to yell loud and long if they did not.

Consequently the typical communications manager's first concern was to avoid problems by providing reliable service. Second, because most communications managers were measured on cost control, they also worked to control the cost of communications, provided that they could reduce costs without harming service. The communications department was not considered a potential source of strategic advantage to the buying organization; it was a utility, a consumer of resources, and something of a nuisance. The prototypical communications manager was cautious and conservative.

By the 1980s communications had considerably more importance, including strategic importance, for buyers and customer organizations needed new skills in their communications managers. Some organizations were investing in training older-style communications managers to handle increased complexity and increased choices. Other organizations were assigning aggressive, able, younger managers to the communications role, and many of the younger managers welcomed the assignment, feeling they could have a visible impact on their organization in communications. Other organizations, however, still had older-style communications managers working in traditional ways.

These managers' individual characteristics strongly influenced their firms' buying behavior. The older-style managers were generally less likely to change vendors. Their conservatism made them likely to remain with the Bell system; it drove the behavior of their organizations toward the lost-for-good end of the spectrum. The communications managers who viewed their jobs as opportunities to make their marks were much more willing and even anxious to make changes.

The communications manager for a chain of department stores provides an example. He had responsibility for communications and for various other service departments, such as alterations. He had spent considerable time (approximately a year) educating himself about the new technologies and the new choices in the marketplace by reading extensively and attending short courses. He had then begun experimenting with lower-priced alternatives to Bell telephones. He had experimented carefully. His organization operated some bargain stores, as well as full-service department stores, and the manager had experimented first in the bargain stores. After those trials were successful, he had proceeded to try a new supplier in some of the department stores.

Some of the more senior communications managers were also willing, or even eager, to experiment. An example was the senior vice-president and treasurer of an especially well-run supermarket chain. The firm's stores were geographically dispersed. Its market stance was one of low prices yet good service; its managers prided themselves on the stores' low stock-out levels, even at the most difficult times of the week—Saturday night and Monday morning. Effective communication between the stores and headquarters was a critical part of this firm's operations. Telephones were not a major expense in supermarkets. One might have expected that the relatively low cost of telephones and their high importance would have made this manager conservative—that he would have experimented only cautiously, if at all, with non-Bell equipment. In fact, however, he had bought a non-Bell switch very early, in 1972. In the late 1970s he had replaced that equipment with newer products from another non-Bell vendor. He considered the whole process rather routine. He explained that his firm had to be extremely cost conscious, that he was sufficiently senior in a rather flat organization to be able to take risks, and that he believed the vendor's role was only to provide the equipment that he, the user, would make work as he wanted.

Clearly this manager's personal characteristics moved his firm's behavior far in the direction of always-a-share. Other managers in other organizations and other industries provided additional examples. Their self-confidence, their willingness to accept risks, and their abilities to manage change and disruption moved their organizations closer to always-a-share. More conservative managers usually influenced their organizations in the direction of lost-for-good.

Types of Switching Costs

The determinants of accounts' behavior—the product category, the customer's usage system, the characteristics of the individual buyer—are thus varied and complex. These factors determine the customer's switching costs. As an aid in identifying and analyzing switching costs, the remainder of this chapter characterizes and describes such costs. It first considers investment actions: the specifics of what the customer does to make and keep its commitment to a particular vendor. The chapter then considers exposure: the risk faced by a customer in its relationship with a particular vendor.

Investment Actions

Investment actions are the relatively more tangible types of switching costs. Customers invest in their choices of vendor and of products in a variety of ways. They obviously invest money to pay for purchases. In addition, customers may hire or train people to work with a vendor and its products. They may build or modify plant and equipment or invest in other lasting assets to use a specific product or group of products. Further, they may design or alter basic business procedures to fit a vendor or a product; for example, a customer may design its procedures for gathering data on hourly employees to conform with a particular software package for payroll, or it may adjust its inventory policies for an important raw material in accord with a vendor's delivery capabilities.

These categories of investment actions are not mutually exclusive. Hiring new employees also requires outlays of cash, and training of existing employees often requires identifiable cash outlays. Similarly investments in lasting assets generally involve specific cash outlays; investments or changes in business procedures may or may not involve identifiable outlays. Further, investments in lasting assets are frequently linked to investments in people; for example, when a firm invests in modifying its production facilities, there is also usually a related investment as people learn how to use those modified facilities, either in a formal training program or in less formal learning as they work with the new environment. Investments in basic business procedures will usually involve at least some learning by people, and they may require substantial new learning. Investments in procedures may or may not be linked to investments in lasting assets.

Thus, a customer typically invests in its relationship with a vendor through some combination of money, people, lasting assets, and procedures. Often the cash outlays for purchases are strongly emphasized in procurement decisions. Most organizations' capital-budgeting procedures emphasize cash flows and are ill-equipped to include other considerations such as required changes in business procedures. Yet investment actions in the other categories, especially investments in lasting assets or in business procedures, can be extremely important in determining the behavior of the account. This disparity between the visibilities of different types of investments and the importance of the effects of those investments offers both a challenge and an opportunity to the vendor.

Investments in People

Obvious investments take place when a customer hires people specifically trained to use a vendor's product. For example, some help-wanted advertisements for data-processing professionals specify people experienced on a particular computer or with a particular operating environment. Similarly an account makes an investment in people when it sends current employees through training programs to learn how to use particular products. For example, a firm purchasing a new type of flexible manufacturing system will have to invest in training its people to operate and to maintain and service that new system.

Other investments in people are less obvious but often even more important in determining accounts' behavior. Those investments involve learning— usually learning the product with use. For example, even if a firm trains operators for a new flexible manufacturing system when the system is new, those employees will not then become fully proficient with the equipment. The initial training may teach them to make the equipment work, but only over time will they become expert with the product, able to use it to best advantage, to recognize its quirks, and to identify and perhaps even correct its problems.

Suppose that a firm begins to buy diesel trucks for its fleet; suppose in addition that the firm does its own repair work, maintaining a repair garage and a corps of competent mechanics. The firm may decide to train its existing personnel to service the new diesel trucks. Although the initial training will provide some competence, the learning provided by actually working on the new trucks will produce considerably more expertise.

In some industrial situations, the accumulated learning of the old-timers in a business can be a substantial benefit to their employer, and the firm can therefore be unwilling to make changes in its processes. Especially where manufacturing processes require substantial judgment and art, buyers can be reluctant to change. Even in cases where a customer's processes involve more science than art, the learning curve phenomenon can create significant reluctance to change; accounts may hesitate to face the lower levels of performance and efficiency in the early stages of their learning curves for new manufacturing processes and products.

Investments in people thus create switching costs. The cash outlays for hiring and training are obvious. Other disruptions can be at least as important. The problems of replacing existing personnel with new people can create reluctance to change. The need to wait for the learning that occurs only over time also creates reluctance.

Investments in Lasting Assets

Investments in lasting assets, such as plant and equipment or other facilities, also create switching costs. Organizations display strong preferences against abandoning past investments in lasting assets, and therefore those investments contribute to a reluctance to change.

In some cases, it does not make economic sense to abandon a past investment. Even in situations where it would make good economic sense for a firm to write off a lasting asset and invest in a replacement, there is often considerable hesitation to change. Managers frequently find it difficult to accept the idea of a sunk cost: the idea that one should make the best decision now for the future, assuming that what is done is done and not feeling wedded to past mistakes.

One example of a lasting asset that has produced substantial real switching costs is applications computer software: the applications programs with which computer users handle accounting functions, plant scheduling, and a myriad of other business functions. Converting software from one computer to another (or from one operating system to another) requires considerable effort.

Conversions have been an important source of difficulty to customers over the history of the computer marketplace. Earlier conversions were especially painful; the conversions to IBM's 360 family from earlier machines in the mid-1960s and later 1960s are still legendary. In addition, both software and the potential disruption and cost of conversions of software have increased in importance. The costs of computer hardware have dropped dramatically, and software costs have made up an increasing fraction of the total cost of a computer installation. In the 1960s, hardware was relatively expensive, and users worked hard to develop software that used the hardware as efficiently as possible. By contrast, by the 1980s software might account for as much as 80 or 90 percent of the lifetime cost of a computer system.

Examples can illustrate the difficulty of changes in lasting assets such as software, even for changes that outsiders might consider relatively trivial. A shoe retailer is one such case. The firm had computerized parts of the merchandise-replenishment system for its shoe stores very early, in the 1950s. Merchandise replenishment—what the firm's executive vice-president called pinpoint replenishment—was crucial in the shoe business. If a particular store sold a specific style shoe in a particular color, length, and width, then generally the same store had to be restocked with another pair of the same style, color, length, and width—quickly.

Since it began computerization in the 1950s, the retailer had added a variety of application programs. Those programs allowed field widths (numbers of columns in printed reports and in data) for prices that could accommodate prices only up to $99.99; it had seemed impossible in the 1950s and 1960s that an individual item would cost $100 or more in a shoe store. By the 1980s, however, the stores were carrying items for over $100. Managers estimated that it would cost approximately $250,000 to fix the programs to handle higher prices. To avoid a succession of such expensive changes to patch old software, they were also considering designing a new, coherent data-processing system. They estimated that the effort would require approximately thirty person-years of work.

Many customers for computers learned about the difficulty of substantial software conversions through personal experience. They have learned the lesson well, as the manager of data processing for a large insurance company explained. That manager recalled the conversion from earlier machines to the IBM 360 family as "awful," requiring hundreds of person-years of effort for his firm and causing problems from the mid-1960s to the early 1970s. He said that his firm had remained with IBM despite the problems because IBM had considerable expertise and "as much of a chance as anyone." He had, however, considered changing vendors at several points in the process.

The manager reported that the trouble caused by the 360 conversions had motivated customers to teach IBM about the importance of avoiding similar disruptions. He said that in the early 1970s, the vendor had begun discussions with some of its leading customers about a possible new operating system. The system provided useful new capabilities in networking and in database management, capabilities that did in fact become important to customers during the 1970s and 1980s. The new system, however, would have required another round of massive investment actions in software conversions. The manager reported that he and others had told IBM that if it introduced such a system, it would have to do so with a new set of customers. The existing customers would not tolerate so much trauma. IBM backed off, he reported.

Investments in Procedures

Investments in a customer organization's basic business procedures—the ways it performs day-to-day business functions—are especially likely to create switching costs. Procedures are difficult to change, and customers are understandably reluctant to change them unnecessarily. If some of a customer's procedures are geared to work with a specific vendor and its products and services and if a change of vendors would require substantial modifications of those procedures, the customer will often be reluctant to change.

The more pervasive the procedure—the more customer employees it involves and the more widely it reaches in the customer organization—the higher the switching costs created by the investment in procedures. The office automation market and the market for local area networks (LANs) in the early 1980s provide an example of customer concerns about investments in basic procedures, investments with widespread organizational impacts.

Many organizations were considering or already investing in equipment for office automation. Generally at the time, customers used their initial purchases as stand-alone equipment, most frequently as work stations for secretaries and others to use in word processing. Even the stand-alone equipment was requiring substantial investments in people and in procedures; employees required considerable training to learn to use the equipment, and the basic work flows and procedures of the organization often required adjustment.

Discussions with a number of managers in a variety of organizations also revealed that they expected office automation to grow in importance to their businesses. They felt that extensive office automation was coming, that their commitments for office-automation products would be very important (operationally and, likely, strategically) to their organizations, and that it was important that the product and vendor choices be made well.

Users and potential users of office automation expected that in the future, individual work stations would be linked through some type of networking. One linking device would be a LAN: a wired (cable) link among a group of electronic devices within some limited geographical area. For example, a LAN might link various devices for office automation within a single building or group of buildings. In the early 1980s, business publications (such as *Forbes* and *Business Week*) and more general publications (such as the *New York Times*) ran special many-page advertising supplements on office automation. These supplements included discussion of LANs as the links that might hold office-automation systems together.

The LAN marketplace was new. Customers used devices of the sort that might be joined with a LAN, but for the most part they did not yet link those devices together. (Alternatively, users might occasionally use slower and less permanent means, such as accoustic couplers and standard telephone lines, to communicate among devices on a far more limited basis than a LAN would allow). Few customers were actually using LANs.

In 1983, although there were few LANs in use in other than experimental ways, there were over fifty vendors in the LAN market. The vendors offered products that differed fundamentally from one another in their technical designs. Discussions of LANs centered on technical issues, such as the design of the physical interface (how, physically, devices would connect with the network) and the choice of network protocol (the rule for determining how devices were allotted turns in using the main network pathways). The discussions were replete with terms like *ring, bus, token passing, time division multiple access,* and *carrier sense multiple access with collision detection.*

Potential users were generally not comfortable with these technical discussions, yet they felt that they would eventually need to link individual devices for office automation. They were extremely concerned with not making mistakes, choices that would require additional unnecessary investments in the future. Adopting office automation was requiring substantial investments in procedures. Buyers and potential buyers of office-automation equipment in general and of LANs in particular were actively concerned that they would move in one direction, making large investments, only to find that the market subsequently turned a different way. They were highly concerned with the core links of an office-automation system, such as LANs.

The discomfort and concern of the group of managers about decisions on office automation and LANs seem sensible given the extent and difficulty of the related investments in procedures. In fact, a major overhaul of an office-automation system, once it was fully linked together, could be even more traumatic than had been major computer changes. Especially during the 1960s (which computer users recalled as the time of the worst conversions), computer conversions tended to be confined within one or a few parts of many organizations—the computer department and perhaps a few user departments such as accounting. Although some organizations had been using computers more extensively than others, at that time few had diffused the use of computers as widely as a typical use of office-automation equipment might be expected to spread. Painful as were many customers' memories of conversions from one computer system to another, such pain pales by comparison with the trauma that could be created by an ungraceful change of office-automation systems.

Investments in other procedures—for payroll, for inventory management and ordering systems, or for administering employee benefits, for example—can also create substantial switching costs. In fact, it appears that even though formal capital budgeting and related procurement procedures may not explicitly consider investment actions in procedures, such investments can be even more important than other investments in erecting barriers to change.

As chapter 6 will elaborate, an established vendor may be able to encourage customers to make additional investments in procedures in relation to their commitments to that vendor. In the process, the customer builds the costs of changing to another supplier. Computers and other types of information technology can be particularly effective tools for getting customers to build investments in procedures.

Characteristics of Investments

Patterns of Investments

When they make an initial commitment to a vendor or to a specific product stream from the vendor, customers may not understand the investments that will follow. They appear especially likely to underestimate the effects of future investments in lasting assets and in procedures.

The computer marketplace provides an example. Interviews explored the histories of purchase and use of computers by a variety of businesses. At all of the sites, computers had grown in importance. The managers reported increasing investments in software; the initial investments by customers had grown almost inexorably into larger commitments. Because the increased investments in software did not readily transfer among the products of different vendors, conversion costs also grew. It became harder and harder for customers to change vendors.

An insurance company provides an example of an organization that did not understand the long-term implications of its investments in its relationships with computer vendors. Over time, the customer did realize the scope and importance of its commitments for computers and found it necessary to change, but by then the switching costs were considerable.

The company had been an early customer for IBM's 650 computer. It had also been a very early Univac customer and had used multiple vendors through the 1950s and 1960s. By 1970 the customer had computers from RCA, Univac, Honeywell, and Burroughs, although no IBM machine remained. The manager responsible for data processing recalled that the choice of Univac over IBM had been based on the specific technical features of the machines available from the two vendors in the mid-1960s. In addition, he said that the decision had not emphasized the idea of upward compatibility (relatively easy transfers of software from one to another of a vendor's machines), which had been a new concept at the time. In other words, he recalled that even relatively sophisticated computer buyers did not then understand the importance of investment actions and conversions enough to emphasize compatibility.

During the firm's multivendor days, its data-processing department had built many separate software systems that interfaced with one another with difficulty, if at all. The manager described the result as a "zoo" whose complexity required especially good technical people.

By 1970, the increasingly large and complex multivendor system was becoming unacceptably cumbersome. Univac, the major supplier, did not offer a newer product that was compatible with the customer's existing machines, so some form of conversion was required. The customer evaluated a change of vendor and chose IBM as a vendor on which it could standardize and with which it could grow. The conversion process was massive. The manager estimated that the firm had about 7,500 software systems and 1,000 databases. Some programs were subjected to what the manager called "gorilla" (line-by-line) rewrites. More major systems were redesigned in the conversion process. Ten years after it had begun, the conversion process was not quite complete.

Initial Investments versus Later Investments

It appears common for customers to emphasize the initial investments required to begin using a vendor or a product and to underestimate possible required future investments. Further, there is often tension between a vendor's ability to provide easy access to its products (with rather low required initial investments in learning) and the vendor's ability to provide fully powerful products for the longer run. In other words, a more powerful product or product stream is often more difficult to learn to use. In designing their products and product streams, vendors face conflicting pressures from shorter-term concerns (to allow customers to adopt them easily) and from longer-term ones (to give customers substantial reasons to commit and remain committed). Customers face conflicting pressures between shorter-term desires for less difficult conversions and longer-term ones for powerful capabilities.

In part, the customer's willingness to make substantial commitments and investments depends on the credibility of the vendor and on the vendor's stance in the marketplace. (Hence, the vendor's ability to choose the longer-term strategy and ask for substantial initial investments by customers also depends in part on the vendor's market position.) A more dominant vendor will often be able to elicit substantial investments that customers would not make for a lesser vendor.

Other factors also influence the customer's willingness to invest. Vendors can help induce substantial investments by providing training, manuals, and other support to customers making such investments. Customers will also be more willing to invest if they expect high benefits from the products. Hence, the product category and the customer's usage system for a product (including the product's role in the customer's own business strategy) influence the willingness to invest.

A department-store organization provides an example of a single customer that adopted a shorter-term orientation (and tried to avoid initial investments) for one product category but took a longer-term view and incurred more investment for another category. The organization was one division of a large department-store group. The division was more advanced in data processing than were some of its sister divisions, and, in fact, it often acted as a test site within the larger corporation for data-processing applications.

The data-processing manager for the division described purchase decisions for mainframe computers and for point-of-sale (POS) equipment. In mainframes, the organization had had a long history of working with IBM and indeed had worked with the vendor to develop a strategy for automation of the retailing industry. Yet the division had switched from IBM to Wang mainframes.

The data-processing manager reported that the parent organization had dictated the change. He felt that IBM would have been the preferable choice for his division. He noted, however, that IBM was not as easy for beginning or less sophisticated users, including the organization's other divisions. The manager believed that IBM products required more initial user investments but then provided more capabilities. He believed the parent organization had wanted the divisions to use the same vendor so that they could exchange and share investments in software and that it had intentionally forced the choice of a vendor that required relatively less initial learning.

The POS purchase provided a contrast. In the late 1970s, the retail division had begun to install POS systems and to emphasize timely information from data processing. The manager said the use of POS was increasing rapidly in importance and suggested that POS was more important than the mainframe used for backroom functions such as accounting and finance.

The parent organization had recommended a choice of vendor for the POS equipment, as it had for the mainframe; it had recommended NCR for the POS choice. The data-processing manager for the division believed that the NCR equipment required a smaller initial investment than would alternative IBM POS equipment. He also believed that the IBM equipment would provide more benefits in the long run, once the organization had learned to use it.

In the POS case, the division managed to get the parent to change its mind; the organization selected IBM. Managers from the division argued that the initial investments were more than worthwhile to obtain the added capabilities of the IBM system, especially its programmability and its ability to function when there were communication problems. Because of the higher perceived competitive importance of POS equipment to the organization, the parent was willing to select higher future benefits, despite the accompanying higher initial costs.

Routine or Watershed Decisions

Literature on buyer behavior has suggested classifying purchase occasions in part on the basis of the customer's previous experience with the product. The work done for this book suggests adding and emphasizing the extent of required investment actions. Customers behave very differently for purchases that require extensive investment actions than they do for purchases that require only limited ones.

The apparent impact of investment actions (or switching costs) is so great as to suggest naming purchase occasions on the basis of the required level of investments. We might define as routine decisions those that require only relatively modest investment actions—in all four categories but especially in lasting assets and in procedures. We might call watershed decisions those that require more extensive investments, especially in lasting assets and procedures.

On routine purchase decisions, customers can emphasize shorter-term issues. As was true in the extreme case of the always-a-share model in chapter 2, they can choose any of the immediately attractive alternatives (assuming that none of those alternatives requires substantial investments). On watershed decisions, customers will generally use a much longer time horizon. As the next two chapters will argue, accounts' behavior on such decisions is fundamentally different from their behavior on more routine, shorter-term choices, and vendors' strategies and tactics should reflect the differences.

Watershed decisions need not involve a change of vendor, and routine decisions may include a vendor change. The preceding discussion mentioned the conversions to the IBM 360 family in the 1960s, a classic example of traumatic change even for users switching from other IBM products. In the early 1980s, some Sperry (Univac) customers were moving from the 90 series of computers to the 1100 series, which would be the company's product line for the future. Such conversions can be classed as watershed decisions, despite the fact that they do not involve a change of vendor.

By comparison, suppose that a customer for video terminals for use in a computer installation switches part or all of its patronage from one vendor to another. Suppose that the customer can select among several suppliers, each of which offers terminals that work with the buyer's system. The new terminals do not require any substantial conversion, and the decision to buy them would be classed as routine.

Some watershed decisions occur because vendors bring out (and shift their emphasis and support to) new products or product lines. Conversions to the IBM 360 family were an example. Other watershed decisions occur because customers decide that they must change their usage systems dramatically; perhaps their existing systems are unacceptably behind, or perhaps increasing importance and future opportunities for using the products dictate a change, or perhaps there is a combination of reasons.

Explorations in the early 1980s considered how a number of organizations had used and planned to use computers. A number of the organizations, including the insurance company discussed above, were undergoing difficult watershed conversions to position themselves for the future. The managers seemed to have decided that it was finally time to rationalize their data-processing organizations. Often they felt that they had been coping (sometimes with considerable difficulty) with an operation that was increasingly cumbersome and difficult to patch; they were accepting a difficult change in order to set up a new structure that would see them through a long period of future use.

In making such watershed decisions, customer managers frequently describe themselves as buying a vendor rather than a product. In the interviews about computer purchases, watershed buyers generally considered the vendor's future capabilities to be key: capabilities to provide continuing streams of useful products and, very important, to allow relatively easy transitions (with relatively low required investments) from one to another of those products over time.

The managers described themselves as commiting to vendors with particular strategies. In some cases, they even said they were committing to a specific product stream with a particular strategic role to the vendor. The following chapter will pursue the topic of just what it is to which the customer commits, especially on important decisions made with long time horizons.

Intervendor and Intravendor Transferability

The histories of computer purchases and usage suggest another important characteristic of investment actions: the extent to which past investments do or do not transfer from one product to another. Past investment actions may or may not transfer readily from one to another of the products of a single vendor. They may or may not transfer readily between products of different vendors.

Intervendor transfers of computer software are usually substantially more difficult than are intravendor transfers. As a result, buyers express strong concerns over the software changes required to change vendors; essentially all such buyers require substantial reasons to undergo a change.

In other situations, buyers may not be actively aware of the extent of their past investments in their current suppliers and of the new investments that would be required for a change. Especially if investments transfer relatively easily from one to another of its own products, an established vendor may want the customer to recognize and value its past vendor-specific investments in people, facilities, or procedures. (The account's decision-making processes may or may not be able to incorporate consideration of such longer-term investments, however.)

Exposure

The preceding discussion considered the relatively more tangible types of switching costs: required investment actions in dollars, people, lasting assets, and procedures. There are also less tangible switching costs: the risks that organizations and individual buyers face in relation to their choices of vendor or product. This book labels such risks *exposure*.

Actually both parties to an industrial marketing relationship face risk or exposure. Thus, we can define exposure as just what it is that the two parties have at stake in the relationship. On each side, exposure affects both the organization and individuals within the organization. It includes issues of dollars invested (by buyer or by seller) and of performance (whether products will work satisfactorily). It also involves reputations of organizations and of individual managers.

The marketing literature on perceived risk and on industrial buyer behavior emphasizes the importance of perceived risk—the exposure of individuals involved in procurement decisions. That literature also suggests categorizing risks as financial risks, performance risks, and personal risks. These three categories prove very useful in diagnosing the exposure of each of the parties to an industrial marketing relationship.

Financial Exposure

Financial exposure for the customer involves the dollar amounts spent on a product category. It also involves the relative differences in outlays the customer would have made with alternative choices. Thus, feelings of financial exposure can involve awareness of possibly acceptable alternatives with substantially different prices in the market.

In the early 1980s, for example, the costs of communications equipment and services were fashionable subjects for managers. Communications bills had risen appreciably as customers increased their usages. In addition, newer suppliers (AT&T's competitors) stressed low price in many of their sales presentations; price was an easily communicated way for them to differentiate themselves from the leading vendor. Senior managers were hearing about alternative suppliers (on the golf course, in a board meeting, or in some other forum) and were asking how their own organizations might save money. For all of these reasons, communications managers were feeling increasing pressure from financial exposure: the risk that their choices would cost their organizations more than was necessary.

The vendor also spends money in its relationships with individual accounts; it also faces financial exposure. In some cases, vendors face the risk that they will not collect their receivables, an obvious form of financial risk. More frequently, a vendor faces the risk that its relationship with a specific customer will not be profitable—that is, that the revenues it receives from the customer (even if all bills are paid promptly) will not cover the total costs of serving the customer, among them, the costs of the products, the selling effort, service, and any unpriced support.

It is still very rare for industrial sellers to be able to provide meaningful estimates of the overall profitability of their relationships with particular customers. They may be able to identify sales histories and even manufacturing margins related to the business of specific customers, but sellers generally do not track account profitability after other costs, such as marketing expenditures. The common lack of knowledge about profitability increases the financial risk that the vendor continues to do business with an account that overall reduces rather than increases the vendor's profits.

Performance Exposure

Performance exposure for the buyer is the risk that the vendor's products will not perform as they should or as the buyer expected. It also involves the risk that the vendor's organization will not perform as expected—for example, that deliveries will be late, that the vendor's representatives will not have adequate knowledge of the buyer's operation to provide proper installation, or that the vendor's organization will not provide satisfactory service.

Performance exposure is a mix of immediate and longer-term issues. In the short run, it refers to concerns about product capabilities in actual use, malfunctions, availability and quality of service, and so on; buyers worry that a product will not work as intended. For the longer term, additional concerns become important. Especially for products that are important to the execution of the buyer's business strategy, performance exposure involves concerns that because of a poor choice, the purchasing firm will not operate as well as it could had it chosen better.

For product categories that entail substantial switching costs, buyers face the risk of painful future investment actions if their vendors do not remain adequately up-to-date technically. Even if the vendors do develop technically, buyers face risks of substantial required investments if the sellers do not provide for intravendor transferability of past investment actions. In the extreme case, the buyer faces substantial risk if the vendor goes out of business.

The computer marketplace provides several examples of these types of performance exposure. An insurance company provided a concrete example of the enormity of some performance exposure. The firm was among the largest computer users in the world. It used computers for standard payroll and accouting functions, for processing claims, and for numerous other purposes. The responsible manager described his data-processing system as a battleship whose basic direction could be changed only gradually. He described extensive planning for backup and recovery after failures or disasters. He had once calculated that if all the firm's computers were to go down for only a few days, the organization might never be able to catch up.

Another firm provides an example of the growing exposure of a customer that felt its vendor had fallen behind technically. The firm was essentially a service bureau that provided time-shared computer power. Because its services were provided on a real-time (on-line) basis, reliability was key. In addition, the firm was a very large user, with an extensive computer installation.

The firm had had a succession of Burroughs products. Over time, the customer had assumed more and more of a role in providing for its own needs, specifically for providing software normally supplied by the vendor. In the mid-1970s, it had decided to develop its own systems software rather than use the Burroughs products. Its own software would be more efficient than the Burroughs version.

In addition, the buyer had become increasingly concerned about Burroughs's ability to provide a satisfactory product stream and to remain up-to-date. By the early 1980s, the firm's computer managers believed that Burroughs was out of date and unlikely to continue to provide adequate products.

The account was making a watershed move to a new, more modular design with which it could mix and match equipment from different vendors and thus reduce its reliance on its current supplier. The manager in charge of hardware referred to one project on non-Burroughs equipment as his "liberation package," but the overall liberation was coming at a substantial conversion cost.

The shoe retailer mentioned previously provides another example of performance exposure for the customer firm—an example of the extreme exposure to a vendor's failing. The example concerns the POS terminals in the individual shoe outlets, which the retailer had installed in the early 1970s. The terminals collected sales information and transmitted that information by telephone to headquarters.

In its initial POS procurement decision, the firm had chosen Singer. The executive who had headed the committee that made the initial choice explained that at the time Singer had been the only vendor offering a product appropriate for specialty stores, such as individual shoe stores, which would use one single stand-alone terminal each. At the time, IBM had been oriented toward department stores, which would each use multiple terminals. Similarly, NCR had not yet introduced a product suitable for specialty stores.

Unfortunately for the customer, the initial commitment created additional exposure over time as the terminals were used more extensively. Then Singer went out of the business. In the early 1980s, another firm was servicing the terminals at what a manager in the retailing organization called ever-increasing prices.

In 1982 the firm evaluated a decision on new POS terminals, using a task force headed by the manager who had headed the first procurement committee. The managers described their key criteria as reliability, the capabilities of the specific products, and, not surprisingly, the viability of the vendor.

Fears that products will not work as intended affect the vendor as well as the customer. Poor performance can hurt a vendor's reputation and prospects for future business—both with the specific customer account that encounters the problems and also with other buyers who hear about the problem (at business or social meetings, through the grapevine, or even in the press). Poor performance can also lead to financial problems for the vendor if it must apply resources, such as sales, service, and engineering attention, to try to fix the situation.

The vendor's performance exposure can be especially troublesome because individuals in the buyer's organization frequently have key impacts on whether a product works as intended. Most obviously, customers can use products incorrectly and therefore cause performance problems. In addition, customers' misperceptions about a product's capabilities can lead to disappointment when the product does not work as the customer mistakenly thought it would.

Personal Exposure

Purchases that involve exposure for the customer organization also create personal exposure for the manager or managers responsible for the procurement. Such managers often believe that they will be blamed if purchase decisions lead to problems. In some cases, they also believe that they will receive credit for successful choices. Often, however, managers worry that they will be penalized for poor decisions and bad news more than they will be rewarded for good decisions and favorable news. The result can be conservatism and inertia caused by feelings of personal exposure.

Although the basic need for a procurement generally arises from overall organizational needs, the degree of personal exposure felt by the responsible manager(s) can significantly affect both the timing of a decision and the choice of vendor. A manager wishing to make an impact may speed up a decision; the previous discussion of forward-looking, often young, communication managers gave an illustration. A manager more concerned with not causing problems may slow down a decision. An example is a communications manager who had recently joined a manufacturing firm after many years managing communications elsewhere. He reported that his new organization needed to consider a major procurement and that he would consider a variety of possible vendors, but that the time was not yet right for him to do so. He believed he was not yet adequately established in the organization to undertake such a purchase.

A less secure or less senior manager will often find it more difficult to choose a nontraditional vendor than will a more secure or more senior one because of the personal exposure involved in the choice. Other details of the procurement process will also depend in part on the exposure felt by the manager(s) involved. The desire of a manager to appear knowledgeable and up-to-date may broaden the set of vendors evaluated on a particular procurement; the manager may want to demonstrate competence and awareness. The more junior or less secure individual buyer may feel it necessary to conduct a more elaborate procurement procedure and consider a wider range of possible vendors than would a more secure and senior buyer.

Purchases and relationships with customers also create personal exposure for individuals within the sellers' organization—for the salesperson who handles the account, the engineer who designs a specific installation for the customer, the trainer who teaches the customer's personnel how to use a product, and so on. Salespeople frequently expect serious harm to their careers if valued customers for whom they are responsible stop buying or significantly reduce their purchases from the vendor. Service people anticipate career damage if the customers they serve are dissatisfied and complain.

As was true for individuals within the buyer's organization, individual employees of the vendor may feel that they face an assymetric reward structure:

that they will be penalized more for bad news than they will be rewarded for good. The result can be considerable conservatism.

Beyond feeling exposure to negative impacts on their careers, individuals are also influenced in dealing with customers by risks to the personal satisfaction they obtain from their jobs. For example, the literature on motivation of the sales force discusses the difficulty of inducing field representatives to make cold calls on unknown potential customers. Even if their organizations strongly encourage such calls and in fact reward the effort, salespeople are often reluctant to face the likely rejection; it is tough not to take that rejection too personally.

Actual and Perceived Exposure

Both customers and vendors face diverse and complex types of exposure or risk. A typical relationship involves a mix of types. For example, suppose that a customer organization purchases a major piece of manufacturing equipment. The buyer will face performance exposure about whether the equipment will arrive and work satisfactorily and also about the equipment's ability to last and to perform well in the future. The buyer may face financial exposure in relation to the specific financing arrangement it selects for the equipment and also in relation to the price it pays. The individual managers responsible for the purchase will feel personal exposure, as may the plant personnel responsible for operating the new equipment and others.

Moreover, not only are intangible switching costs complex and important, but in addition, buyers may not even be aware of some of the risks they face. In other words, the customer's actual exposure may be considerably different from its perceived exposure. For example, because of unfamiliarity with a product, a customer organization may overestimate the exposure it faces. The buyer may agonize over the question of whether a product or product stream will work satisfactorily when in fact the customer's competitor has been using the products satisfactorily in similar ways for some time.

Customers can also underestimate the extent of their exposure. It appears that buyers are especially likely to underestimate longer-term types of exposure, such as their exposure to a vendor's inability to provide an ongoing stream of satisfactory products that do not require extensive conversion costs. (By comparison, buyers may be inclined to overestimate more immediate types of exposure.) Managers in customers for computers, like one of the insurance companies used in previous examples, describe their increased emphasis on compatibility of a vendor's offerings as a response to increasing customer awareness of the actual exposure they face.

When customers actually face more exposure than they realize, vendors may (or may not) want to educate the buyers about actual exposure. The vendor with particularly strong longer-term capabilities may find it useful to do so and convince customers to take a longer-term orientation and therefore increase its own chance of being selected. (This suggestion does not imply a scare campaign. In fact, the next two chapters will argue that tactics such as improper scare campaigns are likely to be harmful to important long-term relationships with customers. Instead it is meant to suggest a professional and fully ethical effort to educate customers to the likely natures of their commitments in the future.) On the other hand, a vendor with less long-term abilities and any vendor without a long-term commitment to a market itself would not want to conduct such education.

Exposure over Time

Both actual and perceived exposures will generally change over time for the buyer and for the seller. The direction of change is not always the same, however; exposure will increase in some cases and decrease in others.

In some situations, increased knowledge of a product category will decrease a customer's feelings of exposure. The increased experience bolsters customers' knowlege and confidence and decreases their perceived risk. In other cases, however, buyers' exposure increases over time. Actual exposure may increase because the customer uses a vendor's products in increasingly important ways and depends increasingly on support from the vendor. Or even if actual exposure does not change, perceived exposure may increase as buyers become more aware of the risks they face. The computer marketplace provides an illustration. Many early customers were not aware of the substantial exposure they faced; over time, buyers learned about the horrors of conversions and of poor choices, often by experiencing conversions themselves.

Actual or perceived exposure of customers can also change because of changes in the technological pace of a product-marketplace. An increase in the rate of technological development can make buyers feel more uncertainty and more concern with suboptimal choices. It can make them more dependent on vendors' specialized technical knowledge. A decrease in pace is likely to allow buyers to rely more on their own judgments and to reduce their feelings of risk.

Buyers' perceptions of exposure depend in part on the relation between past and present levels of choice, uncertainty, and risk. Therefore the history of a general product-marketplace and of individual firms within that market help determine the degree to which customers feel exposure. Customers faced with more diverse and more important choices than they faced in the past will generally feel increased exposure. For example, because of deregulation, most customers for communications equipment in the early 1980s faced substantially increased choices of vendor for PBXs and other equipment—and they felt considerable exposure. A communications-equipment customer in an area that was served by a non-Bell operating company provided a sharp contrast. That firm had always used equipment manufactured by a third party and had had a choice of equipment in the past, and its managers did not feel high exposure in selecting equipment, even for relatively important uses.

The vendor's exposure may also increase or decrease during its relationship with an individual customer. In some cases, the vendor will learn a great deal about its customer, will be better able to serve the customer's needs, and also will be better able to avoid making serious mistakes in the relationship (suggesting the wrong product or not calling on the relevant buying influences, for example). In such cases, the seller's exposure may decrease with time. In other cases, the account may buy more over time and may become increasingly important to the selling firm and to the specific salesperson. In addition, the buyer may become more demanding. The seller's exposure may therefore increase.

Relative Exposure

Customers are frequently concerned with relative as well as with absolute exposure. They do not consider only their own exposure in dealing with a vendor; they are also concerned with the magnitude of that exposure in relation to the exposure faced by the vendor in its commitment to the account. Often a customer feels that it can negotiate, threaten, or cajole far more effectively if the vendor's exposure in the joint relationship is comparable to the customer's. Usually the customer will expect to receive more attention and concern from a vendor that faces a comparably high level of exposure in the relationship.

One banking organization provides an example of a buyer for which relative exposure was an especially important determinant of purchase. The organization, a group of banks, chose an untried vendor for its initial purchase of automated teller machines (ATMs).

ATMs were introduced in the United States in the early 1970s. A vendor named Docutel was the early leader; other vendors then began to introduce products. The banking organization was an early experimenter in ATMs; it became even more of a leader when it pursued its ATM program throughout the mid-1970s recession, which led many other banks to put their programs aside for a while.

The banking organization did not choose Docutel, the market leader at the time. Instead it chose Diebold, a vendor new to ATMs; the bank was one of Diebold's first ATM customers. The bank's data-processing manager explained that Diebold had a good reputation in the bank-vault business. His organization viewed the vendor as a one-industry company; it served only banks. Therefore, they reasoned, Diebold would have to make its ATM work.

In other situations, customers may be uncomfortable if they believe their exposure is high relative to that of the vendor, but they may not be willing to go so far as to change their choice of vendor as a result. Frequently changing to a vendor that would face comparable exposure also means changing to a vendor that is less powerful and less important in its own industry. Customers facing substantial exposure may therefore also face a conflict. On the one hand, they would like to be important to their vendors and to have their patronage involve exposure for the vendor; at the same time, however, they would like to deal with a strong competent vendor with the capability to satisfy their needs.

Similarly, customers may feel conflict between shorter- and longer-term concerns regarding relative exposure. For the shorter term, a customer may favor a vendor to which it is more important—often a smaller or less established one. For the longer term, however, the customer may prefer a stronger vendor that will clearly survive and maintain strong product development for the future.

Different purchasers resolve these conflicting pressures differently. Some feel considerably safer with a lead or dominant vendor, regardless of its size and potential callousness. Others prefer a somewhat smaller vendor that has more at stake in a specific account relationship.

Correspondingly, vendors face different key tasks in regard to customers' concerns about relative exposure, depending on the vendors' positions in their own industries. Because customers may be skeptical of a nondominant vendor's longer-term capabilities, such a vendor will find it useful to work especially hard to communicate competence. While the dominant vendor in a product-marketplace would also emphasize its capabilities, it might find it especially important to combat customers' skepticism about its concern for and commitment to individual customers.

In considering relative exposure, customers weigh the personal exposure of individuals within the vendor's organization, as well as the overall risk of the vendor organization as a whole. The buyer can feel substantially more comfortable if it knows that the career advancement of one or more individuals within the seller's organization depends importantly on keeping the customer happy. This fact can be extremely useful to the strong vendor that is trying to convince individual accounts of its interest and commitment. While the buyer may feel relatively high exposure in comparison with the vendor organization, it may feel that it faces comparable or lower exposure as compared with the individual sales representative or sales team that serves it. To benefit in this way, the vendor will find it useful to maintain reasonable continuity in the sales representative (or at least in the team) that serves a particular customer account.

Summary

The first step toward responding appropriately to—or, better, toward influencing—the positions of real accounts along the behavior spectrum between lost-for-good and always-a-share is understanding the determinants of behavior. Complex factors combine to determine behavior: the product category and the specific product, the customer's business strategy and the role in that strategy of the product category and specific product, other aspects of the customer's usage system, and characteristics of individuals within the customer organization.

In general, switching costs are key to understanding behavior between lost-for-good and always-a-share. Higher switching costs lead to behavior closer to the lost-for-good model; lower switching costs lead to always-a-share. Investment actions are the relatively more tangible costs of change. Exposure is the risk faced by a customer organization and by individuals within that organization in a relationship with a vendor.

A customer typically invests in its relationship with a vendor through some combination of money, people, lasting assets, and procedures. It obviously spends money. It may hire or train people to deal with the vendor or with specific products; additional investment actions in people occur with learning over time about the vendor and/or its products. Customers also invest in lasting assets, building or modifying plant and equipment, writing or buying or modifying computer software, and so on. Finally, in order to deal with a vendor or its products, they may design or alter procedures—the ways they perform day-to-day business functions.

Although formal procurement frequently emphasizes cash flows, in fact the other categories are particularly important in determining behavior of customers. Buyers are reluctant to change past investments and incur new ones, especially in lasting assets and in procedures. Hence, such investments create inertia against change. When investments increase, they can serve to strengthen bonds between customer and vendor. Past investment actions are especially effective for maintaining customers if the vendor can provide intra-vendor transferability of such investments, thus reducing the costs of intra-vendor changes in comparison with the costs of switching vendors.

The categories of investment actions are not mutually exclusive. A relationship between a customer and a vendor generally involves a combination. Together the categories affect customers' behavior extremely strongly, so strongly that this chapter suggests using them to classify purchase occasions as routine or watershed. Routine purchase decisions, which may or may not involve a change of vendor, require only relatively modest investment actions. Watershed decisions require substantial investment actions, especially in lasting assets and procedures. Watershed decisions may or may not involve a change of vendor.

Exposure is risk: the less tangible costs of change. Both parties to an industrial marketing relationship face exposure; the organizations do, and the individuals within those organizations also do. For organizations, we can use the categories of financial exposure and performance exposure. Both buyer and seller face risks that the money they spend on a relationship will not be well spent—that it will not bring satisfactory results or, even if the results are basically satisfactory, that they could have been obtained at lower cost.

Performance exposure for the buyer is the risk that the vendor's products will not perform as they should or as the buyer expected. Buyers face both short-term performance exposure and the longer-term exposure that the vendor will not continue to offer satisfactory products and service. Performance exposure for the seller involves harm to the specific relationship and more widely to the seller's reputation if a product does not work satisfactorily for the buyer or if the buyer is dissatisfied with the seller's service or other aspects of its performance. The seller also faces the possible financial costs of fixing performance problems encountered by the buyer.

Personal exposure is the risk to the individual within the buying or selling organization. Individual managers in the customer organization may face substantial career harm if they make poor choices. Similarly, individuals working for the seller may face substantial career harm of the vendor loses the account or if it simply sees a decrease in sales from the buyer.

The actual exposure of a party to an industrial marketing relationship may be different from the perception of that party as to its situation. A vendor (or customer) may or may not want to convince the buyer (or seller) of the actual exposure it faces.

Levels of exposure generally change over time, but they do not all change in the same direction. In some cases, increasing experience with a product category and a vendor may reduce a buyer's actual and perceived exposure. In other cases, experience may convince the buyer of how substantial its exposure really is; perceived exposure would increase.

Buyers are concerned with relative as well as absolute levels of exposure. In some cases, they will strongly prefer to deal with a vendor whose exposure in the relationship is comparable to the customer's exposure.

References

Choffray, Jean-Marie, and Lilien, Gary L. "A New Approach to Industrial Market Segmentation." *Sloan Management Review* (Spring 1978):17–29.

———. "Assessing Response to Industrial Marketing Strategy." *Journal of Marketing* (April 1978):20–31.

Cox, Donald F., ed. *Risk Taking and Information Handling in Consumer Behavior.* Boston: Division of Research, Graduate School of Business Administration, Harvard University, 1967.

Howard, W.C. *Selling Industrial Products.* Worcester, Mass.: Norton Company, 1973.

Johnston, Wesley J., and Bonoma, Thomas V. "Reconceptualizing Industrial Buying Behavior: Toward Improved Research Approaches." In Barnett A. Greenburg and Danny N. Bellenger, eds., *Contemporary Marketing Thought*, pp. 247–251. Chicago: American Marketing Association, 1977.

Lehmann, Donald R., and O'Shaughnessy, John. "Difference in Attribute Importance for Different Industrial Products." *Journal of Marketing* (April 1974):36–42.

Moriarty, Rowland, T. *Industrial Buying Behavior: Concepts, Issues, and Applications*. Lexington, Mass.: Lexington Books, 1983.

────── , and Galper, Morton. *Organizational Buying Behavior: A State-of-the-Art Review and Conceptualization*. Cambridge, Mass., Marketing Science Institute Report 78-101. March 1978.

Porter, Michael E. *Competitive Strategy: Techniques for Analyzing Industries and Competitors*. New York: Free Press, 1980.

Robinson, Patrick J.; Faris, Charles; and Wind, Yoram. *Industrial Buying and Creative Marketing*. Boston: Allyn and Bacon, 1967.

Sheth, Jagdish N. "A Model of Industrial Buyer Behavior." *Journal of Marketing* (October 1973):50–56.

Webster, Frederick E., Jr. "Modeling the Industrial Buying Process." *Journal of Marketing Research* 2 (1965):370–376.

Webster, Frederick E., Jr., and Wind, Yoram. "A General Model for Understanding Organizational Buying Behavior." *Journal of Marketing* (April 1972):12–19.

────── . *Organizational Buying Behavior*. Englewood Cliffs, N.J.: Prentice-Hall, 1972.

Williamson, Oliver E. *Markets and Hierarchies: Analysis and Antitrust Implications*. New York: Free Press, 1975.

────── . "Transaction-cost Economics: The Governance of Contractual Relations." *Journal of Law and Economics* 23 (1979):233–261.

4

How and What Does the Long-Term Customer Buy?

W hat is relationship marketing? How does the industrial customer with a long time horizon buy? Which marketing tools are most important in winning and keeping commitments from such accounts? How do the buying processes of customers with long-term orientations differ from those of customers with shorter time orientations? How should vendors' approaches differ depending on the time horizons of their customers? How does relationship marketing differ from transaction marketing? This chapter begins the consideration of these questions; the following chapter continues it.

The Time Dimension of Accounts' Commitments

Time is a centrally important descriptor of commitments by industrial customers. In fact, such commitments have two key time elements: their expected characteristics over time and their actual characteristics over time. The first of these aspects involves the accounts' expectations of what will occur in the future: the time period over which the customer expects to remain committed to the vendor and, consequently, the time horizon the customer uses in its commitment. The second aspect involves the actual nature of the commitment: the way the relationship between the customer and its vendor plays out in reality.

The discussions in earlier chapters emphasized expected behavior over time and the time horizon used by the customer. Chapter 1 described the willingness of buyers of shipping services to use short time horizons and make purchase decisions on the basis of immediately attractive inducements to buy; it contrasted the longer time horizons typical of purchasers of major computer hardware and software, who generally expect lasting relationships with their lead vendors. Similarly, in discussing switching costs, chapter 3 noted the importance of the customer's perceived costs of change; switching costs will deter change only if the buyer is aware of those costs. That chapter also contrasted actual and perceived exposure, citing customers in the computer marketplace of the 1960s as examples of buyers that did not perceive the full extent of their exposure and of the switching costs they faced and that therefore did not realize the extent of their reliance on their vendors.

This chapter continues to emphasize the account's expectations about the nature of its commitment. It speaks of long-term customers as buyers that believe their commitments will last; they adopt long time horizons in making and maintaining those commitments. It similarly considers expectations in classifying customers instead as shorter term; such customers expect to be able to change commitments easily and thus believe they can use short time horizons.

As was true when there was a substantial discrepancy between actual and perceived exposure, vendors may or may not choose to educate their customers or potential customers if buyers' expectations of the strengths and durations of their commitments do not match reality—if, for example, a buyer believes it can choose a vendor on the basis of short-term inducements but if in fact high costs of switching will mean that a longer time horizon would be considerably more realistic. The vendor with strong capabilities to serve customers over the long run would have more incentive to attempt such education. This chapter's discussion begins the detailed consideration of those long-term capabilities.

Even the vendor with strong capabilities for the long run may prefer not to educate customers about the switching costs they actually face and the likely durations of their commitments to a vendor. A key reason is exposure. Commitments marked by high switching costs create strong ties between customer and vendor, and they also create exposure and feelings of exposure for the buyer. A vendor may prefer not to stir such feelings; it may decide not to make a customer aware that it is making a watershed decision rather than a more routine one.

Indeed, the preceding discussions suggest linking several key descriptors of accounts' commitments and behavior to the time dimension, as shown in figure 4–1. Commitments made with long time horizons (such as those for major computer purchases) are typified by the lost-for-good model of accounts' behavior. They generally involve substantial investment actions in any of the categories of investments and especially in lasting assets or in procedures.

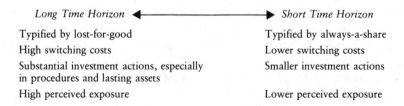

Long Time Horizon ◄─────────────► Short Time Horizon	
Typified by lost-for-good	Typified by always-a-share
High switching costs	Lower switching costs
Substantial investment actions, especially in procedures and lasting assets	Smaller investment actions
High perceived exposure	Lower perceived exposure

Figure 4–1. Time and Accounts' Behavior

They generally also entail high perceived exposure; buyers understand that they are relying heavily on their vendors. By comparison, commitments made with short time horizons (such as those for shipping services) are typified by the always-a-share model of accounts' behavior. They generally involve smaller investment actions and lower perceived exposure for the buyer. The remainder of this chapter will add more descriptors to the scheme displayed in figure 4–1.

Focus of the Account's Commitment

The next basic question about an individual account's commitment is its nature or focus: the question of what the account commits to. There are four major possible foci; an account can commit to a technology, a vendor, a product, or a person. The different foci have strong relations to the time horizon of the buyer and strong implications for appropriate actions by the marketer.

In general, a customer's commitment is characterized by a mix of foci, not by just one of the four possibilities. Thus, a customer's choice can involve more or less focus or emphasis on technology, more or less focus on a specific vendor, and so on. Often, however, the commitment will have one particularly strong focus among the four.

Focus on a Technology

A buyer that focuses primarily on a technology emphasizes the basic (usually technical) way in which products provide desired benefits. For example, a metal-refining company may commit to a particular process for removing sulfur dioxide and sulfuric acid from the stack gases of its facilities. In doing so, the buyer has decided against any available competing processes for removal. It has not, however, decided on a particular vendor to supply equipment and service related to the chosen technology. If more than one supplier is competent to provide equipment and service, the buyer may be able to deal with multiple suppliers. In the extreme case, it may even be able to use equipment from several different vendors together; the use of a common technology may make the equipment sufficiently modular to allow mixing and matching. Similarly, focus on a technology does not necessarily limit the buyer to a particular product or even one product stream over time.

Focus on a Vendor

By contrast, in focusing on a vendor, the buyer ties itself to a specific selling firm. A manufacturer may decide to buy all of its computer-numerically-controlled machining centers from Cross & Trecker. The buyer does not necessarily tie itself exclusively to a specific product or even product line within the vendor's offerings. It may be willing or even anxious to change the specific technology it uses if the vendor develops improved products based on newer technologies.

Similarly a computer buyer might focus its commitment on a particular vendor. In the computer marketplace, buyers generally expect continuing streams of new product offerings from vendors. In committing to a vendor, the customer is committing to such a stream of products and, in fact, is relying on the vendor to offer products that meet the customer's needs over time.

Why would a buyer focus most strongly on the vendor rather than on the technology or on the product itself? Sometimes the full benefits of dealing with the supplier reach far beyond the specific product or particular technology. For example, the buyer's selection may emphasize the seller's combination of product, service, applications engineering, and other capabilities. The buying organization may decide that over time it and the selling organization will learn a great deal about one another—that the seller will learn how to serve the buyer and the buyer will learn how to obtain value from the seller's various offerings and representatives. That learning may provide the basis for a continuing relationship that is satisfactory—perhaps increasingly satisfactory—to both parties. The seller's increasing knowledge of the buyer's organization and usage system may allow the seller to suggest increasingly useful applications of its products and may even lead to new product developments that fit the buyer's needs. In such a situation, the customer is buying a relationship with a total selling organization; its commitment is likely to focus strongly on the vendor.

In other situations, strong focus on the vendor arises because the buyer feels unable to commit to a particular technology. In a product-marketplace that is changing relatively rapidly in technology, customers may feel unable to predict future technological directions. The customers' strategies and usage systems may require that they remain relatively up-to-date technologically as the product-marketplace develops. The customer may therefore have to rely on a vendor to provide a continuing stream of technology over time: to select the most promising potential technologies to explore, to develop good product offerings based on the best technologies, to make those products available on a timely basis, and to provide customers with conversion paths to the new products. In essence, the customer is buying a continuing stream of technology, embodied in particular products, and is relying on the vendor to provide that stream.

Why would such a buyer commit strongly to a vendor rather than simply plan to select attractive products, from whatever vendor, as they are offered? In general, the customer expects higher switching costs if it changes vendors. In other words, it expects that its past investment actions will transfer more readily from one to another of a particular vendor's offerings than they will from a product of one vendor to that of another. The relevant investment actions may, for example, involve learning by people in the customer organization about how to work effectively with the vendor's representatives and products. Or the most relevant investments may involve lasting assets or procedures.

In essence, in such a situation the buyer is relying on the chosen vendor to provide a continuing stream of products and also to provide relatively easy transitions from one to another product in the stream. We can think of the customer as stepping onto the bottom step of an escalator of usage. The customer's usage will change as it adopts new specific products and uses the products in new and likely more important ways. The buyer is relying on the vendor to continue to build the escalator over time—to continue to provide a smooth set of steps to newer and more advanced product offerings. If the vendor does not, the buyer will face a considerably more painful transition to another vendor—a break in the escalator's stairs with no easy place to step next.

Focus on a Product

In other purchase situations, the buyer focuses strongly on the particular product. Consider the buyer of a package of software for a personal computer—perhaps a spreadsheet package for a particular manager to perform financial calculations. In such a purchase, most buyers focus primarily on the attributes of the individual packages that are available: on their power and versatility, on how easy or difficult they appear to be to learn, on the documentation provided with them, and so on. In general, most such buyers do not focus on the vendor of the package. Although they are likely (though not certain) to know the name of the selling firm, buyers do not consider themselves strongly linked to that seller for the future. Although it requires some effort to learn a new software package, that effort is not excessively burdensome and, importantly, the trouble of learning how to use a new package from a different supplier is usually not much greater than is the difficulty of changing from one to another product of the same vendor. Change is not so painful as to produce focus on the vendor. The buyer can select on the basis of features of individual products.

Product-focused commitments can sometimes also involve larger and more important purchases, or they can involve purchases of small items in large quantity. For example, a firm may commit to use IBM Selectric typewriters for all of its office workers, rejecting other typewriter models from IBM or from other vendors. If the firm's primary emphasis in buying is on the particular features of that typewriter, we would categorize the decision as strongly product focused. (If, on the other hand, the decision also rested heavily on the size and capabilities of the vendor's service force, it would also involve significant focus on the vendor organization.)

An electric utility may make a product-focused commitment when it selects a large, new boiler for one of its plants. It may examine the offerings of a variety of vendors and then select the product best suited to handle the mix of fuels and the level of demand expected at the particular site. The next time it needs to buy a boiler, probably for another site, the utility may also choose on the basis of specific product features, choosing relatively independently of what it has done on earlier decisions.

A specific commitment by a customer will generally involve a mix of foci. A buyer that has committed to a particular technology for removing the sulfur and sulfur dioxide from its stack gases will likely also focus on the specific features and capabilities of the products embodying that technology. Similarly, even a customer that is strongly focused on a particular vendor to supply its needs for computer hardware and key software will consider specific product features in making individual purchases, in choosing among the vendor's various individual offerings. Despite involving some focus on the product, however, neither of these decisions would be primarily product focused.

Focus on a Person

Finally, an account's commitment may focus primarily on a person, a particular representative of the vendor's organization. For example, a firm may buy office furniture from a seller because the individual salesperson provides help with office design. A buyer may choose a supplier of specialty chemicals because the seller's technical service representative is especially talented and helpful. A customer may select a vendor for an industrial supply because the vendor's salesperson is effective in teaching new employees of the customer how to use the products.

Although industrial buyers may base some purchase decisions on personal likes and dislikes of vendor representatives, common beliefs appear to overemphasize the importance of personal friendship and to underemphasize the current or future business benefits that the personal relationship may be expected to provide. In other words, the buyer may be relying on personal representatives of the seller to provide important business value, and the personal relationship may be the best available evidence that the representative is interested and committed enough to provide that value.

The marketplace for chemical additives for electroplating provides an illustration of commitments that focus on a person because that person is critical in providing business value to the customer. In electroplating, electrical current is used to transfer a layer of metal onto parts, usually made of plastic or metal. Such plating is used for a wide variety of parts, incuding handlebars for bicycles, knobs for appliances, and bumpers for automobiles.

The electroplating process consists of a series of steps. First, parts are chemically cleaned in tubs (or baths) containing solutions of special cleaners.

Another bath removes the surface film left by the cleaning step. Then the parts are placed in the plating bath itself. Generally all but the smallest parts are attached individually to the cathode (negative electric pole) in the plating bath; bars of metal (such as chromium, nickel, or zinc) are attached to the anode (positive pole). When the electrical current is turned on, a thin layer of the plating metal is transferred from the anode to the parts. After plating, the parts are removed from the bath and dried, often in a spin dryer.

The entire plating operation is difficult; it is something of an art rather than a science, and it is subject to regular and difficult-to-diagnose malfunctions. Finished parts may not have the smooth, level appearance that is desired. Plating may be obviously incomplete. Or later the plated parts may begin to flake or peel. Such problems can be caused by improper cleaning, irregularities in the plating current, or chemical imbalance in the plating bath. Diagnosing the cause of a particular problem can be difficult.

A number of vendors supply materials used in plating. The most obvious (and least complex) supplies are the metals and metal salts used for the actual plating. More specialized are the cleaning chemicals used in the first step in the process and also other chemicals, called proprietary additives, that are used in the plating bath itself. The additives provide desirable properties, such as evenness of the plating layer and smoothness of the finish. (Before such additives were developed, platers used a far more costly process of mechanical buffing to provide a satisfactory finish.)

The suppliers of the more specialized supplies, such as the proprietary additives, provide customers with considerable technical support, including routine monitoring of the customers' plating operations, intended to avoid problems, and troubleshooting help when problems occur. The vendor's service representative will provide regular chemical analyses of the customer's plating bath, collecting a sample of the bath solution (perhaps weekly), having it analyzed in the vendor's lab, returning the results, and helping correct any imbalances indicated by the analysis. The individual technical representative of the vendor is also a first line of defense in solving problems on the customer's line. Those representatives can, if necessary, call on other specialists from the vendor's organization to help diagnose especially difficult problems, but the field representatives usually solve many of the problems themselves. Customers strongly value help in problem solving and want help as quickly as possible when their plating lines malfunction.

Not surprisingly, there appears to be considerable focus on a person, the technical representative of the vendor, in the commitments of customers for proprietary additives for electroplating. The representative is centrally important in making the vendor's offerings work well and work consistently in a specific customer's environment, and the customers value the contributions of those representatives. The technical representatives and the managers of the customers' plating lines are likely to have personal relationships, but it would appear unlikely (and foolish) for a buyer to choose on the basis of friendship rather than because of the ability and willingness of the vendor's representative to provide solutions to important problems.

Focus on the person also occurs in situations with simpler products and considerably less need for technical problem-solving. In fact, the example of additives for electroplating is a bit extreme though not totally unrepresentative. Focus on a person appears appreciably more common in product-marketplaces with simpler, less differentiated products. In such situations, sellers may compete on price, but they may instead compete on the augmentation of their products: on their abilities to provide delivery when desired, to provide current information on order status, to trace any questions about billing, and so on. Frequently, it is the personal representative of the vendor who provides such service to the customer, and the buyer may focus on that personal representative in making its choice. In essence, in such cases the personal representative is the main differentiator among vendors, customizing the vendor's offerings to the buyer's needs.

Similarly, buyers may focus on the person when they are purchasing products that are relatively unimportant to them. Even if a vendor offers products that differ from those of other vendors in features and perhaps also in price, the buyers may not consider it worth while to explore the detailed differences. Instead, they may choose for more superficial reasons, including the personal relationship of individual buyers with the vendor's representative.

Focus and Time Horizon

Customers' commitments made with long time horizons frequently have different foci than do commitments made with shorter horizons. As figure 4–2 shows, long time horizons generally correspond to focus on a technology or on a vendor. Shorter time horizons generally correspond to focus on a product or on a person.

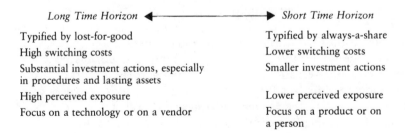

Long Time Horizon ◄——————————————►	*Short Time Horizon*
Typified by lost-for-good	Typified by always-a-share
High switching costs	Lower switching costs
Substantial investment actions, especially in procedures and lasting assets	Smaller investment actions
High perceived exposure	Lower perceived exposure
Focus on a technology or on a vendor	Focus on a product or on a person

Figure 4–2. Time and Accounts' Behavior

Commitments with Short Time Horizons

The essence of the short-term commitment is that the customer is not locked into its choice. The buyer of shipping services can relatively easily change some or all of its patronage to a new supplier. It can experiment with new vendors. It can share its patronage among several suppliers. It can punish one supplier by awarding it a smaller share of that patronage and reward another with a larger share. Similarly, a typical purchaser of carbon steel can rather easily share its business among multiple suppliers and can shift the shares of those suppliers according to their past records or on the basis of some other criterion.

Because the short-term customer is not locked in, it can (and generally will) base its choices of supplier on immediate attractiveness. Frequently such a buyer will emphasize specific product attributes. Suppose a customer buys small copier machines for use in dispersed locations within a large office building. Suppose that the buyer faces low switching costs; its usage system is highly modular, and it does not have substantial reasons to buy its machines from a single seller. In this case, each choice can emphasize the particular features of a specific machine for a particular location in the building. In one instance, the customer might select a machine that can copy on both sides of a piece of paper because the population of users near the location for that machine would value such a feature. In another case, the users might not require any special features, and the customer might base its decision primarily on price. In a third case, the user population might need a machine as quickly as possible, and the customer might base its choice on the speed of delivery. In all of these decisions, the customer has focused primarily on the product—either on specific physical product features or on other aspects of the product such as price or availability.

Other short-term decisions focus primarily on the person. Indeed strong focus on a person is most typical of especially short-term decisions—choices that are sufficiently unimportant that they can be based on the personal representative of the seller. Some purchasers of office supplies or of bulk paper products would display such a focus. The products themselves are essentially commodities, and to many buying organizations they are not very important. The inducements needed to get the customer to choose one vendor or another are often not substantial. The buyer may select on the basis of a sales representative, perhaps because that representative provides some special service or perhaps simply because the representative is courteous and adequately competent and reminds the buyer to buy.

Not all examples of focus on a product or on a person occur in short-term, low-risk purchases; the illustration concerning proprietary additives for plating provides a more important, higher-risk example of focus on a person. Nevertheless, focus on a product or on a person is typical of a shorter-term commitment, the always-a-share model, and low-risk situations and low switching costs.

A customer commitment made with a short time horizon can in fact last for an extended period. Although the customer did not originally expect to remain with a particular vendor, it may in fact stay committed. But even if such a commitment does last, it is better viewed as a series of short-term commitments rather than as one long-term one. Low switching costs mean that the customer could have changed vendors at any purhase occasion. It has remained with the established vendor because that seller offered immediately attractive inducements to do so. Each individual purchase decision is extremely likely to focus on the product or on a person.

Marketers serving customers with a short-term orientation will benefit from understanding the foci characteristic of that orientation and from designing their marketing approaches accordingly. Such customers will generally focus on a product or a person; they will emphasize immediate inducements to buy, such as product features, specific prices, or personal attention from the vendor's representatives. Hence, the key tasks for the marketer are to have immediately attractive offerings and then to let the customers know about the attractions.

Such a vendor should usually view its product policy as a sequence of individual offerings that are not closely related to one another in the customer's eyes, regardless of whether they are closely related in the vendor's plant or in technology. Each individual product will succeed or fail in the marketplace on the basis of its own attractiveness, not because it is part of a successful series or because of the name of the vendor offering it.

In such situations, the marketer's communications program would sensibly emphasize product features. It would not make much sense for the seller to spend time and money on advertising its brand name or corporate image; the customer would not much care. The customer is buying a product, not a company.

Similarly, if the customer is likely to focus on the person, the marketer would want to emphasize its sales force and, in particular, the abilities of its representatives to provide the buyers with whatever immediate service or other inducements might influence their choices. Corporate advertising and other vendor-oriented marketing tools would not seem useful.

It does not make sense for the marketer serving short-term customers to expect its customer relationships to last. It can be dangerous to choose marketing strategies that will prove sensible only if those relationships do in fact last. For example, the vendor should not invest in such customers for the long term, spending resources that will be recouped only if the customer remains committed for an extended period; chapter 1's example about shipping services provides an illustration.

Commitments with Long Time Horizons

The essence of the long-term, lost-for-good-type commitment is the high cost of change. Because the buyer cannot change easily, it is dependent on its choice; it faces considerable exposure to a bad one. Consequently, the customer will want to choose a vendor that will continue to serve it well for the future or else will want to select a technology that will last for a long time. Long-term commitments generally focus on a vendor or on a technology. The customer that is aware of its high dependence on the vendor or technology will view its choice as a serious one, will devote considerable care to choosing, and will work hard to determine the likely long-term attractiveness of the alternatives it faces.

Thus, in selecting a vendor in a long-term commitment, the buyer will try to assess the seller's potential to prove satisfactory for the future. It is likely to consider the vendor's financial prospects, trying to find a seller with a sound financial foundation. It is likely to consider the vendor's ability to develop and market a continuing stream of good products for the future. To do so, it will consider the seller's history of product development. It may examine specifics of the vendor's research and development organization and may want to visit the seller's manufacturing facilities.

Customers making long-term commitments with a strong focus on the vendor frequently describe themselves as buying a company rather than a product, and indeed they are. The customer is stepping onto an escalator that will be built and maintained by the vendor. The buyer is dependent on the seller to build that escalator well, choosing appropriate directions and providing an appropriate pace of change.

Customers find it difficult to judge the vendor's abilities to provide needed development and support for the future, but customers are also aware that they are depending on those abilities. They therefore appear to work hard to understand the vendor's capabilities and to try to assess the vendor's commitment and intentions for the future. For example, explaining their choices in important long-term commitments, buyers frequently included descriptions of their vendors' marketing strategies. The buyers had tried to determine the vendors' strategies and to decide whether those strategies were consistent with the buyer's needs—whether the vendor was likely to continue to serve their needs, under its chosen strategy, for the future.

Chapter 3 distinguished between routine decisions, which involve relatively low required investments, and watershed decisions, which require substantial investments. It noted that a watershed decision might involve a change of vendor but that it need not. Even if they do not entail a change of vendor, watershed decisions are generally made with long time horizons, and, perhaps surprisingly at first, they generally involve substantial focus on the vendor (or technology). For example, suppose that a customer is choosing one or another of a vendor's families of technical equipment (such as computers). Suppose that the vendor provides compatibility among the members of a single family but that different families are not compatible with one another. (In other words, the buyer would have to make substantial investments in order to switch from one family to another; the investments required to change between members of the same family would be much more modest.) A change from one family to another, even from the same vendor, is then a watershed decision.

Interviews with buyers making such decisions, without changing vendor, revealed concern with issues similar to those emphasized on other vendor-focused choices. Buyers talked about long-term capabilities. They frequently explained their perceptions of the role of the particular product family to the vendor's strategy and said why that strategic role was a signal that the vendor would continue to serve the customer well. In such situations we might think of the vendor as offering two or more different escalators of products and usage. In selecting one, the customer must assess the likely future direction, pace, and appropriateness of each of the escalators.

Focus on Technology in Long-Term Commitments

Some commitments made with long time horizons focus more strongly on the basic technology than on the vendor offering that technology. In fact, the buyer can find considerable comfort in being able to commit to a technology rather than to a vendor. The reason concerns exposure.

Buyers frequently (and reasonably) feel uncomfortable and exposed if they are strongly dependent on a single vendor for an important product category. Suppose instead that a customer is able to commit to a technology and that several vendors offer products using that technology. The buyer is less dependent on a single seller. If one vendor fails to offer adequately modern products, the customer can use another vendor without changing basic technology. Or if one vendor's representatives do not continue to offer satisfactory service or other support, the buyer can look for better service or support elsewhere without having to undergo a major change in technology.

Further, the buyer has access to the new product developments of several sellers. Thus, if it is possible to do so, the account can find it very attractive to commit to a technology supported by more than one vendor. In fact, the account may even be able to foster real competition for its patronage among the vendors of the common technology by threatening to switch some of its patronage if a particular vendor does not offer attractive price terms or other immediate inducements.

In the terms of the behavior models, the account has made a lost-for-good-type commitment to the basic technology and, in the process, to the group of marketing firms offering products based on that technology. Within that group of vendors, however, the buyer can appear more like an always-a-share customer. It can switch parts of its patronage and can threaten and cajole in ways typical of always-a-share rather than lost-for-good. The buyer can feel less at the mercy of any vendor and more powerful in its relations with vendors.

The office-automation market provides an example in which, in the early 1980s, customers seemed strongly opposed to committing to single suppliers and instead wanted to commit to technologies that would last. The preceding chapter described buyers' concerns in that marketplace. Changes in office-automation systems would be very difficult for organizations, requiring large changes in basic procedures that would make the substantial and very hard computer conversions of the past seem relatively small. Customers were extremely concerned not to make mistakes and therefore undergo additional unnecessary changes in their systems in the future. They wanted to make commitments that would last.

The preceding chapter also briefly described LANs, the communication links that would eventually hook up the different components of some office-automation and other systems. The LANs would essentially be the glue that would hold some such systems together. Potential customers were especially concerned not to make mistakes in selecting such basic parts of their systems.

In the early 1980s, the marketplace for LANs was developing slowly. There were, to be sure, many vendors—over fifty of them in 1983, offering a variety of different designs based on a variety of different (and frequently incompatible) technologies. Discussions of the differences among the LANs centered on technical issues such as design of the physical interface (how, physically, devices would connect with the network) and choice of network protocol (the rule for determining how devices were allotted turns in using the main network pathways). Potential customers were generally not comfortable with these technical discussions. They were also, for the most part, not buying.

In part, market development was slow because buyers were not clear about the role for LANs; they did not understand the situations in which LANs would be most useful and the other situations in which an alternative (such as communication through a standard PBX) would be preferable. In addition, the business-press coverage of the LAN market suggested that another factor slowing market growth was the reluctance of the buyer to commit to a single vendor on so important a purchase.

Xerox was one of the firms active in the LAN market. A Xerox manager responsible for LANs was quoted in the business press about the importance of customer pressure for adoption of a common technology. He explained that Xerox's original strategy had been to keep its LAN design proprietary.

Individual users and a formal customers' group had, however, been insisting that the manufacturers move toward standardization in technology. The users reportedly said that they had been burned by incompatibility in the data-processing market in the past and that they did not intend to be burned similarly in office-automation equipment and LANs. Xerox had changed its strategy and was urging other vendors to adopt its technology, making it available to them for a token $1,000 fee.

Thus, customers can find it very attractive to be able to focus their commitments on a technology rather than on a vendor. It is not always possible, however, for them to do so. It may be impossible for the vendors and customers to identify the best (or close to the best) technology for the future, even if they are so motivated. Commitment to a single technology can stifle useful innovation. And marketers often prefer to compete using products that are clearly differentiated from competitors' offerings. The vendor that commits to a common technology thereby gives up a potentially important basis for competition and differentiation.

In many other situations, the customer obtains considerable value from the ways that the seller supplements or augments the basic products and technology: from service, applications engineering, pricing terms, delivery arrangements, modifications of the product or technology to fit the account's particular needs, and so on. Often an established vendor will learn how to provide such supplements and augmentations especially well; it will learn, in general, how to work with the customer organization effectively to bring value to both parties. In such a situation, the customer will almost certainly have considerable vendor focus in its commitments; to focus on the technology would be to focus on only part of what brings substantial value to the buyer. The more relatively important to the customer is what the vendor adds to the basic technology, the more focus on the vendor we would expect to find in the account's commitment.

Which Is the Longest-Term Focus?

In general, personal focus is characteristic of the most short-term orientations, and product focus appears to be next in order of time. It is not clear, however, whether technology focus corresponds to a longer time horizon than does focus on the vendor or whether the time order is the reverse. In fact, the relative time ordering of focus on a technology and focus on a vendor appears to vary in different situations.

The difference appears to depend in part on the technological pace of the product-marketplace. It also depends on switching costs and on what we might call switching needs: the needs of customers to be up-to-date technically.

Technological Pace

Effective technological pace depends on the rate of change of the underlying technology or technologies in the market and on the abilities of product developers to translate those underlying changes into new products. Pace also involves the vendors' abilities to deliver new products to market, to service them, and to provide other needed functions.

In some cases, a vendor's willingness to change is key. For example, when it makes a major technological change, a vendor must frequently force at least some trauma and change on its existing customers—its installed base. New products that are incompatible with older ones are especially likely to cause trauma; even relatively compatible new products generally require some adjustments and investments from users. Vendors may be unwilling to cause such problems.

One obvious reason is that customers are frequently vulnerable to approaches by the vendor's competitors at times when the customer accounts are evaluating new product offerings. The benefits of the new products and technologies may prompt the evaluation. Discussions with purchasers indicate, however, that once it has begun an evaluation process, the account will often consider both the negative effects of a change and also possible alternative choices. If changing from one to another of the current vendor's offerings requires substantial adjustment, the customer is likely to feel it might as well also consider the relative benefits and costs of undergoing the adjustment to the products of a different vendor. Thus, times of major procurement evaluations are frequently times of high vulnerability of accounts' commitments.

There is another, more subtle reason for vendors' concerns with the effects of new products on their installed bases. Customers can feel compelled to replace their older products, perhaps because of incompatibility or because they believe the vendor will support newer offerings better than older ones. Customers can therefore feel compelled to face difficult changeovers and financially traumatic write-offs, or, at least, they can feel forced to accept somewhat less burdensome switching costs. If a new introduction requires any substantial adjustments by users, the vendor championing such an advance may be considered to be causing trauma for its customers. Accounts may become worried about their exposure to the actions of such a vendor and may try to reduce their exposure and commitment to that single vendor.

Other factors may also constrain the feasible technical pace of a product-marketplace. For example, a vendor may have to slow the pace because customers cannot obtain financing for worthwhile but expensive new products. Or a vendor may be constrained by the technological rates of other products and services that are related in the customers' usage systems to its own.

Other factors in a product-marketplace encourage relatively rapid technological pace. One factor is the vendor's desire to give users benefits provided by good products: better performance, lower cost, or both. In some cases, changes in customers' needs and usage systems can render older products obsolete so that product developments are not just desirable but actually required.

Vendors may use technological change to try to avoid direct competition with other vendors. The familiar product-life-cycle concept describes tendencies of product-marketplaces to exhibit increasing head-to-head competition and decreasing profitability as vendors offer more and more similar products. Vendors may try to avoid or discourage this type of competition by making frequent technological changes.

Vendors may also want to use technological change to try to build customers' confidence. In technological marketplaces, accounts want their vendors to be credible technically. The account committing strongly to a vendor is essentially betting on the technical capabilities of that vendor. A vendor that does not demonstrate ongoing technical development may not continue to warrant such confidence in the eyes of important customers.

The technological pace of competitors will also influence the vendor. Competitive moves or anticipation of such moves can force a vendor to act. Further, competitors' moves help determine the extent to which customers feel they have credible alternate vendors. Competitors' actions also help determine the real extent of switching costs faced by customers; for example, when a competitor offers products to which the vendor's customers can change relatively easily (in other words, offers considerable intervendor transferability of past investment actions), customers will accept more rapid pace than they would if switching costs were higher.

Thus, a variety of forces help determine the technological pace of a product-marketplace. That pace is one key determinant of the relative time ordering of focus on a vendor and focus on a technology.

Switching Needs

Another major determinant of the ordering of the two longer-term foci is the customer's level of switching needs—in other words, how important it is to the customer to be and remain up-to-date technically. If a product category is important to a customer's basic business strategy and, especially, if the customer uses that category in ways that provide competitive advantage in its own industry, the account is likely to feel strong pressure to remain up-to-date technically. On the other hand, if the product category is useful to the customer but not a major source of competitive advantage, the account will often feel substantially lower needs to switch as technology changes. It may update its products from time to time but it need not try to keep up with every new advance.

In the early 1980s, the marketplaces for mainframe computers and for office-automation work stations appeared to display significant differences in switching needs of buyers. More and more firms were using computers in increasingly important strategic ways. Increasingly buyers either were using computers and related technology to obtain important competitive advantage or were hearing about other firms that were already doing so. Buyers felt the need to remain up-to-date technically in computers.

By contrast, buyers at that time felt lower switching needs in office automation. Certainly managers believed that office automation was coming rapidly and that it would provide important efficiencies to their organizations. They generally believed that their firms would have to adopt office automation and to do so reasonably soon. At the same time, however, most managers in most industries did not feel that they would have to stay absolutely current with technical advances in office automation. The advances might be useful but for the most part would not be strategically important to buyers.

Especially if they face substantial switching costs, customers with lower switching needs can refuse to change; they can elect to remain with a less than fully up-to-date technology rather than incur large switching costs. They can afford to insist strongly that their vendors provide graceful product paths over time.

By contrast, the customer with higher switching needs will feel strong pressure to switch as technology advances, even if the change is painful. Customers for computers were active in pressing vendors to provide relatively smooth transitions from one product to another. Even so, most computer buyers expected conversions to be difficult. In addition, they expected conversions to be necessary. They might push vendors to reduce the pain of change, but they expected substantial pain to remain, and they felt they could not sensibly avoid problems by refusing to change.

Focus on a Technology or Focus on a Vendor

Technological pace, switching costs, and switching needs combine to determine a customer's frequency of change. They also combine to determine whether focus on a technology corresponds to a longer time horizon than does focus on a vendor, or vice-versa.

Customers may find substantial comfort and benefit in being able to focus on a technology rather than on a specific vendor. They may not be able to do so, however. In a product-marketplace with rapid technological pace, in which customers find it important to be relatively up-to-date, they may not be able to focus on any particular technology. Any specific technological choice would soon be outmoded, and the customer could not afford to live with outmoded technology. Instead customers would focus on a particular vendor that they believed would provide sound products in a stream of technology over time. They would be relying on the vendor to identify suitable technologies and to develop products based on those technologies. In such cases, technology flows from the choice of vendor. Focus on the vendor corresponds to the longest-time-horizon commitments. The marketplace for major computer purchases provides an example of strong vendor focus by customers with especially long time horizons.

By contrast, in other situations even if there is considerable technological pace in a product-marketplace, the switching costs and switching needs may make buyers less anxious and willing to remain up-to-date technically. Switching costs may be so high that they outweigh any incremental benefits from moving to newer technologies. In such cases, customers would try to commit to a technology that they expected to work well (if not perfectly) for the long term. They would generally be more confident if several vendors used the chosen technology so that customers would be less exposed to the actions of any single vendor. In such cases, a technology focus would imply a longer time horizon than would focus on a single vendor. The market for office-automation equipment in the early 1980s provides an illustration.

We can sharpen the contrast between the market for computers and the market for office automation by comparing customers' apparent attitudes toward the same vendor, IBM, in the two. Despite the presence of the same strong vendor in each market and the substantial technical and usage links between the two types of products, customers with especially long time horizons differed in the focus of their commitments in the two markets.

In computers, many advanced customers had made strong lost-for-good-type commitments to IBM as their lead vendor for computer hardware and systems software. Those commitments focused strongly on the vendor. Buyers described themselves as buying a company with a strategy. They discussed IBM's technical and market capabilities when they explained their purchase decisions. Customer interviews uncovered especially strong vendor focus in accounts using computers in strategically important ways, where the buyers felt it critical to remain up-to-date technically. In that marketplace, strong vendor focus was typical of especially long commitments made with long time horizons.

By contrast, in the market for office automation and LANs, some of the same customers were unwilling to commit as strongly to a vendor, even the same vendor, IBM. Switching needs were lower, and potential switching costs appeared higher. Buyers did not want to be dependent on any single supplier; they preferred more focus on a technology, which would be accessible to and supported by more than a single vendor. In LANs, for example, large corporate potential users formed the Network Users Association in 1981 to push vendors to adopt standards and reduce the number of incompatible designs in the market. Similarly industry sources reported that a research board of IBM's key customers was insisting that the vendor disclose considerably more about its technological choices than IBM might have wanted to make public. The customers' objective seemed to be to allow and encourage other vendors to offer compatible products based on the same technology. Thus, in this marketplace, buyers with especially long time horizons wanted to focus on the technology rather than on a specific vendor.

Implications for the Marketer

Customers' commitments made with especially long time horizons will thus generally focus either on the vendor or on technology, with the choice between the two depending on the specifics of a particular situation. In either case, marketers would sensibly design their marketing programs to respond to the foci of their customers' commitments and perhaps even to influence those foci.

Implications of Focus on the Vendor

A vendor serving customers that display strong vendor focus in their commitments would want to emphasize the capabilities of the total vendor organization, especially its long-term capabilities to serve customers well. Such vendors would emphasize their technical and research and development capabilities. They would also emphasize their abilities to translate technology into an ongoing stream of good products, to bring those products to market in a timely manner, and to give their existing customer bases relatively easy access to those products. In other words, vendors that are responding to or encouraging strong vendor focus would want to give customers confidence in the soundness of their escalators. They would want to convince the customer that they would choose a sound direction for the escalator and would continue to provide a sufficiently smooth series of stair steps, at an adequate pace, over time.

Corporate advertising will often be sensible for such a vendor because the customer is buying a company rather than a particular product or person. Such a vendor may also find it effective to share with customers and potential customers some of its basic business strategy and its individual product-line strategies. Buyers with strong focus on a vendor tend to be very interested in those strategies and to try to select suppliers whose strategies are consistent with the buyers' needs. Insofar as knowledge about the vendors' true strategies would not create undue competitive harm, vendors might publicize aspects of their strategies, either through discussions between customers and vendors' salespeople or other managers or else through more widespread public relations. The computer marketplace shows evidence of some use of this marketing tool.

In addressing customers displaying strong focus on the vendor, suppliers would also want to emphasize their active concern for the account. Strong vendor focus also generally involves strong dependence on the vendor, and that dependence creates exposure and feelings of exposure for the customer. Chapter 3's discussion of exposure noted the tension between the customer's desire for strong vendor capabilities and the customer's desire for strong vendor concern. Sound marketing requires that the seller be concerned with and communicate both.

Implications of Focus on Technology

If its customers are more likely to focus on technology rather than on the vendor, a marketing organization faces a different set of communication tasks. Its key jobs are to convince customers and potential customers of the soundness of the chosen technology and of its own firm commitment to that technology. To realize actual sales, the vendor must also convince buyers to select its own specific products based on that technology.

One way to convince customers that a technology is sound is to discuss it in detail. Especially if buyers do not feel highly knowledgeable technically, it may be more effective instead to show them that a substantial number of credible vendors have committed to that technology. Adoption of a formal standard based on a particular technology can sometimes be useful for this purpose. The marketplace for LANs in the early 1980s provides an illustration.

Previous discussions noted the technical proliferation and confusion typical of that product-marketplace at that time. They also noted the strong feelings of exposure of customers and potential customers for office automation and for the LANs that would be the backbones of some office automation systems. Many potential customers in the LAN product-marketplace wanted to focus on a technology rather than on a vendor.

Xerox was an active vendor in the general market for office equipment and wanted to be active in the market for LANs. After initially trying to keep its LAN technology proprietary, the firm became an open advocate of standards, apparently responding to strong customer pressures for more openness and more focus on the technology rather than the vendor.

During the 1970s, Xerox's Palo Alto research group developed Ethernet, a technology for LANs. At first Xerox treated the Ethernet design as proprietary. The approach was likely comfortable for the vendor, which traditionally had worked hard to protect the xerography patents backing its basic office products. By the early 1980s, however, Xerox reversed its position. It licensed the Ethernet technology for only $1,000 to anyone who wanted it, and it was pressing for the adoption of the Ethernet design by standards-setting bodies, with some success. Moreover, Xerox had convinced other vendors to join the Ethernet effort. In 1980, Xerox, Intel (the semiconductor manufacturer), and DEC (the computer company) joined forces behind the Ethernet design. Other vendors also signed up.

Xerox began to publicize Ethernet as a many-vendor choice. One advertisement announced "Thirty companies plug Ethernet" and went on to list DEC, Intel, and Xerox on an equal basis (in alphabetical order), with twenty-seven other adopters. Among the twenty-seven were Interlan and Ungermann Bass, two companies that were also manufacturing LANs.

As this example illustrates, marketers addressing customers that focus or want to focus strongly on technology must in a sense make themselves look a bit more like other vendors. The customers want to believe that they will have a choice of vendors, with each vendor strongly committed to the common technology. They do not want their vendors too differentiated technically (or at least they do not want their vendors technically incompatible).

Such desires on the parts of buyers create some problems for the vendor that wants to address the customers' focus but also wants to sell products. Within the group supporting a particular technology, vendors may compete for sales on the basis of particular product attributes, using the types of approaches appropriate for commitments that focus on the product. There can be strong product-oriented competition within that group of vendors; indeed the likelihood of such competition is generally a key reason that the customer wanted to commit to a technology rather than a vendor in the first place.

In the example of Xerox and LANs, the success of Xerox's strategy in terms of its own profitability was by no means clear in the early 1980s. Even if the Ethernet standard were widely adopted, Xerox's own success would depend on its ability to develop and market attractive individual pieces to fit into an office-automation system based on Ethernet. Xerox was stressing competition among vendors as a benefit for customers; one Xerox manager described the firm's strategy as giving customers access to "Route 128" (Boston's technology highway) rather than making them rely on the introductions of a single vendor. Xerox did not yet have an array of products that appeared highly competitive in such a world.

This example highlights the tension faced by a vendor that is motivated by customers' focus on technology to want to appear like other vendors but is also motivated to appear different enough to make a profit. Chapter 6 will return to discuss this difficult tension. In essence, it will suggest that vendors try to provide enough modularity to satisfy customers' focus on technology but that the sellers also offer enough systems benefits to encourage purchases from that particular vendor. This objective often is not easy to achieve. Serving technology-focused customers profitably can be difficult precisely because of one of the key attractions to the customer of such a focus: the fact that it provides access to the products of more than one vendor.

Importance, Investment Actions, and Focus

Yet another basic descriptor of an account's commitment is its importance: how significant it is to the buyer. Commitments can be important to organizations and to specific individuals within those organizations. For the organizations, products and commitments may have day-to-day importance for operations. Some commitments may also be especially important to the customer's basic business strategy—the way it has chosen to compete in its own industry.

A customer's commitments can have strategic importance to the organization, as when a chemical company commits to a particular process technology intended to allow the firm to compete on the basis of lowest cost in its industry. A commitment may have operational importance to the organization, as when a bicycle manufacturer buys proprietary chemical additives for its electroplating baths and those chemicals are central in making the plating operation run smoothly. The organization's commitments can also have personal importance, as when a specific manager in a customer organization successfully pushes the firm to buy a particular type of communications service and that manager's career advancement will be affected by the consequences of the choice. In general, a customer's commitment will be characterized by a combination of these types of importance. It will carry some level of operational importance, some amount of strategic importance, and some personal importance for individuals within the buying firm.

The focus of a commitment by a customer will generally be related to that commitment's importance. More important commitments generally focus strongly on the vendor or on technology; less important commitments are more likely to focus on a product or on the personal representative of the vendor. Indeed the importance of the commitment to the customer is central in determining the nature or focus of that commitment.

Importance and focus are also related to the investment actions associated with that commitment. If a commitment requires substantial investment actions, especially investments in lasting assets or in procedures, then the customer will likely view the commitment as important. Smaller required investment actions allow the customer to assign less importance to its choice.

To probe in more depth the nature of the commitment made by an industrial customer, we can also relate the descriptors of focus and investment actions. In other words, we can ask whether each investment action taken by the customer relates to the basic technology, to a particular vendor, to a specific product, or to a personal representative of the vendor.

For example, consider investment actions in people: actions by the customer to hire or train people or other less formal learning by the customer's employees. Some investments in people may even relate to the personal focus, the person representing the vendor's organization. Individuals in the customer's organization may learn how to work with the personal representatives of the vendor: to communicate the account's needs effectively to them, to obtain desired support from sales and service representatives, and so on. Changing vendors would require new investments, but so would a change in the vendor's personal representatives. Consequently, such investments relate to the personal focus of the account's commitments.

More substantial investments in people are likely to relate to focus on the product, the vendor, or the technology. Suppose, for example, that the customer's employees receive training on a specific product or product line offered by a vendor. If that learning does not readily transfer to other products from the same or different vendors, we could call it an investment related to the product focus of the account's commitments. If, on the other hand, the learning extended to a range of other products from the same vendor, we might instead consider it related to the vendor focus. And if the training really dealt primarily with the basic underlying technology and it would transfer to other products and other vendors using that same technology, we would consider it most related to the technology focus.

Similarly, investment actions in lasting assets or in procedures can relate to any of the foci for an account's commitment. They may relate to the personal focus, making it possible or easy for the customer to work with the personal representatives of the vendor. They may apply only to a particular product (or perhaps product line) and thus relate to focus on the product. They may apply to the customer's dealing with a specific vendor overall and thus relate to vendor focus. Or they may extend to an entire technology and relate to technology focus.

Looking at the account's commitment and investment actions in the light of the four possible foci can be useful because it helps identify switching costs in more detail. The exercise can indicate whether and to what extent the customer's investments are specific to the person, the product, the vendor, or the technology, and, as a result, it can indicate the likely switching costs the customer would face if there were a change of the vendor's personal representatives, the product, the vendor, or the technology. It can provide further insight into how strongly the customer's commitment is likely to focus on a person, a product, the vendor, or the technology.

Long Time Horizons and Short Time Horizons

Figure 4–3 summarizes the characteristics of customers' commitments made with long time horizons and customers' commitments made with short horizons. In general, a change in one of these descriptors will not occur in isolation but will be accompanied by changes in others. For example, when a product category becomes substantially more important to a customer organization, the account is also likely to increase its focus on the vendor or on technology. It will also likely increase its time horizon and feel more exposure in its choices.

The set of descriptors in figure 4–3 is useful and important for analyzing possible marketing actions for vendors. The following chapter discusses re-

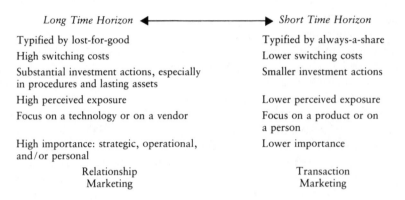

Figure 4–3. Time, Accounts' Behavior, and Marketing Approach

lationship marketing, which is appropriate toward the lost-for-good, long-time-horizon end of the spectrum; it contrasts relationship marketing with transaction marketing, which is appropriate toward the always-a-share, short-time-horizon end.

Before the more complete discussion of the following chapters, however, this section includes one brief example of marketing actions that are sensible in the light of figure 4–3. Suppose that a vendor's marketing approach has strongly emphasized the capabilities and personal relationships of its salespeople; the sales force and especially the individual salesperson have been the vendor's main communication device and at the core of its marketing strategy. Suppose, however, that new breakthroughs in fundamental research have created the foundation for substantially increased technical pace in the product-marketplace. Further, suppose that the increased pace and resulting new streams of products will allow customers to use the product category in increasingly important ways. Suppose in addition that changes from one major product type to another are likely to involve substantial switching costs for customers, even though those changes are also likely to prove competitively useful to buyers. Customers' commitments will become more important. They are also likely to involve longer time horizons, more exposure, and more focus on either the vendor or technology.

Would the vendor's old marketing approach be appropriate for the new situation? Likely not. Even assuming that the older-style salespeople have the abilities to sell and, if appropriate, service the newer, more complex products, the strong personal focus in the older situation does not match the new. Instead the vendor would want to address and perhaps even to encourage stronger focus on the vendor. Its communication program would give more emphasis than in the past to the vendor's general technical capabilities. It would put more stress on the overall abilities of the vendor organization to assure customers that, even if they were increasingly dependent on the vendor, at least they were dependent on a competent, caring vendor.

The seller might also want to change its sales deployment policies. It might, for example, choose to service accounts with teams rather than individual salespeople. It might even begin to rotate salespeople's assignments over time so that no one individual remained on the same account indefinitely. It might begin to offer customers other forms of support, such as training in how to use the vendor's products, provided by other parts of the vendor's organization.

These changes are substantial and should not be made lightly. If appropriate and well executed, they can, however, contribute to more focus by customers on the vendor and less on the vendor's personal representative. The changes may displease customers that have not moved and will not move toward longer-term, more important, and more vendor-focused commitments, and they should probably not be implemented for those accounts. For the accounts whose commitments are undergoing basic changes, however, the steps may fit the customers' future needs far better than would the previous assignment pattern and marketing approach.

The Long-Term Buyer

What Does the Long-Term Buyer Care About?

The discussion to this point has suggested that the buyer with a short time horizon cares primarily (essentially exclusively) about immediate inducements to buy: specific product features, price levels, payment terms, delivery dates, help from the vendor with installation of new equipment or disposal of old equipment, and so on. Because such customers can switch part or all of their patronage rather easily from one vendor to another, they need not be concerned with a vendor's longer-term capabilities, and, in general, they are not in fact concerned with such issues.

Because the long-term buyer, typified by the lost-for-good model, faces substantial switching costs and exposure, such a customer must be concerned with longer-term issues: the vendor's capabilities to provide an ongoing stream of adequately up-to-date products and to provide relatively graceful transitions from one to another of those products, the prospects that a particular chosen technology will in fact prove a sound durable choice for the future, and so on.

Explorations of buying behavior of actual customers with long time horizons does indeed show strong concern with such longer-term issues; however, such explorations show very strong concern with more immediate issues too. In fact, perhaps the best summary of the interests and concerns of long-term buyers is this: *They care about pretty much everything—and they care a lot!*

The nature of the long-term, lost-for-good-type commitment makes concern with longer-term issues appropriate and sensible. The long-term customer's high level of concern with immediate issues requires a bit more explanation. In fact, discussions with buyers with long time horizons suggested strongly that they were, if anything, even more concerned with some of the immediate details of vendors' performance than were customers with short time horizons. Why?

Part of the answer lies in the greater importance of commitments made with long time horizons. Although the customers place special emphasis on longer-term issues, the commitments are sufficiently important for there to be plenty of concern left over for more immediate issues too.

Another explanation appears even more relevant in analyzing the concerns of the long-term buyer. Such a customer is exposed to and concerned about the longer-term capabilities of a vendor or the long-term viability and usefulness of a particular technology. Yet the customer will generally not feel able to assess the capabilities of a vendor or the staying power of a technology. Consider a strongly vendor-focused commitment that is important to the buyer and poses considerable exposure. In such a commitment, the account is relying on the vendor to carry it relatively gracefully into an uncertain future. In fact, the account is relying on the vendor, with its greater knowledge of the product-marketplace, to make decisions that will be good for the customer. If the customer had more knowledge itself, it would not need to depend as heavily on the seller.

Because it is highly dependent on capabilities that it cannot judge well, the customer apparently looks for more measurable or observable signs of competence from a vendor. Generally the buyer is far better able to judge the vendor's performance on immediate issues: whether a product arrives when promised, whether it has the features or documentation it was supposed to, whether the vendor's service representative fixes equipment promptly and effectively, and so on. Although these immediate issues do not relate exactly to longer-term capabilities, buyers seem to use them as one relevant source of useful evidence.

Thus, long-term buyers care about pretty much everything, and they care a lot. They are dependent on their vendors, they know that they are, and they are sensitive to any sign of weakness, inattention, or lack of ability from those vendors.

The administrative vice-president of a multidivision firm provided one concrete example of the impact on a buyer of a vendor's failure to serve immediate needs satisfactorily. The manager was responsible for communications and a variety of other staff functions. A new chief executive realigned the division of responsibilities between line and staff managers, giving the line more work; the administrative vice-president found himself with extra time. He decided that the firm's headquarters' telephones should be improved and began to learn about the options, reading and attending classes. He obtained proposals for a new system from several vendors, decided on Bell, and signed a contract.

Despite a rather thorough procurement procedure, in retrospect the manager said that there had been little chance that he could have chosen any vendor other than Bell. He felt that headquarters' telephones were especially important and that he would have faced considerable personal exposure if there had been problems with a nontraditional (that is, non-Bell) decision. In the terms of this book, his behavior lay toward the lost-for-good end of the spectrum.

Surprisingly, then, the buyer subsequently changed his choice. He reported that he had become increasingly concerned as Bell did not serve his needs satisfactorily. He asked his Bell account executive for information with which he could compare costs of the new and old systems in detail. Despite repeated requests, the account executive was slow to provide the information. Further, Bell tariffs (prices) changed significantly, and the price of the proposed new system increased over 70 percent above the original quotation. The Bell salespeople had not warned the customer about the likely large increase.

In what he described as very uncharacteristic behavior, the manager tore up the original contract and reopened negotiations. He eventually bought a Rolm system for over $1.5 million. Despite his admitted strong initial commitment to Bell, the buyer became increasingly upset over immediate issues of price and of attention from the sales force. He became so concerned over those issues that he finally changed his basic commitment to the vendor.

Serving the Long-Term Customer

Customers that make important commitments with long time horizons are a considerable challenge to serve successfully. To serve them, the vendor must do a variety of things consistently and well over time.

In discussing the two extreme behavior models, chapter 2 noted the apparent attractiveness to the vendor of strong lost-for-good-type commitments from customers. In terms of the current chapter, the vendor would often particularly value commitments with strong vendor focus in which the buyer is relying on the single vendor rather than on a group of suppliers that support a common technology.

In fact, many vendors will find such commitments from customers very attractive indeed; however, the high-quality relationship marketing required for such customers is not easy to carry off well. The customers want many things from a vendor. They want consistent concern for the customer's needs. They want smooth and graceful transitions from one product to another. They want the vendor to be agile in responding to (or, better yet, leading) technological advances. They want long-term capabilities. They want short-term attention and care. They want the vendor to help address the customer's feelings of exposure.

Although the complex tasks of sound relationship marketing can be profitable when used for appropriate accounts, it makes little sense to apply relationship marketing when the buyer will retain a short-term orientation, as in the shipping-services example in chapter 1. Thus, the first step for successful relationship marketing is to make sure that customers behave (or can be induced to behave) in ways suitable for that approach. The concepts of this and the preceding chapters can help importantly with that determination, although they will by no means provide formula answers; the analysis of customers' behavior requires considerable thoughtfulness and insight.

After determining that relationship marketing in fact makes sense, marketers can then proceed to the task; the following chapters suggest some principles to use in doing so. Alternatively the marketer can instead work toward successful transaction marketing, where that approach makes sense. Either approach can provide profitable market success where it is suitable, but trying to use one where the other in fact fits is a sure prescription for serious problems.

Summary

Time is a centrally important descriptor of industrial marketing relationships. This book speaks of long-term customers as buyers that believe their commitments will last; they adopt long time horizons in making and maintaining those commitments. It speaks of short-term customers as buyers that use shorter time horizons and that expect to be able to change commitments rather easily. Long-term customers and short-term customers behave in fundamentally different ways and require substantially different marketing approaches.

The long-term buyer is typified by the lost-for-good behavior model. Such customers generally make commitments that focus most strongly on the technology or on the vendor (with switching costs, switching needs, and technological pace determining which of these foci corresponds to the longer time horizon). Long time horizons generally are accompanied (in fact, caused) by high switching costs, substantial investments (especially in lasting assets or procedures), high perceived exposure, and high importance (strategic, operational, and/or personal). Relationship marketing fits such customers.

The long-term customer can be very attractive to the seller that wants close, lasting relationships with its accounts. In general, however, the long-term customer can also be a real challenge to serve successfully. Such customers appear to care about everything, and they appear to care a lot. They care about longer-term issues such as the vendor's abilities to provide a sound, smooth escalator of usage for them for the future. They also care about immediate issues, in part because their relationships with their vendors are so important overall and in part because they use information about a vendor's immediate performance as evidence about the vendor's critical but harder-to-evaluate longer-term abilities.

The always-a-share model, by contrast, typifies the short-term buyer. Commitments made with short time horizons are generally characterized by lower switching costs, smaller investment actions, lower perceived exposure, focus on a product or on a person, and lower importance. In such commitments, buyers emphasize the immediate attractiveness of the available alternatives; they display little concern with longer-term issues. Transaction marketing fits such customers.

The focus of customers' commitments is an important determinant of key communication tasks for the marketer. For commitments that focus strongly on the personal representative of the vendor, marketers should stress the capability and concern for the customer shown by those representatives. For product-focused commitments, they should stress specifics of the product (features, prices, delivery, availability, detailed capabilities, and so on). For vendor-focused commitments, marketers would want to communicate the overall, longer-term capabilities of the vendor organization as a whole. With technology-focused commitments, they would stress the soundness and staying power of the chosen technology and their own strong commitment to that technology.

Sensible marketing strategies differ in other basic ways for long-term versus short-term customers. The discussion of buyers' behavior to this point has provided concepts and ideas (such as those in figure 4–3) to use in understanding the behavior of actual customers. The following chapters pursue in detail suggestions and principles to use in marketing successfully to those customers.

References

Raiffa, Howard. *The Art and Science of Negotiation.* Cambridge: Belknap Press of Harvard University Press, 1982.
Schelling, Thomas C. *The Strategy of Conflict.* New York: Oxford University Press, 1963.

5
Relationship Marketing and the Time Dimension of Marketing Tools

We can now shift emphasis to the question of what to do with an understanding of the time horizons of industrial customers: how to serve customers with different time horizons and different other (related) characteristics and how to affect the time horizons of customers and potential customers. This chapter focuses primarily on serving customers with various time horizons; it generally assumes that those time horizons are given, not determined by the vendor. The next chapter considers ways that sellers can act to influence the time horizons of their customers.

Thus, the basic topic for this chapter is transaction marketing and relationship marketing. The first suits the needs of short-term customers, the second of longer-term buyers. What does it take to be successful in each? What are common pitfalls for vendors that are attempting transaction marketing? For those trying to succeed at relationship marketing?

The Individual Account, the Full Marketing Mix, and Time

Emphasizing the Individual Account

The first key to success in either relationship marketing or transaction marketing is to focus on the individual account, to consider the behavior of that customer over time, and to weigh decisions about all tools in the marketing mix at least in part according to how they affect that industrial customer.

This book differs from much other marketing literature (and a surprising amount of marketing practice) by emphasizing the individual customer account rather than the market segment. For too long, the individual account has been the focus of the sales force but not the marketer. Salespeople have considered it their job to cultivate individual customer relationships, but other marketing choices (such as the basic product-policy choices of a firm) are too often made with heavy emphasis on rather abstract market segments and too little concrete attention to real individual customers. Market segmentation is certainly a useful and important technique, but it is, after all, the individual account that buys. Purchase orders are signed by customers, not by market segments.

At times, marketing practitioners argue that emphasizing the account is characteristic of a sales orientation rather than a more complete marketing view of customers, their needs, and the segments to which they belong. In practice, those practitioners are often right; emphasis on the account in practice often does correspond to almost total emphasis on the sales relationship with the individual, rather idiosyncratic customer. Such emphasis is not what this discussion means to suggest, however. Instead, this book argues that the marketer will benefit importantly from analyzing all marketing decisions in terms of their effects on individual customers over time. Sales-force decisions are often analyzed in that context in practice, but product-policy decisions and other major marketing choices often are not. They should be.

Marketers will have to go beyond the analysis of how actions might apply to individual accounts. It will not usually be feasible to design separate marketing strategies for individual customers or even for small handfuls of accounts. The suggestion here is to do the individual analysis thoroughly first. Then if a strategy or tactic appears promising in its effects on a few individual customers, the marketer can work to determine whether there are enough adequately similar customers to justify deploying the strategy or tactic.

The reader may ask whether the suggested approach is not really equivalent to using a market segmentation based on behavior of customers—in other words, on grouping into a segment accounts that will behave similarly and will respond similarly to the various tools of the marketing mix. The answer is yes; that is precisely the suggestion. Usually, however, segmentation is based on variables that are more accessible than behavior—on Standard Industrial Classification (SIC) codes or on geography, for example. This book argues instead for analysis (and perhaps segmentation) based on behavior and, importantly, on behavior over time. True, it will be considerably harder (perhaps impossible) to estimate the size of such a segment than it would a segment based on SIC codes or other more accessible variables, but the segmentation based on behavior and time will frequently be so much more effective in suggesting and identifying promising marketing actions that it will be worth while.

The individual account relationship is especially important in situations suggesting the lost-for-good model: long-term, important customer commitments. Therefore it is especially important for marketers to emphasize the individual account when they are attempting relationship marketing. Similarly it is also important for vendors in such situations to emphasize and analyze customer behavior over extended periods of time. By comparison, the challenge in transaction marketing to customers with short time horizons is often for the vendor to avoid taking too long a time perspective; the vendor should not assume, for example, that the relationship is likely to last.

The Marketing Mix

In analyzing marketing strategies and tactics in the context of the individual account over time, vendors will benefit from construing the term *marketing* very broadly. A leading industrial marketing practitioner, Charles Ames, has written that in industrial firms, marketing is a general management activity because almost all functions in the vendor organization are, or should be, importantly involved in serving customers' needs. Thus, research and development, manufacturing, and other functions serve critical marketing roles regardless of whether those areas are closely linked to marketing within the vendor's organizational structure.

Long-term customers making important, high exposure, lost-for-good commitments care a great deal about the vendor's longer-term capabilities, such as its general technological direction and its abilities to provide a continuing stream of satisfactorily up-to-date products. Especially in such situations, the marketing mix includes everything the vendor does that matters to the customer and affects the relationship—in other words, almost all that the vendor does.

The importance of the full marketing mix in long-term relationships makes it especially important in such situations to make the individual account the focus of the full marketing effort, not just of the sales force. The sales force does not control the full marketing mix; it generally cannot, for example, make product-policy moves in support of account strategies. In addition, the sales force often tends to have a shorter- rather than a longer-term focus, and a long time orientation by the buyer generally requires a long time orientation from the seller. The long-term customer generally cares about the full marketing mix. Successful relationship marketing requires the involvement and coordination of a wide range of tools and people from the vendor's organization.

Thus, this book stresses a concurrent emphasis on three elements: the individual account, the full marketing mix, and time. This combination is especially important for understanding and developing long-lasting relationships between industrial vendors and individual customer accounts—the attractive relationships that have received surprisingly scant attention in other literature and even in practice. It is especially important for successful relationship marketing.

Time Dimension of Marketing Strategy

Nature of the Time Dimension

Another key element in successful marketing to individual accounts, whether short-term buyers or long-term ones, is what this book calls the time dimension of marketing stratgy. The *time* in this concept is used in a special way; it denotes time as measured on the clock of the individual account. The clock monitors the account's history of purchases and use of a particular product category.

In serving customers, vendors make choices (implicitly or explicitly) about when in the account's history to try to establish a relationship and, perhaps, when in that history to stop trying to maintain one. Suppose that customers typically purchase increasingly complex products from some general category; they begin by purchasing simple versions and using them in relatively simple ways. Then their uses of the products grow in size and complexity; they buy increasing numbers of increasingly complex individual products.

Some vendors serving those customers may choose to try to grow with the accounts, offering wide assortments that can serve the buyers' changing needs over extended periods. At any one time, such a vendor can serve some customers that are just beginning to use the product type and that have rather simple needs; they can also serve some considerably more advanced users with far more complex needs and usage systems.

Other vendors may concentrate on less extensive product offerings that will meet customers' needs during only portions of their histories. Some may offer simpler product variants and expect some of their customers to outgrow them. Others may focus on more sophisticated or complex product variants, waiting for customers' needs to evolve to a point at which the more sophisticated offerings fit.

There are other key dimensions of marketing strategy, too. E. Raymond Corey suggests considering two key dimensions in market selection and planning. One is what he calls the horizontal dimension: the choice of which market segments to address (or, in other words, how broad a market to approach). His other dimension is the vertical: the choice of which particular end products or intermediates, from a possible vertically integrated production process, to offer for sale in the market. In correspondence with these two dimensions, the third (time) dimension might be called longitudinal: the choice of when, in an account's history of usage of some product category, to try to enter the account and of how long to try to continue to serve the customer.

Choices on the Time Dimension

Although it might appear at first that marketers would essentially always want to win an account early and stay in the account for the long term, in fact that is not the case, especially if the buyer's needs change importantly. Accounts whose needs change significantly can require substantially different marketing approaches at different times in their histories. It can be very difficult for the vendor to deploy a wide enough range of marketing tools, effectively and efficiently, to serve the range of customers' needs effectively and well. Problems of choosing and coordinating resources can become complicated when considered in the light of individual account histories.

Suppose that customers typically show increasingly important uses for a product category and increasingly long time horizons in their commitments as they use the products. Their initial rather small and unimportant purchases suggest behavior toward the always-a-share end of the spectrum. The buyers then focus primarily on immediate inducements to buy. Over time, the buyers' behavior becomes less like always-a-share and more like lost-for-good. The uses become more important, and the buyers become more aware of their dependence on their suppliers. They emphasize longer-term issues when they buy.

What should be the approach of the marketer that wants to serve such buyers for extended periods? Consider the sales force. Suppose that a sophisticated sales force is needed for selling in later but not in earlier stages of the typical account's history.

One choice for the vendor is to use the same sales force for all products and for accounts in all stages of development. This choice might make sense if accounts were likely to focus their commitments on a person and if they wanted continuity in the person serving them. It would, however, create a problem by using a more sophisticated and expensive sales tool than was necessary early in the customer's history. The strategy might be highly vulnerable to cost competititon for less complex products.

Another choice would be to use two sales forces, with a less sophisticated and less expensive group selling to customers in earlier stages of usage. This choice matches the cost and complexity of the marketing tool with the stage of the customer. Its disadvantage is that it involves a change of representative at some intermediate stage. Further, customers might interpret the lower sophistication of the initial sales representative to mean that the vendor was overall less able and less sophisticated.

A third choice would be to use third parties (agents or distributors) for the earlier, simpler sales to a particular customer and for the vendor to use its own more sophisticated sales force for later, more complex sales. This choice is sensible in terms of matching marketing costs with products and with accounts' commitments at particular times on those accounts' clocks. On the other hand, it may be inadvisable because the account must be handed off in mid-history and because the account's early experience with a third party may prejudice it against the vendor.

Thus, considering the time dimension of marketing strategy makes the marketer's task appear even more complex. Yet considering that dimension can also be important for marketing success because time and the customer's time horizon are important in determining how buyers behave. The first step in dealing with that time dimension is to address it explicitly: to use the concepts of the preceding chapters to explore customers' likely time orientations and interests at different times in their individual histories. The next step is to consider and use the time dimension of marketing tools. The final step is to put the appropriate marketing tools together in a consistent way over time.

Time Dimension of Marketing Tools

The full marketing mix contains a wide variety of individual tools. It includes product (widely defined to include design, engineering, and even the vendor's general technological stance and direction), channels of distribution (including logistical systems), communications (including sales, advertising, public relations), and price (including payment terms and conditions). For long-term customers, the vendor's basic business strategy becomes an important basis for purchase behavior, and thus strategy can usefully be considered a marketing tool too.

The individual tools in the marketing mix have important characteristics in terms of time, as do all of the other key components of the individual account relationship. Different marketing tools take different lengths of time to deploy. They also have effects of different durations.

In general, tools with especially long-lasting effects also take long times to deploy. Shorter-acting tools can generally be used more quickly. Therefore we can describe individual tools with single time descriptors: long-term tools, medium-term tools, short-term tools. A long-term marketing tool takes a long time to deploy and has effects in the marketplace that last. A short-term tool takes only a short time to apply but has effects that are short-lived.

This book speaks of the time dimension of marketing tools in terms of the effects of those tools on customers. The concept of the time dimension would also contribute to a consideration of the competitive effects of tools, but this discussion does not pursue that topic. It is worth noting in passing, however, that the time ordering of tools in regard to competitive effects is not always the same as the ordering in regard to effects on customers. For example, the following discussion classifies price as primarily a shorter-term tool. When used competitively to drive another vendor out of a business, however, price acts as a medium- or long-term competitive weapon.

Relative Time Ordering

To some extent, the time dimension of tools and the relative ordering of various tools on that dimension will depend on the specifics of a product-marketplace: on characteristics of the products and usage systems for those products, on needs and capabilities of buyers, and on needs, capabilities, and traditions of sellers. Therefore it is not possible to suggest one universally valuable time ordering of marketing tools. Nevertheless, consideration of a wide range of product-marketplaces suggests an ordering that appears to apply widely. (In order to apply this concept in a particular situation, however, it is important to consider the durations of effects and the times to deploy tools in that specific situation; the initial generally useful ordering may require some modification to fit the specific situation.)

Figure 5–1 shows a range of time effects for each of five broad categories of tools: price, advertising, sales force, distribution, and product. These broad categories cover many but certainly not all marketing tools. For example, in some situations, it is important to consider the service force as a tool separate from the sales force. The tool of general technological direction does not appear in the figure. Neither does the tool of basic business strategy.

Figure 5–1 classifies the main effects of the tools in terms of time. *Short term* means that the tool's effects can be felt almost immediately after the decision to use the tool. *Long term* means that there is a substantial delay between the decision to deploy the tool and the observation of effects of that tool. Because the time to impact of a tool is generally strongly related to the duration of that impact, *short term* also means that the tool's effects last a relatively short time; *long term* implies longer duration for the effects.

Figure 5–1 gives a range of time values for each broad category for two reasons. First, each category contains a variety of specific mechanisms, and those mechanisms have somewhat different time characteristics. Second, the same basic tool can serve considerably different purposes in different situations.

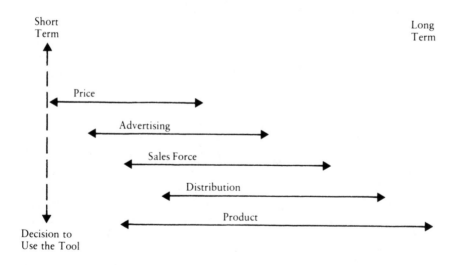

Figure 5–1. Time of the Main Effects of Major Categories of Tools

Short- to Medium-Term Tools

Figure 5–1 indicates that price is the shortest term of the major categories of tools. Next comes advertising, then sales force, and then distribution. Product can be the longest-term category of the five; it also has the widest range of different time impacts, ranging from short or medium to very long term.

Simple price moves are especially short-term tools. Price changes can be deployed easily—perhaps by printing a new price list, perhaps simply by notifying salespeople or price administrators of a new multiplier to be applied to an older price list, or perhaps by changing pricing rules or formulas.

Simple price moves are also easy to copy. The competitors can also print new lists, establish new multipliers, or promulgate new rules or formulas. In addition, simple price moves generally have short-lived effects. Today's price is not likely to determine a future purchase decision unless that price is also in effect in the future.

So-called long-term price contracts would often have somewhat more extended durations. They might be medium-term tools, taking a bit longer to deploy than simple price moves, providing effects that last more, but not lasting for really extended periods as compared with truly long-term tools.

Advertising is generally a short- to medium-term tool. It takes longer to create and execute a new advertising campaign than it does to make a simple price move, but the advertising tool can be deployed relatively quickly when compared with longer-term tools. Similarly, advertising campaigns appear to have some effects that last beyond the actual end of the campaigns. Although marketing practitioners and marketing academics continue to study and debate how long and how strong are the impacts of advertising over time, it seems clear that those effects do not last for truly long periods.

Medium- and Long-Term Tools

The sales force is usually a medium- to longer-term tool. Sales force capabilities are hard to build. Training takes time; the valuable informal learning that takes place on the job takes even longer. Especially because strongly individual people and their abilities and motivations are involved, it takes time and effort to change substantially a sales force or its direction. In situations in which customers care about and focus on the vendor's salespeople, salespeople can build important trust and commitment from the buying organization. They can adapt the vendor's products to fit especially well into the customer's usage system. They can create or facilitate smooth day-to-day working relationships between the two organizations by handling orders, status checking, delivery, billing, and so on. Although the effects of the sales force are not as long lasting as those of truly long-term tools, they are not as short as those of simple price moves either. In general the effects are short- to medium-term ones. Especially for complex or technical products that must be adapted to the customer's particular situation, the sales force can have medium-term effects.

Vendors and customers often have close, lasting relationships with channel intermediaries. Those relationships generally involve substantial knowledge by each party of the other. They often include establishment of procedures to let the two organizations work smoothly together. Consequently channels of distribution are frequently a long-term tool. Selecting and obtaining the desired set of distributors, giving them necessary knowledge of the vendor and its products, establishing smooth working relationships between the two organizations, and in general creating a sound partnership with distributors is a challenging and lengthy task for an industrial-marketing firm. Making substantial changes in its distribution channels will also take a vendor a long time. By the same token, distribution changes are difficult for the vendor's competitors. Investments in channel relationships usually pay back dividends to vendors for long periods of time. Other aspects of distribution (such as logistics systems) can have medium- to long-term effects depending on how much disruption changes would create for the customer and for the vendor.

Figure 5–1 shows a wide range of possible time characteristics for the broad category of product policy. Relatively minor product changes are often short- or at most medium-term tools. To the extent that they emphasize specific product features in their choices, buyers will generally weigh the specific characteristics of the array of offerings available at the time of a choice. Rather minor product differences may influence a specific decision, but, especially since they are not likely to induce or require strong vendor-specific investment actions by the customer, they are not likely to do much to discourage a change of vendor. Buyers can select another vendor (perhaps to obtain some other immediately attractive minor product feature) rather easily on the next choice. Such product moves thus have rather short-term effects. They can also usually be made rather quickly.

By comparison, a vendor's general product policy, technological stance, and technical capabilities are long-term tools. It takes a long time to change product directions by building the needed skills and making them work effectively to produce specific products. Even the development of a major new product that extends a vendor's offerings without a major change of direction frequently takes many years. An example is the development of a major new tractor design. By the same token, however, such developments are hard to copy.

The preceding chapters described the strong interest of long-term buyers in the general product directions and capabilities of their vendors. Buyers work hard to assess those abilities. They make up their minds carefully, and then they are generally slow to change their assessments. Consequently, impressing customers and potential customers with its long-term product capabilities is likely to provide a vendor benefits for a considerable time thereafter. The vendor's general direction of product policy is an especially long-term marketing tool.

The vendor's general marketplace image in part cumulatively reflects all of the vendor's other capabilities. In product-marketplaces where customers care strongly about the vendor's long-term capabilities, those capabilities are especially important in creating the vendor's general image. In such marketplaces, the vendor's image is especially hard to build and to alter. By comparison, in product-marketplaces where buyers emphasize shorter-term tools, the vendor's image is primarily determined by those tools: price, specific product features, or perhaps the sales force. In such marketplaces, it is considerably easier for a vendor to change its image.

Exposure for the Vendor in Long-Term Tools

Long-term tools involve exposure for vendors. When a vendor decides to use or change a long-term tool, it must generally begin to invest resources. For example, it might start to build technical competence in a new area or start a major new thrust of product development. By the natures of the longer-term tools, the vendor must wait, sometimes for a considerable period, until it can begin to reap benefits from the new deployment of a long-term tool. In the interim, the vendor faces risk that the investment it is making in deploying the tool will not pay off satisfactorily in the marketplace.

Matching Marketing Tools and Customers' Commitments

The preceding discussions of short-term customer commitments noted that in making such commitments, customers emphasize immediate inducements to buy. In the terms of this chapter, they strongly emphasize or are influenced by short-term marketing tools. In buying individual stand-alone copying machines, routine office supplies, carbon steel, or shipping services, the customer generally is most influenced by price, product features, delivery, and similar short-term tools. Therefore the vendor should emphasize such tools in addressing that type of customer commitment.

Transaction marketing thus requires shorter-term marketing tools. Longer-term tools are not of high interest to customers effectively addressed through transaction marketing, and they would therefore not be emphasized by vendors addressing such customers. For example, advertising specific product features can be useful in transaction marketing; corporate image advertising to convince customers they are buying from a strong, able vendor organization is not particularly useful in such situations.

By comparison, customers making long-term commitments care about longer-term issues: a vendor's general technological capabilities and direction, its financial ability to survive, the staying power of a particular technology, and so on. In selling computers, aircraft engines, communications equipment, heavy construction equipment, and other products to such customers, vendors would sensibly emphasize the longer-term issues that interest customers; they would use and emphasize longer-term marketing tools. Relationship marketing thus requires longer-term marketing tools.

Thus, the preceding discussion of customers' behavior suggests a first basic principle to use in managing the time dimension of marketing strategy: *Use and emphasize marketing tools with time dimensions that correspond to the time horizons of the customers you are trying to serve: shorter-term tools for shorter-term customer commitments and longer-term tools for longer-term customer commitments.*

In fact, discussion with customers making especially strong long-term commitments suggests an even firmer statement of principle. Such customers consistently emphasized long-term tools when they discussed and explained their choices of products and vendors. Many, for example, said they were buying companies with specific strategies for the very long term. This emphasis on longer-term issues was so strong as to suggest the following principle: *Serving customers with especially long time horizons requires long-term marketing tools. Such customers will not buy on the basis of short- and medium-term tools alone.*

Mismatching Marketing Tools and Marketing Tasks

This last statement may seem reasonable and even straightforward, especially in the light of the preceding discussion of the behavior of buyers, but in fact it conflicts with a considerable amount of apparent marketing practice. Faced with less than satisfactory results from the marketplace, many marketers almost automatically try to adjust price or else fiddle with the sales force's compensation. In general, even if they do not face specific disappointment in the marketplace, marketers often appear to ask a great deal of the sales force and of price. Yet, the concepts of this book strongly argue that short- and medium-term tools cannot carry the burden of winning and maintaining long-term customer commitments. Those commitments require long-term tools, and fixing problems in long-term relationships often also requires using long-term tools.

There appear to be several reasons for this type of mismatch, of relying too heavily on shorter-term tools in long-term relationships. In a sense, it is easy to understand why marketers would want to use shorter-term tools. Those tools act quickly; the fast action is attractive. Given problems in the marketplace in general or in a specific customer account, it is hard to be patient and wait for the impact of a significant change in product policy, especially when a price change could be implemented so rapidly.

Similarly, marketers appear to be influenced by the exposure they face as they deploy longer-term tools (for example, the resources a firm must pour into product development before it can implement a significant change in product policy and bring new products to market). Further, the relatively short time horizons used for measurement and evaluation in most businesses contribute to a bias toward shorter-term tools. Many managers feel they must show results this quarter.

In addition, longer-term tools are usually partly or completely outside the control of the marketing function in a vendor organization. Therefore, deploying longer-term tools requires a coordinated effort within that organization. By contrast, the sales force and price are often directly controllable by marketing or by sales.

There is considerable temptation, especially in the heat of competitive battle, for vendors to ask too much of short- and medium-term tools in longer-term relationships. Vendors are tempted to use shorter tools for firefighting and to neglect longer-term tools. Yet shorter-term tools cannot do the job alone. They can help, but long-term commitments require longer-term tools. Resisting the natural temptation to overemphasize shorter-term tools is a challenge for vendors trying to win and maintain commitments made with long time horizons.

The reverse problem appears less prevalent, although it does also occur in practice. Vendors may try to use medium- and longer-term tools to build lasting relationships with customers that are not likely to make lasting commitments—customers whose behavior is much more like always-a-share than lost-for-good.

Consider a vendor of time-sharing computer service that invests substantial resources to learn about its customers' businesses and to help them (without charge) to create computer programs supporting those businesses. Investing to learn customers' businesses in depth and to help them plan for the future is often very sensible in longer-term relationships, but it can be risky in a situation where customers face low switching costs and are likely to buy on the basis of immediate inducements. After one vendor has spent resources and helped it develop useful programs, the time-sharing customer can relatively easily switch to another vendor to save money on the actual computer cycles used to run those programs. It may not make sense, therefore, for a time-sharing vendor to invest in customers as if relationships will last.

The problems of mismatches of tools and commitments are different in transaction marketing and in relationship marketing. In transaction marketing, the challenge for the vendor is not to invest too heavily in longer-term tools and not to invest in individual account relationships as if they will last. In relationship marketing, the challenge is not to overemphasize short- and medium-term tools but instead to pay adequate attention to the long-term tools that are key to long-term relationships.

Combining Marketing Tools

Shorter Tools in Longer Relationships

Although short- and medium-term tools cannot alone win or maintain longer-term commitments, those tools still have useful roles in longer-term relationships. On the positive side, they can provide important support for long-term tools. On the negative side, misuses of short and medium tools can severely damage longer-term relationships.

Short- and medium-term tools can be extremely useful in supporting longer-term tools, in tailoring them to the needs of particular customers, in communicating them, and in making them more concrete. A competent and professional sales force or service force can support and make more concrete a vendor's general reputation for technical competence. Medium- and short-term communication tools can publicize longer-term capabilities. Those tools are especially important because longer-term capabilities are complex and difficult to communicate to customers and potential customers. Announcements of planned product developments (subject to legal restrictions on such announcements) can help communicate a vendor's general direction of product policy. Public relations can communicate a vendor's capabilities in technology and other important areas.

At the time of the breakup of the Bell system, many of AT&T's customers were feeling exposure about what would happen to their vendor over the longer term; they were concerned about product continuity and upgradability. Some actions by AT&T at the time could be viewed as assuring its customers of continuity. In a set of product announcements in May 1982, AT&T stressed its future product plans, such as plans for enhancements to the software of its main (Dimension) products.

On the negative side, misuse of shorter-term tools can ruin even substantial customer relationships, as shown clearly in the example at the end of the preceding chapter describing the loss of a lost-for-good commitment for communications equipment. Customers appear to take a vendor's performance on immediate issues (and shorter-term tools) as useful evidence of important but hard-to-judge capabilities on longer-term tools.

Customers in long-term relationships generally have long memories. Vendors that apply short-term tools as immediate expedients can find themselves living with the after-effects of those actions for a long time. An example is what some customers call a political campaign: an attempt to go over an individual buyer's head in the customer organization to influence a choice. Another example is a scarce campaign: an attempt to convince customers that specific competitive offerings will not work. If such campaigns are based more on wishful thinking than on fact, they can be extremely harmful to a valuable long-term relationship. The customers are likely to catch on eventually. When they do, they are likely to question the vendor's good faith and integrity and to become seriously worried and perhaps resentful of being linked in an important relationship to such a vendor. Honesty and integrity appear especially important in long-term relationships.

Together the positive and negative roles of short- and medium-term tools discussed in this section provide the following principle: *Medium- and shorter-term tools can support longer-term tools in longer-term relationships. They cannot win long-term commitments alone. They can, however, lose such commitments alone.*

Different Uses of the Same Basic Tool

Short- and medium-term tools are important both in shorter-term relationships (transaction marketing) and in longer-term relationship marketing. Actually the same tool or similar tools often serve somewhat different purposes and act in somewhat different ways in serving customers with different time horizons.

Consider the sales force, for example. In serving customers with short time horizons, the sales force would sensibly emphasize specific product features, details of specific pricing analyses, and other immediate issues. In serving customers with somewhat longer time horizons, the same sales force might (instead or in addition) provide help with training, installation, or financing arrangements. It might also have a more substantial role in product selection and in giving the customer confidence that the vendor is committed and cares. The sales force might serve to tailor the vendor's general approach to fit the needs of specific accounts. In long-term relationships, the salesperson can also be an important means of communicating and explaining the vendor's long-term direction of product policy and its long-term concern for the buyer.

As a result, vendors serving customers with a range of time horizons may need to use the same tool especially flexibly. If, for example, a vendor uses a single sales force, that sales force will have substantially different tasks in customer accounts with substantially different time horizons.

Challenges in Serving Long-term Customers

Challenge of Coordination

Because short-, medium-, and long-term tools have useful roles in serving long-term customers, vendors face a challenge of coordination: *Winning and maintaining commitments made with long time horizons generally require coordination of longer- and shorter-term tools.*

The long-term customer is especially sensitive to any sign of weakness from the vendor on which it depends. Lack of smooth coordination can be one sign of weakness. One example is a sales force and a service force that do not communicate well. Another is a failure to inform the sales force quickly and thoroughly about a new pricing policy, with the result that the customer is told one thing by the sales representative and another by the vendor's headquarters.

Relationship marketing requires doing a wide variety of things well and consistently over time. It generally incorporates a wide range of marketing tools. Those tools should individually be applied well, and they should also be coordinated well with one another. Vendors are considerably more likely to succeed at such marketing if they plan coordinated programs by specifically assigning roles to the different tools and planning for their coordination.

Often a vendor serves customers with a variety of different time horizons. Some may use the vendor's products in more and some in less important ways. Others may be in early stages in their uses of the product category; they may evolve to use the products in more important ways and to have longer time horizons. The vendor therefore faces another challenge of coordination: *To serve customers with different time horizons, the vendor must often manage different uses of the same short- and medium-term tools.*

Building and coordinating a variety of tools aimed at different types of customers can be difficult and expensive. One problem is that in attempting to do too many different things, a vendor organization may end up doing none really well. A vendor may decide that it cannot simultaneously be outstanding in low-cost products for price-oriented, short-term commitments and in high value-added products for commitments made with longer orientations. The vendor may be better off trying to be outstanding in one area only.

Tools best suited for one job can be inefficient or even dysfunctional in other situations—for example, using the same sales force to sell to a range of customers with different needs. A vendor may need a sophisticated sales force to sell complex products to customers making longer-term commitments. It may be inefficient or even unprofitable to use that same force to sell simpler products to customers making product-focused commitments.

For such reasons, vendors may prefer to target only limited types of customer commitments. Such a choice has the advantage of allowing the vendor to concentrate on a less complex array of marketing tools and uses of those tools than would be required to serve a broader group of accounts. On the other hand, the choice may limit the vendor's size and thus deny it substantial scale economies in manufacturing. Very important, the choice may be inappropriate if an individual customer is likely to show a changing pattern of commitment and if there are benefits to a vendor that can meet the customer's needs over an extended portion of its history.

Often a vendor offers customers an assortment of products. An especially good example is a vendor that sells equipment (perhaps heavy construction equipment or offset duplicators) and also sells parts, service, and/or supplies for that equipment. To this point, the discussion has avoided the additional complexity of such groups of offerings, but chapter 7 returns to the topic of satisfying what this book calls *cascaded demand*. It is worth noting here that the vendor offering such an assortment faces additional challenges of coordination; the later discussion elaborates.

Challenge of Consistency

The challenge of coordination in serving long-term customers is made even more difficult because such customers often want consistency from their vendors. They want vendors to be consistent in their concern for customers' needs, and they want vendors to provide smooth escalators carrying customers upward into the future. At the same time, however, the same customers want vendors to be agile in responding to (or sometimes creating or leading) changes in technology or other forces. Especially if the customer feels pressure to remain up-to-date, it will want its vendor to be dynamic and creative. Such a customer becomes highly concerned if it feels that the vendor on which it depends has fallen behind.

Thus, buyers do not want static consistency. They want vendors to appear consistent in their concern for customers but dynamic in their responses to changing conditions. The combination creates tension for the vendor, which will feel pressure to be agile but will also find that desires for consistency limit its abilities to move quickly.

There are no simple answers to these challenges of coordination and consistency. At best, I can offer some suggestions for addressing them. First, vendors should be aware of them and manage them actively. Second, they should consider the time dimension of marketing and use a long enough time horizon to consider such longer-term challenges. Third, they should consciously communicate to customers evidence of coordination, consistency, and concern.

Dealing with Customers' Exposure

Much of the long-term customer's concern with consistency and caring from its vendor stems from the buyer's feelings of exposure. Therefore an important part of the secret of successful relationship marketing is for the vendor to deal with and address those feelings. Since the customer will generally be correct in perceiving that it faces exposure, the vendor probably cannot eliminate those feelings, but it can work to alleviate them.

The vendor can try to convince buyers of the selling firm's long-term capabilities and commitment. Image advertising and public relations can tell customers about a vendor's general capabilities. So can plant tours, circulation of articles written by the vendor's technical personnel, descriptions of the vendor's strategic approach and level of financial commitment to a market, and many other tactics.

Contacts by vendor representatives, especially senior managers, with top managers from customer organizations can help convey both competence and commitment. Such contacts have traditionally been considered important in markets such as those for computers and for electrical generation equipment.

Customers and potential customers can be reassured if a vendor has won and is successfully serving other substantial customers. Technologically advanced customers can be valuable as showcase or demonstration accounts. For example, many purchasers of non-Bell communications equipment found it important to know that the vendors they were considering had already been selected by other substantial customers; customers in the same industry were especially important as reference or showcase sites. Especially in product-marketplaces with less technical pace, accounts can be useful showcases even if they do not lead technically. For example, an account that has developed mundane but effective manufacturing processes to reduce its usage of a particular chemical might be a showcase for the supplier of the chemical.

In trying to sell to other accounts, the vendor's representatives would describe the uses of its products by showcase customers. The vendor might even be allowed to describe the showcase in sales literature or in articles for the relevant trade press, and it might be allowed to have potential customers tour the showcase site. Word of mouth in the user industry in some cases may spread the story of the choice of visible, respected showcase accounts even without active vendor involvement in telling the story.

The sales force can be especially important to a vendor trying to demonstrate interest and concern for a specific account. The general vendor organization provides longer-term capabilities, such as product development. The salesperson becomes the advocate for the specific customer, representing the customer's interests within the vendor organization.

Vendors sometimes deal with customers' concerns with exposure by making their products compatible with the products of another particularly strong vendor. Through compatibility, the lesser vendor allows the customer to focus its commitment more on a common technology and less on the specific vendor. Such a choice is not without risk for a vendor; it will generally create increased competition for particular customer orders among the group of vendors backing the same technology. The choice can, however, be sensible, especially if a vendor could not otherwise convince customers to accept the exposure of buying its products.

Deploying Long-Term and Shorter-Term Tools

Relationship marketing appears unavoidably to be a complex, challenging task. It requires using a variety of tools and coordinating those tools effectively. It requires addressing customers' feelings of exposure. It requires taking a long enough time horizon in marketing to address customers with long horizons. It also requires a long time horizon so that the vendor can plan its marketing moves, whenever possible, with enough lead time so that it does not appear abrupt and inconsistent to customers.

Although it appears impossible to avoid complexity in relationship marketing, a few principles and practices can make the task more manageable. The first principle is to be explicit about the time dimensions of marketing tools and of marketing strategy. The concepts presented in preceding chapters (such as switching costs and focus) can be used to analyze the apparent and likely future behavior of customers. It will not, in general, be possible to place customers with precision along the behavior spectrum between lost-for-good and always-a-share; the determinants of time horizon and the customer's time horizon are too complex and difficult to assess. Nevertheless, precision is not necessary. Just placing customers' behavior in some range along the spectrum will provide important insights about the buyers' time horizons and, from that information, about the key marketing tools and key marketing tasks in serving them.

Vendors working for longer-term commitments from customers will need to adopt longer time horizons in their own marketing strategies. Long-term customer commitments require long-term marketing tools, which take a long time to build and to deploy effectively. Thus, changes come about relatively slowly in relationship marketing. To make appropriate changes at the right times in their marketplaces, relationship marketers will have to plan moves well in advance. They will find it especially important to have as much advance understanding and warning as possible of the future directions of customers, competitors, and other factors in their markets. The desires of long-term buyers for consistency make such a long marketing horizon even more important. Such customers will frequently be frightened or disturbed by abrupt changes on the part of their vendors. The vendors will generally need considerable advance planning to provide smooth changes that communicate consistency and concern.

A third general principle can help in making it possible to put together a coordinated relationship-marketing program; that principle provides an order for the deployment of marketing tools: *In deploying complex groups of tools for relationship marketing, select the longer-term tools first. Add medium-and short-term tools to support the longer-term ones.* Thus, in relationship marketing, the vendor would think of the harder-to-build-or-change longer-term tools as the foundation for strategy. Changes in such tools are particularly difficult, require longer time periods, and therefore would be managed with a long time horizon. Medium- and short-term tools would supplement the longer-term tools, and frequently they would tailor the longer-term tools to the needs of specific customers. Further, especially because the medium- and short-term tools can be changed and deployed more rapidly than can long-term tools, the shorter-term tools can sometimes be used tactically to respond to smaller, more immediate perturbations in the marketplace—perhaps to a particular price or communications campaign by a competitor. Such uses of shorter-term tools are sensible and can be very effective as long as the marketer does not assume that such tools can substitute for, rather than supplement, the longer-term tools central to long-term relationships.

Account Specificity of Marketing Tools

Another related concept can assist in the successful deployment of marketing tools, especially in the complex situation of relationship marketing. That concept concerns the *account specificity* of tools.

Individual products, sales programs, and other marketing devices can apply to large groups of customers, or they can be specific to a few customers or even to one account. In other words, marketing tools have different degrees of account specificity. One vendor of computer software may offer a general package for payroll calculations, useful in a wide range of organizations with a range of rules for salaries, benefits, and deductions. Such a product is very general, not account specific. Another vendor might offer payroll packages specifically tailored to different types of factory environments, with the capabilities to handle different bases for compensation, deductions, and benefits and with the ability to report productivity results as an aid to the factory's management. That product is not completely general but it is also not fully account specific; it applies to a group of customer organizations. Finally, consider another vendor that writes customized software to handle the payroll and other functions of one large customer. That product is highly account specific.

In general, the following principle applies to the deployment of marketing tools: *The more general building blocks or tools come first. Account-specific tools fill in the gaps to make the less specific tools fit individual accounts.*

Frequently the vendor's longer-term tools are more general. Medium- and shorter-term tools are or can be made more account specific. Therefore the concept of the time dimension of marketing tools combines with the idea of account specificity of tools to produce the following principle: *Medium-and short-term tools can combine with account-general long-term tools to form effective account-specific vendor strategies.* The medium- and shorter-term tools can fit the vendor's general longer-term capabilities to the needs of groups of accounts (such as industry groups) or to individual customers. For example, a vendor's field representatives might configure general product building blocks to meet the needs of specific customers. Or industry specialists in a vendor's sales force might help groups of customers obtain additional value from generally applicable products.

Sensibly, vendors would determine whether it was appropriate to deploy a particular marketing tool in part by considering the account specificity of the tool and the likely benefit the tool would provide for the accounts to which it applies. They will find it useful to develop and deploy more general building blocks only if those tools apply effectively to large groups of customers. Similarly, somewhat more specialized tools (such as a special educational program for customers in the metal fabrication business) can be justified only if they are useful for a large enough base of accounts. Account-specific tools would be justified by the benefits they provide for a specific customer.

Notice that in this discussion, the individual account still remains the focus of analysis. The vendor considers the effects of tools on individual customer accounts, but for more general tools it then adds up the effects of the tool on the individual accounts to which that tool usefully applies.

Sales Orientation or Marketing Orientation

This chapter began by arguing that the individual account for too long has been the province of the sales force rather than the concern of the marketer and of the vendor organization as a whole. Much of the rest of the chapter explains why this idea is so important, especially for successful relationship marketing. Long-term customer relationships require long-term marketing tools. Many of those tools are not the focus of the sales force and are not within the control of the sales force. Moreover, successful relationship marketing requires consistency and coordination. The vendor organization must pull together, in a coordinated and consistent way, to serve the needs of individual customer accounts over extended periods.

Thus, especially in relationship marketing, marketing strategy should focus on the individual account over time, and the term *marketing* should be broadly construed. The individual account should not be the province of the sales force alone; decisions on product policy should not be made at the product-manager level for one product at a time. Instead, top managers should insist that sales, marketing, product development, R&D, and other departments consider the individual account, the marketing mix, and time. Top management involvement will generally be needed to ensure the necessary coordination of these efforts and to establish measurement systems consistent with overall longer-term goals. In essence, this suggestion makes marketing to the individual account the job of the entire vendor organization.

Relationship marketers will also frequently find it useful to try to give the sales force itself a somewhat longer time horizon than is typical in shorter-term transaction marketing. One would not want to forget that the job of a sales force is to sell. At the same time, however, in relationship marketing, the salesperson can be effective as a manager of a lasting relationship by helping the customer plan for the long term, tailoring the vendor's offerings to the customer's needs, and in general working to create lasting links between the customer and the vendor organization. Compensation schemes, sales practices and sales objectives, and training and feedback to the sales force can help encourage this longer-term view and discourage salespeople from thinking of themselves as pushers of individual products.

Summary

Key to success in serving industrial customers is to consider together the individual account, the full marketing mix, and time. The individual customer—not the market segment—buys and is fundamental to marketing. (The market segment is simply a useful shorthand for describing a group of individual accounts.) Time is central in relationship marketing; marketing strategy has an important time (or longitudinal) dimension. In serving customers, vendors make choices (implicitly or explicitly) along that time dimension—deciding when, in an individual account's history, to try to establish a relationship and perhaps when to stop trying to maintain one. Especially in long-term relationships, customers care strongly about a wide range of vendor capabilities, and, therefore, especially in such situations the term *marketing* should be construed widely. The full marketing mix includes almost everything the vendor does.

Marketing tools have a time dimension. Long-term tools take a long time to deploy, and their effects last. Shorter-term tools take less time to deploy, but their effect are less long lasting. In general, price is usually a short-term tool (in its effects on customers), advertising a short- to medium-term tool, the sales force medium-term, distribution medium to long. Product-policy tools cover a broad range of time characteristics, with general product policy being an especially long-term tool.

In general in effective marketing, the critical tools are those with time dimensions matching the time horizons of customers' commitments: short-term tools for short-term commitments and longer-term tools for longer-term commitments. Serving customers with long time horizons requires longer-term tools. Medium- and shorter-term tools can support longer-term tools in longer-term relationships. They cannot win longer-term commitments alone, despite the rather frequent temptation for marketers to rely too heavily on such tools, such as price or the sales force. Short- and medium-term tools can, however, lose longer-term commitments alone, apparently because buyers take the shorter-term tools as evidence of the vendor's harder-to-judge longer-term capabilities.

Winning and maintaining commitments made with long time horizons generally require coordination of longer- and shorter-term tools. The shorter-term tools support the longer-term ones and frequently make them more account specific. Long-term customers feel considerable exposure in their relationships with vendors, and they are therefore especially anxious that the vendor appear consistent and caring—but also agile—over time.

Although the complexity of relationship marketing appears unavoidable, some principles can make the effort more manageable. Vendors will generally benefit by addressing explicitly the issues of the individual account, the marketing mix, and time. In relationship marketing, they will benefit from adopting long time horizons in their marketing strategies and from trying to anticipate marketplace changes so as to have enough time to make their own changes smoothly and adequately consistently. And in deploying marketing tools, they will find it useful to think of deploying longer-term tools and more account-general tools first. Shorter-term and more account-specific tools can then be applied in coordinated support roles.

References

Ames, B. Charles. "Trappings vs. Substance in Industrial Marketing." *Harvard Business Review* (July–August 1970):93–102.

Borden, Neil H. "The Concept of the Marketing Mix." *Journal of Advertising Research* (June 1964):2–7.

Corey, E. Raymond. "Key Options in Market Selection and Planning." *Harvard Business Review* (September–October 1975):119–128.

6
Strengthening (or Weakening) Customers' Commitments

Chapter 5 discussed principles for industrial marketers to use to respond effectively to the time horizons of their customers and potential customers. Understanding those time horizons provides a sound foundation for marketing decisions. Vendors can deploy marketing tools in accord with that understanding, using long-term tools in key roles in winning and maintaining long-term commitments from customers, using shorter-term tools in support roles in long-term relationships, and using shorter-term tools as the key marketing mechanisms in shorter-term relationships.

Useful as it is for the marketer to respond effectively to time horizons of customers, it can be even more profitable for the vendor to be an active determinant of those time horizons. Vendor actions can be important in determining customers' switching costs, in affecting customers' perceptions of exposure, and, in general, in influencing the positions of customers along the behavior spectrum between lost-for-good and always-a-share. This chapter explores the topic of vendor actions aimed either at strengthening customers' commitments (and moving the buyer toward the lost-for-good end of the spectrum) or at weakening commitments (generally in order to move a competitor's customers away from lost-for-good and toward the always-a-share end of the spectrum).

Acting to Change Commitments

Other Influences and Constraints

The actions of a vendor attempting to influence time horizons and behavior will be only one of many forces that act to change customers' commitments. Some changes occur relatively inexorably—for example, as customers gain experience with a product category and therefore become more knowledgeable about the products and more adept at using them effectively. Other forces are created by developments outside a particular product-marketplace. Examples are legal and regulatory developments, such as changes in the enforcement of the antitrust laws. Similarly, the environmental movement has created changes for a variety of industrial customers in switching costs, exposure, and the seriousness of purchase decisions.

Sometimes customers act consciously to change or influence the natures of their commitments to and reliance on vendors. The example of potential customers for LANs, described in chapter 4, provides one illustration. Those customers were pressuring vendors for more standardization and for more open communication about the vendors' technical designs. The customers said they wanted to avoid being harmed by incompatibility, as they had been harmed in the past in other related markets. In other words, customers were pressing vendors for actions to allow buyers to commit with less exposure to the individual vendor and more reliance on a basic technology.

Similarly, in the 1980s many advanced users of computers are implementing network architectures: overall plans for their data-processing systems that make clear and explicit conventions for interfaces between different components of the systems and that therefore allow relatively easy mixing and matching of components from different vendors. In describing their network architectures, managers for customer organizations said that one key motivation was to reduce the buyer's reliance on any individual seller. The network design allowed buyers to select individual components on a shorter-term, more product-focused basis, confident that those products would fit into the long-term network design.

Other players also consciously act to affect the strengths of the commitments of customers to their vendors. Actions of competitors are often intended to weaken the ties of a competitor with its customers. Further, legislation and administrative governmental actions can be designed to keep the links between customers and competitors from becoming too tight; rules against tying arrangements are an example.

Thus, a variety of forces influence the time horizons of customers and constrain the ability of any one vendor to change customers' commitments. The nature of a product category and of customers' usage systems for that product category also constrain the types of changes in commitments that vendors can induce. Commitments for shipping services, for example, are not likely to be as strong and lasting as are many key commitments for computers, regardless of vendors' actions.

Nevertheless, within all of these constraints and in the face of all of these additional influences on the behavior of accounts, there often remain substantial opportunities for vendors to change the strengths of customers' commitments. Some such actions can be extremely attractive to the vendor.

Changing Switching Costs

The basic principle for analyzing and evaluating possible changes in customers' commitments and behavior is a rather simple extension of the earlier discussion of the determinants of accounts' behavior. Switching costs (both tangible investment actions and intangible exposure) are key to understanding the positions of accounts along the behavior spectrum between lost-for-good and always-a-share. The basic idea in changing location along that spectrum is to change the customer's switching costs. Raising switching costs moves the account closer to the lost-for-good end of the spectrum; reducing switching costs moves the customer closer to always-a-share.

Figure 4–3 lists a set of characteristics of customers' commitments made with long time horizons. Such commitments generally involve high importance, substantial switching costs (with high levels of exposure and substantial investment actions, especially in lasting assets and in procedures), and focus on the vendor or on a technology. Vendors can think about actions intended to increase customers' time horizons in terms of any of these characteristics. For example, in some situations, a vendor will find it helpful to think in terms of importance—perhaps to try to identify ways to help the customer use that vendor's products to reduce costs appreciably as part of a customer strategy of competing as a low-cost producer or perhaps to try to find ways to use the vendor's products to help a customer that competes on the basis of service to provide its own customers with faster response to their orders.

In other cases, vendors act to change the customer's time horizon and behavior through communications programs about exposure. An established vendor like AT&T in communications or IBM in computers can strengthen customer ties by educating or reminding customers about the levels of exposure that they face. For example, an IBM print advertisement showed a pillow and suggested that dealing with IBM would provide the buyer with sound, peaceful sleep; dealing with competitors presumably would not. (By comparison, less established vendors sometimes try to communicate other types of customer exposure in relationships with strong vendors as an argument for dealing with an alternate supplier. One advertisement in the early 1980s from Rolm, an AT&T competitor, showed a meeting room, perhaps a board room, with everyone around the table looking questioningly in the same direction and with the caption, "You mean you didn't consider Rolm? How embarrassing!")

A variety of marketing tools can help to influence the account's location along the behavior spectrum. Long-term tools such as product policy turn out to be especially effective, as should not be surprising, given the key importance of longer-term tools in winning and maintaining long-term commitments. Similarly, although all types of switching costs can build inertia in the customer organization and strengthen ties to a vendor, investments in lasting assets and changes in procedures are especially effective in changing customers' time horizons, again not a surprising result given the central role of such investment actions in creating long time horizons.

Thus, long-term tools, customer investments (especially investments in lasting assets and procedures), and exposure are key levers for changing customers' behavior. Those levers can be used to decrease time horizons and encourage behavior more like the always-a-share model, or they can be used to increase horizons and move behavior closer to the lost-for-good.

Winning Commitments with Modularity

Effects of Modularity

In discussing the determinants of switching costs and of customers' behavior, chapter 3 described the spectrum running between modularity and systems. That spectrum applies to customers' usage systems, and it applies as well to vendors' decisions about product policy. A modular usage system is one in which a customer can combine pieces or parts from different vendors, mixing and matching them rather freely. In a system usage pattern, the customer cannot freely mix and match; the system is a more closely integrated whole. Similarly, in a modular product policy, the vendor's own products mix and match rather freely with one another and frequently with the individual products of at least some other vendors. In a systems-oriented product policy, the products cannot be freely mixed and matched.

This spectrum between modularity and systems is key for product policy and for understanding and managing the effects of product policy on the time horizons of customers. The basic reason is that the modularity-systems spectrum relates closely to the level of swiching costs faced by a customer if it tries a new vendor.

Modularity in product design and modularity in usage by customers allow a customer to make a smaller initial purchase from a vendor; the customer can identify a relatively contained, low-risk modular experiment as a first step in dealing with a new vendor. The modular usage pattern allows the customer to conduct a relatively isolated (and hence lower exposure) initial trial of a vendor's products. The buyer is not forced to make a major initial commitment.

Consequently modularity in product design and modularity in usage by customers make it easier for a vendor to break into new accounts. They allow the vendor to obtain a toehold in the account. The toehold, or low-risk initial commitment, gives the customer a chance to get to know the vendor and to test its performance. For example, the buyer can obtain first-hand experience about the seller's abilities to meet promised delivery schedules, to install a new product smoothly, or to provide maintenance service after installation. The vendor would hope that the account's initial experience would give the buyer the confidence necessary to make subsequent, more substantial investments.

These insights about modularity and systems can provide guidance to vendors as they select targets for their selling efforts. A vendor can try to identify as targets potential customers with usage systems that allow low-risk initial modular experiments. Often the vendor's salespeople will be key in identifying the possible experiments and inducing the potential customers to experiment. If the likelihood of eventual more substantial commitments is sufficiently high, the vendor can justify giving the customer immediate inducements to make the experimental purchase—perhaps a special price or special delivery arrangements.

The behavior of AT&T's competitors in the PBX market in the late 1970s and early 1980s clearly showed active use of this sales pattern. Although many communications customers were interested in the new choices they had been provided by deregulation, many were reluctant to change vendors. The buyers worried about exposure. Often they were most concerned about reliability of products and about vendors' abilities to provide adequate repair and maintenance service. Initial relatively low-risk modular experiments were extremely effective ways for non-Bell vendors to begin relationships with industrial customers.

One retailing organization provides a rather typical example. Its communications manager was a young person who felt that he could make a mark by saving his firm money on communications. His personal characteristics and his attitude toward risk encouraged him to experiment with lower-priced alternatives to Bell. But telephones were important to the retailing organization, so the manager felt that he had to move carefully.

He decided to consider only vendors he believed were well established and, because service was so important to his organization, to consider only vendors that provided their own service (as opposed to using a third party). The organization had a modular usage pattern; many of the stores had their own separate switches. Therefore the manager could use individual stores in relatively isolated lower-risk experiments. He was also able to control the risk in his experiment by selecting the sites; the organization operated some bargain outlets, as well as its full-service department stores, and he selected three bargain outlets.

The customer bought two of the three experimental switches from Rolm and the third from another vendor. He was pleased with Rolm's performance and gained considerable confidence in that vendor's ability to provide service. The confidence he gained from the initial experiments then allowed him to commit to the new vendor for more important parts of his usage system. He chose Rolm to supply telephones for three full-service department stores. Next he decided to consider Rolm for what he considered an important and higher-risk purchase: communications equipment for the organization's headquarters.

In this example, Rolm apparently used price concessions as an investment to induce the customer to make those initial experiments, apparently hoping that the effort would lead to larger purchases. The two Rolm switches in the initial experiement were considerably more powerful than the stores required and at full price would have been too expensive. At the time, however, Rolm did not have a switch that was better suited to the stores' needs. The manager reported that Rolm had provided a special buying program to the retailer's parent and that the vendor had also provided another special program to a retail trade group. The combined discounts made the purchases of the initial Rolm switches economical and helped induce those trials.

Intervendor and Intravendor Transferability

Chapter 3 discussed the role of intravendor transferability of past investments in encouraging a customer to remain with its current supplier. By contrast, intervendor transferability allows the customer to change vendors without forfeiting any substantial past investments.

Vendors can use this concept of transferability in thinking about and providing modularity. Suppose that a new vendor begins offering products for preparing text for printing; the new equipment automates parts of the preparation process that had not previously been automated. This vendor will likely benefit substantially if it can make its product work smoothly with the existing printing equipment of many different potential customers with different usage systems. In other words, the vendor would want to allow potential customers to buy and benefit from its new product without having to change any of their previous investments in automating other parts of their printing operations.

The marketplace for plug-compatible computers provides another example. Vendors such as Amdahl have based their marketing approaches on products that use the customer's past investments in software for IBM computers but that offer the buyer a price break as compared with IBM. In other words, the plug-compatible vendors design their products to allow intervendor transfers—from IBM to their own products.

Maintaining Commitments with Systems Benefits

Risks of Modularity

Modularity allows an account to experiment without having to make a substantial lost-for-good-type commitment. More modularity allows a customer to move toward the always-a-share end of the behavior spectrum. It makes it easier for a vendor to enter new accounts.

By the same token, however, that same modularity also makes it easier for the new vendor to be displaced in turn. The vendor therefore faces considerable tension between desires for modularity to help win commitments and fears that modularity will jeopardize existing ones. Ideally the vendor would like to create modularity so that it can enter an account but then make the modularity go away so that it is more likely to remain in the account. Creating such a pattern is sometimes impossible, but sometimes the vendor can use systems benefits to approximate the desired pattern.

Similarly, vendors face tension because of desires to provide intravendor transferability of past investments by customers but to avoid intervendor transferability of those same investments to the products of competitors. Frequently, providing intravendor transferability requires the vendor to be more deliberate and predictable in its product changes than it otherwise might be. The deliberateness and predictability make it easier for competitors to keep up with the vendor's designs, or at least to keep up adequately to provide intervendor transfers.

Strong leading vendors that stress relationship marketing and serve customers wtih high switching costs are especially affected by this tension. Such a vendor has a large base of established customers. The high switching costs make those customers especially anxious to obtain intravendor transferability. Providing such transferability generally reduces the vendor's agility and makes it an easier target for competitors.

Essentially the leading vendor's choices for technology and product design become de facto standards for at least part of the vendor's industry. Competitors can copy enough of the technology or the product designs to offer customers intervendor transfers of past investments to their own products. The lead vendor may want to make frequent substantial design choices so as to stay ahead of competition, but the need to provide smooth, graceful transitions to its established customers can severely limit the vendor's ability to do so.

The tension between the desires to provide modularity and to avoid modularity and the tension between desires to have intravendor transferability but to avoid intervendor transferability are important and difficult. They cannot be resolved easily (and generally the vendor's best decisions about them will be strongly affected by specifics of a particular product-marketplace and of the position of the vendor within that market).

Managing for the Short-Term and the Long-Term

Those tensions illustrate a general tension that faces the relationship marketer: managing simultaneously for the short term and for the long term. A long time horizon is necessary for the marketer serving long-term customer commitments. At the same time, managers in the vendor organization will usually feel strong pressure for immediate profitability. The vendor organization as a whole must also be sufficiently successful in the short term to survive and prosper.

This general tension between managing for the short term and for the long term is an issue of general concern in U.S. business in the 1980s. It exists in many situations, not just those involving relationship marketing. It appears, however, to be even more important, more complex, and more difficult for the relationship marketer.

This book cannot provide definitive answers to this fundamental tension, but it can raise the topic and note its special importance in relationship marketing. It can suggest that the vendor explicitly plan marketing strategy and tactics with concern for both the short run and the long run. It can also suggest one helpful general approach for tackling the issues of modularity or systems and of intravendor or intervendor transfers. That approach involves the idea of systems benefits.

Systems Benefits

A systems orientation in a usage pattern or in a product policy stresses integration. The user cannot freely combine components to form different patterns, mixing and matching at will. The system is an integrated whole. In the extreme case, the customer must replace all or none of it; it must purchase an entire system or nothing.

Previous discussion noted that there is a spectrum running between end points of modularity and systems. The spectrum applies to usage patterns and to product policies. Actual situations usually correspond to intermediate points on this spectrum.

At times, the customer can elect to treat the same group of products as more or less modular. On the one hand, the physical parts of a usage pattern may be sufficiently basically compatible for the customer to do some mixing and matching. At the same time, however, there may be some features or benefits that the user can obtain only by buying all or at least substantial parts of the usage system from one vendor or one product family. We can call these additional features or benefits *systems benefits*: the added value to the user of the full system. The idea here is that the benefits provided by the whole can be greater than the sum of the benefits of the individual pieces, treated as modular building blocks. Those incremental benefits are systems benefits.

An actual sales example can illustrate this idea of systems benefits and show the effectiveness of systems benefits in keeping customers committed. The example concerns communications equipment, specifically PBXs. Previous discussion noted the substantial inherent modularity in the basic communications network of the United States. Once deregulation allowed competitors to AT&T to enter the PBX market, they could relatively easily offer products that interfaced smoothly with that basic network. At the same time, however, PBXs from different vendors are not completely compatible. The switches contain computers, and those computers use both hardware and software. Modularity of the basic communication network allows substantial hardware compatibility and enough software communication for devices to talk to one another. There is not, however, complete software compatibility among the offerings of different PBX vendors.

The software in a switch provides a considerable amount of its functionality. Some functions depend on having the same software on more than one of a customer's switches. An example is AT&T's ETN (electronic tandem network), which provides for networking of a customer's long-distance traffic among the customers' multiple switches so as to reduce long-distance charges.

The sales situation illustrating the use of systems benefits involved a division of a larger firm, located in a separate city from the firm's headquarters. Rolm, a leading competitor of AT&T, had been especially successful in selling to companies in the division's industry in the division's city. In fact, the division appeared to be the last organization in its industry in its city that had not changed to Rolm. The division was evaluating the procurement of a new telephone system.

A national-account salesperson for a Bell operating company was assigned to the firm's headquarters. (The example occurred just before the breakup of the Bell system, so the operating company was still joined to AT&T corporate.) That salesperson told managers at the customer's headquarters that the Rolm switch would indeed work with the basic telephone network but that she believed that they should choose Bell.

At the time, the organization's other divisions had Bell switches; a Rolm switch would not be fully software compatible with those switches. The salesperson argued that the customer would obtain substantial benefits from full software compatibility of the switches at its different divisions. She argued that the compatibility would provide immediate benefits of ETN for efficiency on long-distance calls. Further, she explained that in the future Bell would provide new features through software to its switches. An example was a message-store-and-forward capability that would be used for electronic mail. If one of the organization's divisions had a noncompatible Rolm switch, it would not be able to participate in ETN or in a future electronic-mail system based on Bell software.

The headquarters managers insisted that the division remain with Bell; the division selected a Bell Dimension switch. The customer decided that the systems benefits, immediate and future, made that choice appropriate.

This example is an especially good example of a sound sales approach for relationship marketing. The salesperson was truthful to the customer and made no attempt to claim the competitor's product would not function. Inaccurate scare campaigns in relationship marketing can be damaging to a vendor that tries them; customers are likely to catch on eventually to the truth and to resent the vendor's tactics. (By contrast, attempts by some AT&T managers early in the deregulation process to convince buyers that competitive or interconnect equipment would harm the basic communications network seem dysfunctional, especially for relationship marketing.)

At the same time, the salesperson successfully differentiated her firm's offerings from those of the competition. She sold on the basis of real benefits that her customer would value. She sold both immediate systems benefits and the promise of additional systems benefits for the future. The time horizon was right, the benefits were real, the pitch was professional, and the customer bought.

In this and other examples, systems benefits provide the glue that turns components into a system with the whole greater than the sum of the parts. Systems benefits increase switching costs. If the customer changes only part of a usage system from one vendor to another, it loses at least some systems benefits.

Systems benefits that are real and valuable to the customer therefore move the customer closer to the lost-for-good end of the behavior spectrum. A product policy or a usage pattern toward the systems end of the spectrum would be attractive for keeping customers' commitments once they have been won. A systems usage pattern and systems product-policy choices mean that customers can make either substantial choices or none at all. In response to high switching costs, customers will generally adopt long time horizons in their commitments to vendors. Once won, such commitments are generally won for a long time. A vendor that is established in a particular account would generally prefer the account to have a system-oriented usage pattern. The problem is that the commitments of such customers are so difficult to win in the first place.

Product Policy over Time

Vendors would prefer the ability to win accounts with a modular product policy and then the ability to keep the same accounts with a systems-oriented product policy. On the clock of the individual account and the individual account relationship, the seller would like a product policy that moves toward the systems end of the spectrum.

Implementing such an approach is by no means easy, but, perhaps surprisingly, it is not impossible in at least some situations. The basic idea is for the vendor to allow and encourage initial modular experiments as far as is allowed by technology, usage patterns, and other relevant factors. Once it has used modularity to gain a toehold in the account, the vendor would use the potential of systems benefits to encourage the customer to buy more and more from the same source and to build systems interdependence in its usage pattern. In terms of the behavior models, the vendor would first use modularity to move the account away from the lost-for-good end of the spectrum and induce the buyer to change its prior commitment. The vendor would then use systems benefits to move the account closer to lost-for-good (won-for-a-long-time) behavior again.

For such an approach to work, the vendor would need to offer attractive modular ways for a customer to try the seller. Generally the vendor would want to instruct and motivate its salespeople to help identify promising opportunities for low-risk initial modular experiments. The initial modular placements should be sufficiently attractive on their own to induce customers to buy. The attraction might involve special capabilities that competitive products did not offer, special price or delivery availability, or any of a wide variety of other benefits.

The marketer would not want to make the initial sale contingent on the customer's acceptance of a larger system; to do so would negate the benefits provided to the customer by modularity and a low-risk initial trial. On the other hand, the seller in some situations will want to tell the customer about the potential for systems benefits in the future. The buyer may find it an added attraction to have the opportunity to use a low-risk initial trial purchase to try out a vendor with which it might want a more substantial future relationship.

Highly credible vendors might find it especially useful to inform potential customers of possible systems benefits as an added (but not necessary) inducement to make the initial purchase. A less well-established vendor might prefer not to press the issue of potential systems benefits when it worked for an initial trial. It might find it preferable to avoid discussing the customer's possible but not required higher future dependence on the vendor until experience had made the buyer more able to contemplate such dependence.

The systems benefits offered by the vendor should thus be valuable but optional capabilities, ones that the account could decide to add or not to add. There are other legal reasons why the benefits should be optional; optional benefits would appear far less likely to run afoul of the antitrust laws, such as those against tying arrangements. The account would obtain those benefits by obtaining a major part (or, in some cases, all) of its system from the single vendor.

The additional power provided by software compatibility of PBXs in the preceding example provides an illustration. Customers can use individual switches for many routine purposes without such compatibility, but, at the same time, the additional power can bring real benefits to the user.

Two general approaches can allow vendors to offer initial low-risk modular experiments where the technology and the customer's usage pattern allow. First, vendors sometimes offer stand-alone products that interface as little as possible with other parts of the customer's operations. In other situations, the vendor can instead or in addition provide intervendor transferability of the customer's past investments. In other words, the vendor can offer products that fit as components into customers' established usage systems.

Compatibility with the products of dominant vendors are often especially well suited for this purpose.

Such desires for compatibility with the products of a strong vendor are a strong force in making the designs of leading vendors become de facto standards in some markets. In some other marketplaces, groups of vendors adopt formal official standards. Those formal standards also allow compatibility and modularity and can therefore be part of vendors' strategies to combine modularity and systems benefits over time to individual customers.

Industry Standards

Formal Standards

Industry standards are protocols or conventions used by many vendors that can allow products to interface. In practice, the technological and design choices of an especially strong vendor often become a de facto standard that is followed and copied by other vendors. The process by which a group of vendors agree to a formal standard is generally considerably more complex (unless a potential formal standard is also the preferred choice of a vendor with the power to create a de facto standard); usually members of the group of vendors and other parties (such as customers, other members of professional technical organizations, and government employees) are involved.

In understanding the role of standards in affecting modularity, it is important to note that standards can be established at various levels in a system of products. For example, consider two relatively familiar industrial product categories: computers and grocery-store scanners. In each case, there is some standardization in the basic encoding of information but not full compatibility of the products of different vendors.

For computers, standards-setting professional bodies have established codes for recording alphanumeric information in groups of digital (0/1) bits. Those codes allow some transfer of information from one computer to another—for example, on magnetic tape. Similarly, the universal product code has established a basic language used by grocery-store scanners. That code allows food manufacturers, scanner manufacturers, and others to produce products that can be used within a single grocery store.

These necessary agreements on encoding information do not mean, however, that physical products of different vendors in either market can necessarily be joined together. The computer codes do not mean that computers from different vendors will have all of the necessary matches in physical design, timing, and operating systems to allow them to link together closely during operation. The universal product code does not guarantee that checkout stations with scanning devices made by different vendors can link to the same controller within a store or that store systems from different vendors can link together within a retail chain.

Thus, there can be many different levels of standardization, and products can be compatible at some levels but not at others. Further complexity arises because customers (and vendors) are often unclear as to how much compatibility actually exists in a product-marketplace. For example, press coverage about personal computers has noted that products supposedly compatible with IBM's PC in fact differ in some details of timing or software. Consequently, some customers have encountered serious difficulties when they have tried to take advantage of "compatibility."

The product category of LANs discussed in chapter 4 provides additional detail about possible levels for standards. By the early 1980s, several organizations had tried to define possible levels of interface in a network. For example, the ISO (International Standards Organization) had defined a seven-level scheme for describing protocols for networks. The lowest level was a physical one, describing the actual physical connections of devices with the network cable. The next levels concerned conventions for packaging information (into what were called packets) for transmission onto the network. An intermediate level defined conventions for what were called sessions—essentially conversations between two networked devices. A session protocol would specify how a device could initiate a session, what procedures would be used by one device to acknowledge receipt of a packet of information from another, and how to end a session. The top levels in the ISO standard were most concerned with applications software: conventions to allow programs on the various physical devices to communicate successfully through the network.

Similarly, IBM developed SNA (System Network Architecture), another multilevel set of definitions for use in networks. SNA did not use exactly the same set of levels as did the ISO standard, although there was considerable similarity between the two. SNA also ranged from levels concerning physical connections to higher levels dealing with applications software.

In general, standards at higher levels require standards for the lower levels as well. For example, devices cannot provide usefully compatible applications software on a network if those devices cannot physically plug into the same network. An industry can adopt standards for one or more lower levels, however, without standardizing at higher levels. Within the developing market for LANs, most serious discussions about adopting standards focused on the bottom few physical levels of compatibility. The serious discussion of standards that might actually be adopted did not proceed all the way to the upper levels of software compatibility.

Standards and Customer Confidence

Technological uncertainty frequently creates strong customer feelings of exposure. Such uncertainty may occur in product-marketplaces characterized by rapid technological pace. It can also occur in the early stages of many product-marketplaces. Especially if customers believe that they will be making long-term commitments with high importance, they will feel considerable exposure in making a choice in a market that they do not understand and that is still unsettled in technology and even in terms of which will be the key (or surviving) vendors.

The LAN market provides a good example. Since office-automation systems would involve a user firm's basic procedures and, when fully adopted, would reach into essentially every corner of the organization, the looming investment actions in procedures were monumental. Customers in the early 1980s described themselves as lacking knowledge and, often, as being worried and afraid.

The obvious objective for vendors trying to develop a new product-marketplace would be to give potential customers enough confidence to begin to commit. Similarly, in an established market going through a period of substantial technological change, vendors would also want to give customers confidence that choices they make today will not be obsolete unreasonably soon. In either case, the vendor's objective is to give customers confidence that they are stepping onto a sound escalator that will carry them smoothly to future usage. Customers want to be sure they choose an escalator that will continue smoothly upward. They want to avoid escalators based on poor technologies or escalators that vendors will not continue to build.

When an especially strong vendor selects a technology and begins to offer products for sale, those actions alone may give customers confidence to commit. The vendor may also create a de facto standard, adopted by other vendors in the marketplace. The fact that other vendors adhere to the standard will frequently give potential customers even more confidence.

Formal industry standards also create customer confidence. Suppose that an entire industry or a sizable group of vendors adopts a particular standard. In doing so, the vendors in the group would be telling the market that they had enough confidence in the technology embodied in the standard to be willing to commit to it themselves. Such actions are likely to reassure customers that the technological bases of escalators built on that standard are sound. Similarly customers can be reassured that they will have access to a variety of vendors; the entire group committed to the standard would contribute to building the escalator over time.

Standards and Modularity

In product-marketplaces in which customers' usage systems are combinations of separate parts, standards establish common conventions for joining those parts. In the process, they increase modularity. They allow customers to focus their commitments more on a technology and less on any particular vendor.

In committing to a standard technology that is followed by multiple vendors, the account can make its fundamental lost-for-good commitment to the technology on which the standard rests. Within the group of vendors, the account can share its business, appearing more as an always-a-share customer to any particular vendor.

Chapter 4 described the efforts of Xerox and other vendors to make the Ethernet design a formal standard for LANs. Potential customers for office automation and LANs did not feel it would be worth while to undergo ungraceful change in such systems unless absolutely necessary. The potential benefits of keeping an office-automation system completely up-to-date technically would easily be outweighed by the costs of any but a very graceful evolution. Customers wanted to step onto sound, smooth escalators. The Ethernet standards effort can be viewed as an attempt to provide customers with confidence to commit; it would also provide substantial modularity.

Vendors' Attitudes to Standards

Vendors in a new or changing product-marketplace will value the ability of standards to induce customer confidence. The problem is that standards have other much less attractive effects. The modularity provided by the standard creates more competition for a buyer's business, allowing customers to show always-a-share-type behavior within the group of vendors committed to the standard. In deciding whether to accept or to advocate a movement for formal standards, the individual vendor will need to balance the positive and the negative effects.

The choice will depend on the strengths of customers' desires (or demands) for standards and modularity. The more unwilling the customers are to commit without standards, the more attractive will be the standards effort.

The vendor's choice will also depend on its position in its market (or, in a developing market, on its likely future market position). The stronger the vendor is or can reasonably expect to be in the market, the more likely it is to be able to convince customers to commit to it without formal standards. In general, vendors will prefer lost-for-good-type commitments made specifically to them over always-a-share-type commitments made to a group. Therefore a dominant or potentially dominant vendor will often be reluctant to accept a formal standard unless it is necessary to do so.

Small vendors generally will not have enough clout and credibility in the market to induce high-exposure lost-for-good commitments. Thus, some such vendors would favor standards for facilitating commitments—essentially for allowing them into the game. At the same time, however, a small vendor is unlikely to have enough power or resources to lead an effort toward formal standards. The best strategy for a small vendor favoring standards would therefore likely be to support and encourage efforts by others toward standards.

The medium-sized vendor in a new marketplace with expected long-term high-exposure commitments is the most likely player to lead in an effort for formal standards. Such a vendor may have substantial resources, but those resources may well be insufficient to induce lost-for-good (won-for-a-long-time) commitments. Hence, it can be extremely sensible for the medium-sized player to work to rally a group of vendors in a drive for standardization that will give customers the confidence to commit to the group.

There is a large component of education and persuasion in any such formal standards effort. Advocates must convince vendors of the value of supporting and adopting a standard; they must convince vendors that the individual vendor will be better off if customers can commit to a technology that has been certified by standardization. Often vendor advocates must also convince some customers that they should prefer products based on the formal standard to alternatives, perhaps including the de facto standard of an especially strong vendor. Advocates might emphasize that the formal standard would give customers access to the products and innovations of a group of vendors, including entrepreneurial firms that could provide special value in individual parts of a system based on the standard.

An effort toward formal standards is likely to involve a professional organization, such as the IEEE (Institute of Electrical and Electronic Engineers). Such an organization brings together representatives of various vendors, often representatives of customers, and other specialists such as academics. It provides a forum and some sense of impartiality in selecting a technology as the basis of the standard.

Many such organizations have standing committees on standards or form special committees for specific considerations. A vendor trying to lead a move toward standards would first need to win the interest and attention of an appropriate committee. It would then want to work with that committee, providing information and other support to facilitate progress. In that process, the medium- or large-sized player would often be working hard to convince other vendors that its own technology was in fact best for the group.

Xerox's effort toward an Ethernet standard provides an example of the apparent attractiveness of standards to a medium-sized player in a developing marketplace characterized by high levels of customer exposure. Although Xerox is a large company, it is a medium-sized player in the office-automation market as compared with potentially dominant IBM or AT&T. Alone, Xerox could not induce many strong customer commitments. The firm could, however, provide the rallying point for a drive toward standards. Xerox was using commitments to Ethernet by other vendors to leverage its own efforts to develop the market and to help induce important customer commitments focused on technology rather than on a single vendor.

Profitability Despite Standards

A successful standards effort facilitating modularity can accelerate market development and provide market access to vendors that could not induce substantial commitments on their own. But standards also create less desirable longer-term consequences for vendors, putting them into a relatively rough-and-tumble, always-a-share world. Thus, the vendor faces tension between desires for the short-run benefits of standards and desires for the long-run benefits of incompatible systems.

The vendor may be able to use systems benefits as a way out of the dilemma; systems benefits may allow it to enjoy the immediate advantages of standards but also to enjoy the longer-term profitability of strong commitments from customers. To do so, the vendor would use the concept of different levels of standardization.

Suppose that a vendor decided that it was necessary or useful to advocate standards to facilitate modularity and encourage initial commitments from accounts. That seller would work for standards on only as many of the possible levels as necessary. It would then make its own products compatible with one another at the higher levels, too, and build systems benefits based on that higher-level compatibility.

In LANs, for example, the vendor would push for standards at the bottom few levels only—physical connections and network protocols. Devices meeting the standard would not necessarily be compatible at higher levels. For example, it would be very unlikely for devices from different vendors to be software compatible with one another. Therefore a particular vendor that supported the standard could use software compatibility to build systems benefits among its own products. Buyers would not have to buy all, most, or many of the components of their usage systems from a single vendor, but doing so would provide additional benefits that would not be available in more mixed patterns.

Xerox's future success in the office products and LAN markets is not entirely clear. Xerox's profitability will depend on the firm's ability to develop and market pieces that fit into an office-automation environment based on Ethernet. It is not clear whether Xerox's planners will develop enough individually attractive components, and it is also unclear whether they will provide systems benefits as an inducement for customers to buy substantial amounts of equipment from Xerox. Nevertheless, a strategy of standards for physical levels and systems benefits among individually attractive components seems sensible for Xerox to use in its standards effort.

Inducing Customer Investments

As another cut at the problem of strengthening commitments, marketers can consider how to induce and use customers' investment actions as a way of building switching costs. Chapter 3 described investment actions in dollars, people, lasting assets, and procedures. Substantial investment actions in any of these categories can create switching costs for a buyer, particularly if past investments transfer more readily among the products of a particular vendor than they do from the products of one vendor to those of another. Actions by vendors can encourage such investments and thus induce customers to raise their own switching costs.

The previous discussion considered a variety of switching costs, including investments in people. Customers may hire or train people to work with a vendor or its products. In addition, there is frequently considerable less formal but highly useful learning over time as the buyers' employees learn to get the most out of products and services that have been purchased.

Although some such training and learning occurs without specific encouragement of the vendor, the vendor's choices can also be an influence. Consider a vendor of equipment that requires reconfiguration and maintenance over time. The vendor must make decisions as to how much of the reconfiguration and maintenance it will perform for customers (with or without a specific charge for the service) and how much it will allow, encourage, or require the customer to do.

There are arguments for and against heavy involvement of users in the processes. One argument for their involvement is that in learning to work closely with the equipment, the customer's employees will be creating an investment and switching costs, especially if their learning transfers more readily to other products from the same vendor than it does to competing products. This factor may or may not convince the vendor to involve customers heavily in reconfiguration and maintenance, but it certainly ought to be one consideration in the decision.

Investments in lasting assets and in procedures are especially likely to create inertia in customer organizations. As an example, consider a vendor for carbon steel. A traditional carbon-steel customer is likely to behave much like the always-a-share model. Switching costs are low, and the customer can buy on the basis of immediate inducements. Suppose, however, that the vendor helps a customer implement a just-in-time (JIT) inventory system to reduce inventory and costs of inventory. Such an inventory system requires considerably closer coupling of the vendor and the customer. Ordering and delivery procedures must mesh closely and smoothly. Buyer and seller invest in procedures to coordinate closely with one another.

A buyer that has established a JIT policy is not likely to change vendors easily, even for a relative commodity such as carbon steel. Changing would require another substantial investment in learning to work with a new vendor. Moreover, such a customer will be less likely to use multiple suppliers than would a more typical carbon-steel purchaser. (Use of multiple suppliers with JIT is not impossible, and, in fact, it appears to be common in Japan, where JIT is well established. In the United States, however, neither customers nor vendors are experienced with JIT. Working out such a system with one vendor may be enough of a challenge for a buying organization.)

Increasingly in the 1980s, substantial investments in procedures are involving information and information technology (computers and communications) in key roles. Thus, information technology has become an important marketing tool for building switching costs and strengthening the commitments of customers. The following sections examine the now-classic example of American Hospital Supply's ASAP (analytical systems automated purchasing) systems.

American Hospital Supply's ASAP Systems

Hospital Supply Industry

In 1975, just before the introduction of ASAP, there were 7,000 hospitals in the United Staes. The 1,800 largest hospitals (with 200 or more beds each) accounted for 50 percent of the market for medical equipment and supplies. Equipment and supplies were also sold to laboratories, individual physicians, and others. Approximately two-thirds of the dollar volume of manufacturers' sales of equipment and supplies went through distributors (local, regional, and national). Just over one-fourth of the dollar volume was sold direct to health-care institutions, and the remainder moved through a variety of other channels (such as drugstores).

Buying processes within hospitals were complex, and it was often difficult to determine who in fact made the purchase decision. The primary contact of a salesperson (from a distributor organization or from a manufacturing organization that sold direct) was generally a doctor, nurse, technician, or pathologist. The hospital administrator might also ask for advice or information from department heads or purchase committees. For especially large purchases, the hospital's board and various government agencies might also become involved. The government role was increasing as agencies tried to help control costs of health care and to avoid aggregate overcapacity among the health-care institutions within the same geographical area.

Hospitals bought many different items, ranging from inexpensive relative commodities such as syringes and hospital gowns to elaborate, costly instruments. Historically distributors had been especially strong in selling the thousands of common supply items required by the hospitals. The distributors emphasized their abilities to provide the desired assortment of products and to give customers service. The distributors were considerably less successful in selling instruments. Approximately three-fourths of the medical instruments sold in the United States in the mid-1970s were sold direct; in general, only less expensive, more standard instruments were sold through distributors.

Although many manufacturers of instruments were skeptical of distributors' abilities to sell complex instruments, large distributors were working hard to obtain instrument lines from manufacturers. American Hospital Supply, by far the largest distributor, was also building its own manufacturing divisions. It was obtaining perhaps 40 percent of its sales dollars from products it manufactured.

Recent (1984) sales literature from American Hospital Supply describes the need for a system to reduce hospitals' ordering and inventory costs. That brochure describes problems that also faced the hospitals in the mid-1970s and were needs addressed by the ASAP systems. The brochure describes an endless shuffle of paperwork, purchase orders, and invoices and the shuffle of receiving, storing, and delivering products. It suggests that for each dollar a hospital spends on an actual product's cost, the buyer also spends up to an additional dollar for acquiring and storing that item. It states the average cost of a purchase order as $25 to $50—approximately 75 percent for people and the remainder for supplies.

The brochure also describes the cost of inventory, giving the holding cost of inventory as 27 percent of the unit cost of the item. Inventory, it says, earns nothing, must be counted and controlled, and can be obsolete, outdated, lost, or improperly appropriated. High inventory, it explains, reduces cash flow, operating revenues, and working capital. Especially difficult to control is the department inventory in laboratories and other locations outside the main hospital inventory. That inventory is not entirely visible, is often vary large, and is frequently controlled by the end user rather than by the hospital's materials-management function.

First ASAP System

In the late 1960s, American Hospital Supply's new chairman, Karl Bays, decided that the firm should computerize its own inventory. In retrospect, in an interview fifteen years later, Bays recalled that many of his managers had not been happy with the move and that he himself had not been able to explain fully why it made sense. He did, however, insist on the computerization. The automated inventory was needed as the firm later introduced a series of automated systems for the entry of customers' orders: the ASAP systems.

The first ASAP system was introduced by an American Hospital Supply division in 1976. The suggestion apparently came from a salesperson on the West Coast who believed his customers could use help ordering more efficiently. That ASAP 1 system provided automated order entry, either through a touch-tone phone (and seven-digit product numbers) or through a wand that could read bar codes from the sides of packages or from a catalog of the codes. Some of the early versions also used prepunched plastic cards to provide automated dialing of preset orders.

Over time, ASAP was used by all six of American Hospital Supply's distribution divisions. Systems improvements created ASAP 2, 3, and 4, but

ASAP 1 also remained in use, generally by small hospitals or single departments within larger ones.

ASAP 1 provided benefits to customers in convenience of ordering and in the reduction of ordering costs and time. In theory, there was no reason for those benefits to apply only to products from American Hospital Supply. Other vendors could have offered automated entry using the same idea, the same ordering wand, or certainly the same telephone. In practice, however, American's competitors could not respond quickly; the first response came two years after the ASAP introduction. Much of the delay was caused by the need for the competitors to computerize their own inventories in order to offer a computerized system to their customers.

American's next system was ASAP 2. It contained the order-input capabilities of ASAP 1 plus the ability to accept orders from a deck of computer cards and a card reader. ASAP 2 also added a teleprinter that could be used either to input orders or to obtain a printback of an order for verification. Printback (in a fixed standard format) was useful to help catch errors.

ASAP 2 was a standardized offering that in theory should not have been difficult to copy. Competitors could have accepted orders from the same devices and provided the same types of outputs to customers. If they did, the customers would find it quite easy to mix and match orders, obtaining parts of their requirements through the automated systems of several vendors. In practice, the competitors eventually offered similar services, allowing hospitals to order by teletype from many different suppliers. The responses took time, however. By that time, later versions of ASAP had provided a service somewhat more tailored to the needs of the individual customer account and, very important, had built real systems benefits into the offering.

Later ASAP Systems

ASAP 3, the next offering, added several features to customize the system to a particular hospital's needs. The system allowed users to create and then use repeatedly computer files of purchase information, thus reducing the amount of input subsequently needed to send the order. A user might create a standing-order file for regular orders of routine items; the file would contain the list of items and quantities, as well as information about the timing of orders. A user could also establish repetitive files: listings of items ordered as a group, although they might not be ordered completely regularly. Such files could contain economic order quantities (EOQs) to determine reorder decisions for individual items. Users could also define basic files or more complete lists of items; on any specific order, the user would select some, though generally not all, of the items in the basic file. EOQs could be included for the individual items.

ASAP 3 also provided customization of output. Customers could specify their own purchase-order formats, which would be programmed by American Hospital Supply; they could thus obtain ASAP purchase orders in the same formats as their other purchase orders. Further, ASAP 3 inputs were automatically separated by American Hospital Supply's computer into sets of items processed by each of the company's six distribution divisions. Customers received copies of purchase orders and invoices from each of the divisions.

In November 1983 American Hospital Supply introduced ASAP 4, which provided a computer-to-computer link from the hospital's computer to American Hospital Supply's mainframe. It was appropriate only for hospitals using computerized materials-management systems. ASAP 4 linked directly to such systems, providing for automatic ordering (subject to override) as the materials-management software determined the needed purchases. (The actual physical link involved telephone communication between machines.) Before ASAP 4, hospitals had had to take information from their computerized materials-management systems and rekey it into a teleprinter for transmission.

Each hospital placed its ASAP 4 orders at a prearranged time of the day; the system was not designed for emergency orders. The original ASAP 4 system linked to mainframe computers within hospitals; American Hospital Supply had also announced plans to introduce a system for hospitals' microcomputers during 1984.

Customers did not pay for the use of any of the ASAP systems (or for the necessary software customization, which might take up to eight hours of programming effort). Salespeople were not charged for software customization; however, the sales force was otherwise compensated entirely on the profitability of their accounts, with no base salaries. All costs, including their automobile costs and the costs of computer terminals, were borne by the salespeople (from their gross commissions).

The later ASAP systems built clear systems benefits for the customer. In ASAP 3, the standing-order files and repetitive files listed groups of items ordered at one time. Essentially those files grouped the products into a system for ordering purposes. Although customers could split up such a group and order parts from different vendors, much of the convenience and cost reduction provided by ASAP would be lost if they did so.

The systems benefits for the customer contained in ASAP 4 were even stronger. That system provided all of the benefits included in its predecessor. In addition, by linking the American Hospital Supply computer to the customer's materials-management software, ASAP 4 essentially joined all of the customer's purchases into an efficient ordering system. The customer could certainly choose to obtain products from even a wide variety of sources, but it would give up substantial benefits if it did so.

Additional Developments Related to ASAP

Important developments in American Hospital Supply's market after the first ASAP introduction made the systems even more appropriate for serving customers' needs. Perhaps the most significant was a major change in the way that the U.S. government reimbursed hospitals for the costs of treating Medicare patients. Previously hospitals had been reimbursed on the basis of the actual costs they incurred in serving those patients. The cost-plus system did not reward the hospitals for efficiency. Federal legislation signed in April 1983 provided for a change (over a four-year period) to what was called a prospective-payment approach based on diagnosis-related groups (DRGs).

DRGs had been developed at Yale University, initially as an aid in reviewing and predicting the lengths of patients' stays in the hospital. The idea was to create major diagnostic categories (MDCs) and subgroupings (DRGs) that identified patients with sufficiently similar conditions to produce similar patterns of length of stay, treatment, and consumption of hospital resources. The initial project was intended to help review and manage capacity utilization. A revised system of DRGs was later developed as a tool for predicting the amount and type of resources that would be used in treating patients. The system used in the 1983 legislation contained 469 DRGs.

Under the new reimbursement system, the payment to a hospital would be based on national and regional costs for each DRG, not on the hospital's own costs. Moreover, the national and regional averages would be updated over time, so that if hospitals overall improved their cost performance, they would be subject to stricter DRG-related payment limits. For the phase-in period, the hospitals would be compensated by a fraction of their cost-based rate and the complementary fraction of the DRG-related rate. Over that period, the fraction based on the DRG rates would increase to 100 percent.

This fundamental change made hospitals substantially more conscious of costs, including inventory and ordering costs. It was creating increased interest in materials management and in systems like ASAP.

Another important development in the health-care industry that was also heightening concern of hospitals about costs was the growth of alternative forms of health care. In part because employers and third-party insurers were increasingly concerned with controlling the costs of care, there were high interest and growth in health-maintenance organizations and other alternatives to the traditional health-care institutions. Hence, for the first time, many hospitals felt they faced competition in their businesses; they felt the need of improved management (including control of inventory costs) to avoid pricing themselves out of the market.

American Hospital Supply promoted the ASAP systems as tools for productivity and cost containment and used a theme of productivity in much of its overall marketing. For example, in 1984 the firm staged a product exposition, "Productivity through Technology," that displayed many of the products it handled. The exposition emphasized equipment to produce high-quality clinical analyses at low cost. Only one of many booths contained information about ASAP, and one of many seminar presentations considered the ordering systems.

The following are two brief excerpts from one of the brochures about ASAP that were used at the 1984 exposition:

> The endless shuffle . . . is an expensive shuffle.
>
> The shuffle of determining what, when, and how many to order. The shuffle of paperwork, purchase orders, and invoices. And the shuffle of receiving, storing and delivering products. Endless? Yes. And expensive. Much more expensive than the unit cost of each item reveals. For every dollar you spend on the unit cost of an item you can expect to pay up to one additional dollar acquiring and storing that item.

> ASAP ends the endless shuffle.
>
> The American ASAP System is a complete, automated order entry system, designed to provide rapid order entry, order confirmation and ensure efficient product delivery. It puts an end to the endless shuffle while supporting effective materials management and aggressive cost containment.

Systems Benefits through Information Technology

The ASAP example is widely cited as an example (perhaps, *the* example) of the use of information technology for strategic advantage. There are an increasing number of other examples. The basic idea is for the vendor to use information technology—computers and, especially, communications—to link closely to customers. The vendor uses the link to provide substantial real benefits to buyers; the value of those benefits induces the customer to allow or even encourage the strong link to its vendor.

In the terms of this book, the strategic uses of information technology provide systems benefits: real and valuable reasons for the account to do a substantial amount of business with a single vendor. Those uses of information technology increase the customer's switching costs and move the buyer closer to the lost-for-good end of the behavior spectrum.

The basic principle to use in marketing efforts to build systems benefits and switching costs is that the benefits must be real and valuable to buyers. Customers will not make real and substantial investments, building switching costs, without correspondingly solid benefits.

Actual marketing efforts to induce investments in procedures (whether or not those efforts are based in information technology) have provided an assortment of benefits. Some, such as the ASAP example, have concerned ordering and inventory management; those areas appear particularly suitable. In other situations, vendors have induced investments and higher switching costs by addressing different aspects of their customers' businesses. The example of McKesson, a major distributor to pharmacies, provides an example in which the vendor first offered benefits relating to ordering and then offered additional benefits using the communication link it had established with its customers.

McKesson (formerly Foremost McKesson) began this story as a traditional distributor to pharmacists. Its salespeople called on customers, manually took their orders for a range of products, and delivered the ordered products. McKesson's first information-technology link to customers used terminals in the customers' locations for ordering. Customers entered their own orders when they wanted something. The orders were transmitted over telephone lines to McKesson, which provided rapid delivery. That initial system reduced the work load for the McKesson salesperson and also provided the customer with the real benefit of more rapid service; the buyer did not have to wait for the next visit by the salesperson to place an order.

McKesson then began to add further capabilities for customers using the same terminal in the customer's location. For example, the vendor offered help to pharmacists in planning and managing the allocation of shelf space in their stores. Next, McKesson added a service that addressed what was probably the most unpleasant and troublesome issue facing many pharmacists: the handling of forms for reimbursement of insurance claims. The vendor learned to work with the claims procedures of the different paying organizations. It offered to take claims processing off the pharmacists' hands for a fee. The pharmacists sent McKesson the information about each claim and received prompt payment from McKesson. McKesson then handled the rest of the dealings with the payer of the claim and eventually received payment.

Over time, McKesson thus served an increasing set of needs of its customers. In the process, it induced customers to adapt their basic procedures to the vendor, and it established very strong links with them. The benefits provided to the buyers were certainly real and valuable, addressing the particularly pressing concerns of pharmacists.

Singles and Home Runs

Not all strategic marketing moves to build switching costs and systems benefits involve information technology, and not all marketing uses of information technology build substantial switching costs and systems benefits. Some uses of technology, which we might call home runs, build extremely strong links between vendors and customers. Others, which we might call singles, may be very useful marketing tactics but do not provide lasting links between buyer and seller. Two examples illustrate this distinction.

First, consider a vendor of insulation materials that sold through building distributors and contractors. It offered its customers access to a computer program to help them determine how much insulation they needed to provide specified levels of performance in different particular buildings. The customer used a terminal to enter information about the building and the desired insulation results. The program then calculated and provided the customer the amount and type of insulation that was appropriate.

The vendor's program provided definite benefits to customers, and customers likely appreciated those benefits, especially at a time when their customers were highly concerned with energy costs and with insulation. At the same time, however, this use of information technology did not create a system. The customer could provide the recommended level of insulation by using some or all of the required materials from the products of another vendor. In fact, a rating (or standards) system for insulating materials helped the buyer determine the equivalencies among the products of different vendors.

This use of information technology is a single. It appears a sound marketing tactic, but its effects are not likely to keep the customer highly loyal for an extended period. The vendor may be able to keep considerable interest and patronage from buyers with a series of such offerings, but the buyers are not linked closely to the vendor by the particular program.

By contrast, consider a Dutch firm that sold pigments for auto bodies to body shops throughout Europe. When they painted only one part of a car after repairs of some sort, employees of the body shops faced the challenging job of matching the color of the rest of the car. Although they might be able to determine (and buy or mix pigment in) the original color of the car, the car would not have remained precisely that original shade over time. Moreover, different cars of the same original color would change color differently over time, depending on the climate of the area in which they were kept, whether they were garaged, and other factors.

The pigment maker offered all of its auto-body customers terminals that accessed a computer program for determining how to match the colors of cars. The customer input data on the original make and color of the car and additional information about location, garaging, and other relevant factors. The terminal then printed out a suggested formula for matching the car, using the vendor's pigments.

This use of information technology is a home run, not just a single. The customer cannot freely mix and match the pigments of different vendors; the program refers only to the precise colors of the offering vendor's palette. In addition, the customer needs a full range of pigments to use the system. Even if another vendor offered a similar program, the customer would need a second complete set of pigments to use the second system. It seems highly unlikely that a buyer would choose to deal with two such systems. There is room for one terminal and one system in a body shop.

The ASAP example is noteworthy in that it started as a single but ended as a home run. To continue the baseball analogy, we might call it an inside-the-park home run. American Hospital Supply was fortunate in the sense that it had the luxury of a long time—years—to build systems benefits for its customers. The early ASAP systems did not build strong enough systems benefits to have made customers strongly prefer dealing with a single vendor for ordering; other vendors did not offer ASAP strong competition at the time simply because they were not yet prepared to do so. By the time other distributors were offering automated ordering systems, American Hospital Supply had introduced more and more real systems benefits for its customers.

Vendors trying to use information technology to build systems benefits and strengthen links to customers frequently do not have the luxury of time today as American Hospital Supply did in the 1970s. Such marketing moves are very frequently preemptive. Getting there first is critical; being second often is not worth a great deal.

The behavior models help explain why. When the ASAP systems were introduced, the behavior of hospitals lay toward the always-a-share end of the behavior spectrum. Buyers could rather easily shift some or all of their purchases from one supplier to another. The ASAP systems moved the customers closer and closer to the lost-for-good end of the spectrum. Those systems helped customers with some of their most pressing problems; they thereby provided substantial real benefits to customers. They also built switching costs very appreciably.

In general, the idea of being the first vendor to move customers from always-a-share toward lost-for-good can be extremely attractive in a particular product-marketplace. It is relatively easy to induce changes in a customer whose behavior approximates always-a-share, provided that the vendor can offer substantial real benefits to the account as inducements. Once the customer moves toward the lost-for-good end of the spectrum, however, big changes are much more difficult to induce. A second vendor will find it difficult (though not always impossible) to dislodge the first. And as the example about pigments for body shops illustrates especially clearly, there is often not room for more than one vendor in the customer after it has moved along the behavior spectrum.

Thus, timing is critical. An increasing number of marketing firms are looking for effective and legal ways to build strong customer relationships through information technology and other means. They are motivated in part by the fact that such strong relationships are economically attractive to them. They are also motivated in part by a fear that some other vendor will reach the customers with real systems benefits first—and hit a home run.

Because of this increased interest in building links through information technology, it appears that there will be less and less room in the future for inside-the-park home runs. They may not become impossible, but they will not necessarily be a readily available approach for future marketing moves as they were for American Hospital Supply. Thus, the good news is that information technology can help a vendor build close, lasting relationships with customers. The bad news is that the vendor's competitor may get there first.

Winning versus Maintaining Commitments

Vendors face a tension in dealing with new customers as compared with established customers. Frequently the marketing approaches best suited to winning new commitments from customers are different from those that would be ideal for maintaining and strengthening commitments from existing customers. Although the concepts of this chapter provide some suggestions for dealing successfully with this tension, that tension remains.

The tension includes pressures toward modularity for winning customers through low-risk initial experiments and pressures for systems benefits to strengthen links to existing ones. It can include desires by vendors to use standards to help win customers but to avoid standards for the business of an established customer. It includes pressure toward more technological pace so that the vendor appears dynamic and creative and attracts new buyers but pressure toward a more controlled pace so that the seller can offer existing customers graceful transitions from one product to another. It includes the pressure concerning how much initial investment the vendor should ask of customers. Higher initial investment makes it harder for the new customer to commit, but frequently, requiring more initial investment allows the vendor to offer more powerful products and additional benefit for established buyers.

In part, the tension is one between managing for the short run and managing for the long run. It is by no means an easy pressure to resolve and in many situations is simply a continuing fact of life for the marketer.

This book cannot provide clear, easy answers to coping with this tension. It can simply suggest that vendors deal explicitly with the issues and use some of the concepts provided here to help. For example, they can consider the pressure involved in decisions on whether to invest substantial resources to win new customers. Concepts about switching costs and customer behavior can help the vendor make an educated guess about how a customer is likely to behave over time. Concepts of modularity and systems benefits can help the vendor find promising ways through low-risk modular experiments to induce initial commitments that may grow. And explicit consideration of the whole question can help the vendor avoid making up-front commitments in potential

customers that are likely to remain more like the always-a-share model—
customers that are not likely to move toward lost-for-good.

Summary

Vendors can profit not only from understanding the time horizons and commitments of their customers but also from acting consciously to influence
buyers' behavior. A variety of forces and constraints limit a vendor's ability to
determine the behavior of its customers, to be sure, but within the feasible
limits, the marketer can sometimes strongly affect buyers' behavior.

Changes in switching costs change customers' time horizons and their
locations along the behavior axis between lost-for-good and always-a-share.
Vendors can use many different marketing tools, such as the sales force or
public relations or advertising, to help change the switching costs of industrial customers. Especially because of the importance of longer-term tools
in longer-term relationships, long-term tools such as product policy can be
especially effective for lengthening short or medium commitments or for
shortening long-term ones.

Modularity in product design and in usage allow a customer to make a
relatively low-risk modular experiment as a first step in dealing with a new
vendor. Modularity is therefore frequently an effective way to win new commitments. The problem for the vendor is that modularity can also subsequently allow other competitors to enter an account. Modularity can therefore hurt a vendor's chances of maintaining commitments.

By contrast, a systems approach is an effective way to keep customer
commitments, but such an approach makes it harder to win new buyers.
Ideally the vendor would like to have a product policy that changes over time,
as perceived by the individual account. It would like to offer modular initial
experiments to win new customers. Once established in an account, it would
like to offer real (though optional) systems benefits to encourage the account
to purchase more from a single source and to form stronger links to the seller.

Formal industry standards can be one route to modularity, allowing vendors to offer relatively modular initial experiments with their products. Vendors may be able to combine adherence to a standard with a policy of systems
benefits at design levels not covered by the standard. In doing so, they may effect a product policy for the individual account of modularity to win business
and systems benefits to keep and increase it.

The vendor that can use the offer of substantial real benefits to convince
customers to invest in lasting assets and procedures is especially likely to
build strong links to customers. Recently information technology (communications and computers) has been one important way for vendors to link
strongly to their customers' procedures. American Hospital Supply provides
an illustration; there are an increasing number of others.

Some uses of information technology are adequate as marketing tactics but do not build high switching costs; this chapter calls those uses singles. By contrast, home runs are applications of information technology that build strong links and high switching costs. They can also be extremely painful for other vendors in the same marketplace. Increasingly marketers are aware that such uses of information technology are more often than not preemptive moves; many marketers are working hard to be first rather than second in their markets with such an approach.

In general, the possibility of influencing the time horizons of customers can be attractive to vendors. Awareness of that possibility also creates tensions, however. Actions well suited to winning commitments are frequently not well suited to keeping commitments. Actions that seem best for the short term are frequently different from those best suited for the long. The problem is a complex one that is not amenable to easy general solutions. The concepts of this book for understanding and for action can help, as can the vendor's determination to face the issues squarely and explicitly.

Reference

McFarlan, F. Warren, and McKenney, James L. *Corporate Information Systems Management: The Issues Facing Senior Executives.* Homewood, Ill.: Richard D. Irwin, 1983.

7
Cascaded Demand

T
o this point, this book has essentially ignored one additional element of complexity in extended industrial marketing relationships. It has concentrated on the key or major purchases in the history of dealings between the customer and the vendor. For example, in discussing computers, it has emphasized the purchases of the computers themselves, with their key operating software. In discussing copiers, it has focused on purchases of the copiers themselves.

Extended industrial marketing relationships generally contain a series of purchases of key items such as computers or copiers. Frequently, however, those histories also include other purchases, sometimes of supplies for the major purchases, sometimes of maintenance, sometimes of parts. These follow-on purchases are also important to the relationships between buyers and sellers.

In an especially common pattern of follow-ons, an industrial vendor first sells a customer some equipment and then over time sells the customer follow-on products and services in connection with that equipment. A vendor might sell a customer an item of heavy construction equipment. Subsequently the vendor would sell replacement parts and service for that equipment. Similarly a vendor might sell an office copier and then sell supplies, parts, and service for that equipment. This book uses the term *cascaded demand* for such patterns of purchases by customers: the purchase of an item of equipment cascades into demand for various follow-on products and/or services.

The presence of cascaded demand in an industrial marketing situation adds to its complexity. There are obviously more different factors for the marketer to consider and coordinate. Especially in relationship marketing where it is so important to have a coordinated marketing approach, cascaded demand increases the complexity and the challenge for the seller.

Cascaded demand can also increase the vendor's opportunities to carry out effective and creative marketing approaches. In offering a cascade of products, a seller has a variety of levers available to affect the customer and the relationship—in general, more levers than would be available to a vendor that offered a more limited line (such as equipment only, with no follow-ons).

Thus cascaded demand provides both additional challenge and additional opportunity in relationship marketing. This chapter discusses aspects of cascaded demand that are key in long-term relationships.

Cascaded Demand, Pricing, and Profitability

Most discussions of cascades of demand emphasize issues of pricing and of how much profit the vendor should try to earn on each part of the cascade. That topic has been an especially current one for practitioners in the late 1970s and early 1980s. Vendors offering cascades of products often assign different roles to the elements in generating profits. Recently many vendors have become increasingly aware of those roles and have reassessed their past pricing practices.

Frequently vendors use a razor-and-blades analogy in discussing pricing with cascaded demand. Marketers suggest, with this analogy, that they should sell equipment at relatively low margins to consume supplies, parts, and/or service on which the vendor earns considerably higher margins. Vendors often justify such a pricing policy by arguing that customers are more sensitive to price on the larger equipment sales than they are on the more routine purchases of follow-ons. True, sometimes the total dollars spent on follow-ons are considerable. Even so, customers often purchase those follow-on elements of the cascade in smaller individual orders than the order for equipment. As a result, the argument goes, they are likely to be less price sensitive in purchasing follow-ons, even in cases in which the customer has a choice of vendors for these elements.

The razor-and-blades analogy is a sensible one in some marketing situations. In other cases, however, higher margins on equipment and lower margins on supplies would give the vendor more overall profit from its relationship with a customer. For example, the customer's procurement procedures for the two types of purchases can make it easier for the seller to obtain higher margins on the equipment sales.

The equipment procurement often requires a major capital-budgeting exercise and other special procedures. On some equipment purchases, nonprice factors may be central. For example, on a technical procurement of equipment, the opinions of a firm's engineering and manufacturing personnel will often be weighed especially heavily, and performance issues may outweigh price (although price would generally also be included in an evaluation).

By contrast, supplies are frequently purchased in a more routine manner by lower-level managers. In such cases, the customer may appear more price sensitive for supplies and other follow-ons than for the more expensive equipment. For example, the managers of reproduction departments in businesses are frequently evaluated on the basis of cost control; their departments are cost centers. Managers of such departments would of course want to avoid buying supplies of such low quality that they would cause performance problems. At the same time, however, the managers would have strong inclinations to save money and might buy lower-priced follow-ons of acceptable quality.

One aspect of pricing in cascaded demand has received special attention from practitioners of late: the pricing of service (maintenance and repair). Industrial vendors appear to be increasingly aware of the costs they incur in providing service. That interest is sparked both by the rising costs of trained people to perform service and by a general tendency in business to use sharper pencils in figuring costs and profits. In addition, marketers seem increasingly aware of how valuable good service is to their customers. A number of firms have changed their service departments from cost centers, their more traditional role, to profit centers. Other vendors have not gone quite that far but have taken steps to monitor and control the costs of the service they provide.

Questions of pricing in cascaded demand are frequently challenging, requiring considerable analysis and insight. This chapter does not pursue the topic or some of the other aspects of cascaded demand in detail; instead, it focuses on those aspects of cascaded demand that are especially important and challenging in relationship marketing and that might be missed in a discussion that was not emphasizing long-term industrial-marketing relationships.

Roles of Elements of the Cascade

Different items in a cascade of products can have substantially different roles in winning and keeping commitments from industrial customers. Understanding and actively managing those different roles can be important and useful for the relationship marketer. This discussion uses the example of Xerox copying machines to demonstrate that point.

The Cascade for Copiers

For decades Xerox has marketed copy-duplicating machines and also paper and other supplies (particularly toner) for those machines. Originally Xerox only leased its copier products; more recently, it has also offered equipment for sale. The vendor provided service to leasing customers as part of the basic lease package. Customers that bought machines did not automatically receive such service; they might purchase it from the vendor. Thus, the cascade of products in this example consisted of a copier followed by paper, toner, and other supplies and (for customers that purchased) service and parts.

Xerox faced competition for all major follow-ons. Those elements of the cascade had different economic impacts for Xerox; they also had different roles in influencing customers' commitments.

Xerox machines could operate with paper of different types, but the vendor believed that some papers worked considerably better than others. Xerox itself had worked with paper manufacturers over the years to develop production processes for making paper the vendor considered to have important performance benefits with its machines. Xerox purchased such paper and resold it to customers.

Sale of the paper could not be restricted to Xerox for legal reasons; it was also sold to paper merchants. Despite that direct competition, the scale of Xerox's purchases and its extensive logistics systems for distribution gave Xerox a strong position in the market. Although paper was available, often at lower prices, from alternative sources, Xerox historically obtained considerable shares of its customers' commitments for paper and reportedly earned considerable profit on that business.

Toner was a supply item especially important to the performance of the copying machine. Low-quality toner resulted in low-quality copies and might also make a mess of the machine. Users spent substantially less on toner than they did on paper. For example, a customer might make 125,000 copies per year on a machine. In 1983, a medium-grade Xerox paper for the copies might cost $750 per year. The Xerox toner might cost about $95. The equipment might cost $7,000.

Competitors entered the toner business in the late 1960s with products that varied significantly in quality. Some of the competitive toners produced high-quality copies, but others produced distinctly inferior ones. Xerox's response to the competitive toner products, even the low-quality ones, was decidedly restrained. Apparently in part for legal reasons (concern over antitrust laws), Xerox had a strict policy that forbade its field representatives from commenting on the quality of competing products, even if asked. On occasion, however, the vendor ran tests for customers to compare the performance of Xerox's toner and of competing toner on the copying machine at the customer's location. The tests were expensive because they required thorough cleaning of the machine and other setup and because they required time. The vendor did not run many such tests.

The final major follow-on for the Xerox machines was service. Customers that leased received service, without additional charge and without any choice of source, from the vendor. For purchased machines, customers could buy service from Xerox. They might pay on an hourly basis for the service time they actually used. Alternatively, they might buy a maintenance contract, which covered all of the machine's service needs for a specified period of time (such as a year). In 1983 a maintenance contract might cost $1,700 for a year.

Several factors reduced Xerox's service business from customers that purchased machines. Customers might reduce the frequency of service for their machines, calling in service people only for more extreme problems. Alternatively, customers might purchase service from other sources, often small businesses founded by former employees of the copier vendors. Finally, the customer could elect to have its own employees service the machines.

The most likely result of too little service was a degradation in copy quality. The machine was not as likely to stop working, at least not immediately. Instead, it produced successively lower-quality copies, until it did stop working or until the lower quality finally prompted the customer to call for service.

Roles of the Elements

The elements of this cascade had very different roles, both in generating immediate profits for the vendor and in influencing customers' commitments for the longer term. The vendor's actions appear to have reflected the different roles in influencing commitments in part, but only in part. Fuller recognition would likely have allowed the vendor to avoid some important problems in its marketplace.

Paper sales were apparently economically important to Xerox, and loss of some or all of a customer's paper business could have a negative immediate economic impact. Paper did not, however, have a high impact on the performance of the machine; non-Xerox paper could work quite satisfactorily. As a result, the customer's paper business—and its retention or loss by Xerox—did not have a strong impact on the likelihood that the customer would remain committed for the long term. This point is made clear by a comparison of the far different roles of toner and service in influencing commitments over time.

Sales of toner apparently provided the vendor with considerably less immediate total profit dollars than did paper, although the percentage margins on toner at the time of competitive entry to the market were apparently high. Because of its strong impact on the performance of a Xerox machine, however, toner was important in influencing customers' commitments over the longer term.

When low-quality toner caused a degradation in performance, the customer was not likely to attribute the change to the toner; customers were instead likely to blame the machines. As a result, the customer would become less satisfied with Xerox. It might reduce the degree of focus of its commitment on the dominant vendor or even purchase its next equipment (at the start of the next cascade) elsewhere, perhaps from a competitor that offered lower-priced, lower-performance equipment.

Xerox faced increasing competition from vendors of lower-priced, lower-quality machines in the 1970s and 1980s after the introduction of competitive toner products. It was therefore particularly harmful to Xerox to allow low-quality toner to weaken customers' faith in Xerox and to make them more willing to deal with competitors for major machine sales.

Xerox can be faulted for not acting forcefully enough to head off competition for toner or to keep competitors from harming important long-term commitments once they had entered the market. In essence, Xerox apparently did not take a sufficiently long-term account-oriented view of the importance of toner.

High margins on toner apparently attracted competition in the first place. One option that Xerox had was to drop its prices to counter competition. The advisability of such a move is not entirely clear. Even if it had been effective (and legal) against competition, it might have raised customers' suspicions about how much profit Xerox had been earning. Abrupt marketing changes can shake the confidence of strongly committed customers. But a price change was also not clearly inadvisable, and the importance of toner to long-term commitments suggests that a careful consideration of the option would have been worth while.

Alternatively or in addition, the vendor might have been more willing to run tests for important accounts to demonstrate the superiority of its own products. The cost and bother of the tests might not have been justified by the immediate profit on the toner sales, but they might well have been highly appropriate moves to protect the relationships with (and longer-term profits on equipment sales from) important customers. (It is worth noting that the competition for toner was especially harmful for the vendor because the toner competitors entered the market at a time when all Xerox machines were on lease and the vendor was responsible for service. Hence, the vendor faced short-term expense to clear up problems with the machines, in addition to the short-term loss of profits from toner and the longer-term damage to customers' commitments.)

Xerox's actual actions in regard to service appear to fit better with what would be suggested by a thorough consideration of impacts on long-term customer commitments. Inadequate or infrequent service had impacts much like those of low-quality toner. The customer was likely to observe a degradation in performance and was also likely to attribute that decline to the machine itself.

Xerox would therefore want to do what it could to encourage customers to use adequate service. It would want to keep prices for its service reasonable (in customers' eyes and especially in comparison with the prices of service from alternative sources). In addition, it would want to encourage customers to select maintenance contracts rather than hourly service charges. With hourly charges, the buyer might feel an incentive to skimp on service in order to save money. With a maintenance contract, the buyer would not have such an incentive and would be considerably more likely to use adequate service.

Xerox's pricing of hourly service versus service contracts does appear sensible in the light of this analysis. The vendor encourages maintenance contracts and thus encourages customers to use adequate service.

Implications for Marketers

In general, vendors will find that the elements of a cascade serve different short-term roles in generating profits and different medium- or longer-term roles in influencing the commitments of buyers. Marketers will benefit from recognizing those different roles and from making policy decisions and deploying marketing tactics in the light of the differences.

In particular, it is important to distinguish between follow-ons (such as toner and service for Xerox machines) with strong performance implications for the vendor's equipment and follow-ons (such as paper for Xerox machines) without such effects. Performance problems can damage and reduce the extent of a customer's focus on the vendor; customers become less confident in relying on that vendor.

Vendors therefore should be especially careful to monitor and, if possible, to anticipate competition for follow-ons with important performance implications. If competitive offerings are (or are likely in the future to be) of unsatisfactory quality, the vendor will have strong and sensible motivation to counter the competition or to head it off. By contrast, on follow-ons with fewer long-term effects on accounts' commitments, a vendor may sensibly charge higher prices or make other marketing decisions that might allow competition, provided that the vendor's immediate profits from the resulting share would still be attractive.

Because different follow-ons in a cascade serve different roles in terms of generating profits and of winning or maintaining commitments, sensible marketing decisions should consider both types of impacts. Failure to recognize the differences in roles can harm profits and commitments in the short term and in the long term.

Offering a Full Cascade

Desires to Offer and Protect the Full Cascade

Many industrial vendors attach considerable importance to offering all items in a cascade, even, in some cases, individual items on which they lose money. Such desires appear sensible if the elements of the cascade have important performance implications and if competitive offerings are likely to degrade performance. Vendors' desires for full lines appear more widespread, however, occurring in situations in which follow-ons do not have strong implications for performance or in which competitive offerings are of adequate quality. We might ask why and whether such desires make sense.

A case study on Deere & Co. provides an example. Deere offered crawler tractors and bulldozers for a variety of applications, including construction use. It marketed its equipment through a network of dealers (433 for industrial equipment alone in 1976, the time of this description). For the most part, dealers offered only Deere products. They sold new equipment, older (used) equipment, parts, and service.

As a rule of thumb, a crawler tractor used 65 percent of its initial purchase price in parts and service during its first three years of operation. During a life of 10,000 operating hours, it used parts and service costing approximately 90 percent of the initial price.

Parts were important to vendors in terms of profit. Industry practice was to try to obtain higher margins for parts and accessories than for the basic tractors.

Deere's managers classified parts as captive, competitive, and highly competitive. Captive parts might be manufactured by Deere, or they might be purchased and resold by Deere; their distinguishing characteristic was that they did not face competition in the marketplace. The competitive and highly competitive parts faced competition from alternative parts vendors, called *will-fitters* in the industry. (In other industries, the term *pirate parts* is used to describe parts that are offered in the after-market in competition with parts from equipment vendors to be used with the equipment originally sold by those equipment vendors.) Will-fitter competition occurred for the highest-volume parts, such as the undercarriage parts that required frequent replacement.

The case study gives costs (factory standard costs) and net prices to Deere of a variety of parts. The ratio of cost to price ranges from 45 percent (or a 55 percent margin) to 73 percent for the engine and drive-train parts included in the relevant case exhibit. For the highly competitive undercarriage parts, however, the case includes examples in which Deere's costs exceeded its prices, including one example with a cost that is 137 percent of the price.

The case states that the parts were priced in this way because of intense competition. The case does not suggest that will-fitter parts performed unsatisfactorily. Why, then, would Deere offer parts at prices that were competitive with those of the will-fitters if doing so lost money for the vendor?

Reasons for Protecting the Full Cascade

Deere's decision to offer some parts even at a loss certainly seems surprising when evaluated only in terms of immediate economic impact. In the context of customers' commitments and exposure over time, however, the decisions may be considerably more sensible. In this instance, the commitments of Deere's first line of customers (its dealers) may be the issue.

In 1976 most Deere dealers handled Deere products exclusively and thus were strongly committed to Deere. If a dealer were to buy some highly competitive part from a will-fitter, that purchase could be an initial low-risk modular experiment. In the future, that experiment could lead to the dealer's obtaining additional parts, more attractive to Deere in terms of cash flow, from other vendors. Initial modular experiments can be very effective in letting accounts move closer to always-a-share behavior, loosening their ties to a single, established vendor. Such initial experiments could give dealers confidence to alter their commitments more substantially.

Thus, Deere's policy might make sense. Pricing to the market on competitive parts even if the sale of a particular part thereby generated losses would make sense if it were effective in keeping dealers committed to Deere with no economic reason to switch. On the other hand, the policy might not make sense. It would not make sense if buying from a will-fitter the parts that were unprofitable to Deere would not in fact lead the dealers to obtain other more attractive parts elsewhere. Even if pricing to the market did keep other profitable business for Deere, the policy would not make sense if the profit on the additional parts did not match the losses.

Cascades and Modularity

In general in situations involving cascades of demand, customers' feelings of exposure may make them extremely reluctant to try new vendors on purchases of major items of equipment. The same customers may feel considerably less exposure in their purchases of follow-ons. They may be much more willing to focus such purchases on the product, emphasizing shorter-term issues such as price.

Sometimes a vendor can use an initial modular sale of a follow-on such as parts or supplies to gain a toehold in an account. If the vendor can build the customer's confidence in the vendor organization and its sales or service representative, the toehold may become a more substantial position. In other words, the customer may gain enough confidence in the vendor to try a more substantial longer-term commitment, perhaps for a piece of equipment, with more focus on the vendor.

Follow-ons will not always be able to serve such a role. For such a strategy to work, the follow-on must offer the customers what they consider adequate information about the vendor and its representatives to justify additional commitments. The follow-on must be sufficiently low risk for the customer to be willing to experiment in the first place. It must also, however, be sufficiently important (in terms of the product's role and performance, for example) to build the customer's confidence. In those cases in which follow-ons can provide a meaningful initial experiment, they can be an effective tool for a vendor trying to win new commitments.

Thus, follow-ons in a cascade can be important in keeping accounts more or less strongly tied to a vendor, as well as in direct cash flow implications. A vendor's decisions about follow-ons help determine the position of its product policy on the spectrum between modularity and a systems orientation.

A vendor may, for example, try to change the designs of its parts and supplies frequently and to make its follow-ons incompatible with those for other equipment. Such a policy can be effective in discouraging competition. The frequent design changes might deny competitors and potential competitors enough aggregate sales on any specific part to justify the investments needed to make that part (investments in tools and dies, for example). By contrast, the equipment vendor would make the part for the original equipment as well as for replacement sales and would therefore face a more favorable cost and volume situation. In discouraging competition, this policy also moves the vendor toward a system orientation. Customers would have to buy entire cascades from the single vendor.

To protect valuable long-term, vendor-focused commitments of its customers, an established vendor may find it worth while in the long run to offer whatever short-term concessions are needed to keep accounts from having the immediate incentive to obtain specific follow-ons from alternative vendors. On the other hand, such decisions would have to be made carefully and would be sensible only if the longer-term results of keeping customers committed were sufficiently attractive.

The Challenge of Coordination

A consistent, coordinated approach by a vendor is important in maintaining long-term commitments from customers. The vendor can face difficulty in coordinating marketing approaches for different products needed by the same customer at different points in its history. Cascaded demand makes the problem even more difficult. The vendor must coordinate marketing approaches for different products, frequently for extremely different products, to a single customer at the same time.

The topic of coordinating marketing approaches for the elements of a cascade is one of strong current interest to many industrial marketers. Cost is the key motivator for that strong interest. Especially as the costs of an industrial salesperson and an industrial sales call appear to soar, marketers have been exploring ways to limit the use of field salespeople to situations that really require them. They have been experimenting with 800 numbers and internal salespeople, with catalogs, and with a variety of other approaches to try to sell efficiently.

Effective as they can be for controlling costs, mixed marketing approaches for the elements of a cascade can present considerable challenges in coordination. Different elements of the cascade are likely to involve substantially different marketing jobs. The problem is especially likely to involve human resources, such as the sales force and/or distributors.

Selling equipment is likely to involve different skills and a different process than would selling supplies, for example. A direct sales approach might seem appropriate for selling equipment. In some cases, distributors might seem better suited to sell supplies because of their abilities to provide rapid delivery of small orders to customers.

In general, equipment sales and supply sales require very different selling tasks. Equipment sales usually involve the customer's formal capital-budgeting procedures, require more sales calls per order, and involve more members in the decision-making unit than do purchases of supplies. Equipment sales tend to be occasional but important events. Supply sales tend to be more regular, smaller purchases that become important only in the aggregate. Selling supplies often requires frequent calls on the account and may emphasize issues such as delivery. Often vendors feel that the equipment sales force is too technical and too expensive to fit the job of selling supplies.

For these reasons, vendors may use separate sales forces for equipment and supplies. The approach matches the marketing tool with the specific marketing task.

Customers may, however, find it inconvenient to deal with multiple representatives of the vendor. Buyers may also feel they lack a committed representative in the vendor organization. In addition, a vendor that uses different salespeople to sell equipment and supplies risks losing one of the benefits of cascaded demand: the frequent presence in the account of someone who is likely to recognize the signs that the customer is ready to consider buying another item of equipment and who can then sell that equipment. Because equipment sales are generally infrequent though important purchases, equipment-only salespeople are unlikely to be in the accounts as often as would a supplies salesperson; if they were, much of the cost advantage of using separate forces would be lost. With two representatives for the account, the supplies salesperson would be most likely to know when the account might purchase new equipment. The vendor needs to coordinate the flow of information from the account, ensuring that the supplies salesperson helps the equipment salesperson know when to call.

Similar problems can arise when different representatives are used for sales and service. Using different representatives matches the marketing tool with the specific marketing task. The service person can be a specialist who is especially adept at solving problems; the salesperson can specialize in selling. The specialization raises a risk, however, because it separates the person likely to obtain information about likely sales from the person assigned to act on that information. The service representatives are likely to know more about usage, especially problems in usage, of the customers. They will learn when older equipment is likely to be replaced. They will learn when customers are using current equipment so heavily that they may be receptive to purchasing additional units. They are also likely to know the special problems or abuse to which equipment will be subjected in a particular customer's operation. And they may learn about the customer's experience and any problems with competitive equipment. All of this information is useful to the salesperson in deciding when to call, what equipment to recommend, and how to sell that equipment (both for its own characteristics and because of its comparison with competitive offerings).

Thus, using multiple representatives to serve a single customer offers benefits in terms of costs and of specialized skills. It also creates risks that information will be lost. In essence, the challenge of coordination arises because vendors can benefit importantly by understanding, monitoring, responding to, and influencing commitments of individual customers. The idea is to view the customer relationship as a whole, not as a disjointed series of separate transactions. Especially in relationship marketing to customers that make long-term, lost-for-good-type commitments, vendors need to collect and use consistently and effectively as much information as is practical about individual accounts. Tailoring marketing tools to specific tasks makes coordination more difficult, despite the other more positive effects it can offer. Thus, the vendor faces conflicting pressures for specialized marketing tools and for unified approaches.

The necessary coordination in relationships with individual accounts has become even more difficult as vendors have added new tools to their approaches. As field sales forces have become increasingly visible expenses to vendors, many firms have begun to use alternative lower-cost marketing tools—usually, in addition to a field sales force, to take over some of the salesperson's work and allow the field force to concentrate on those jobs for which it is essential. For example, many firms are using telemarketing for some of their products and/or some of their customers. Often telemarketing is used for selling smaller, more routine items, such as supplies, while the more expensive field sales force is used for larger, more technical sales.

Wright Line, a vendor of computer-room and related supplies and furniture, provides an illustration. Originally the vendor used only a field sales force that called on customers with major computer installations. Then Wright Line added a catalog and telemarketing to its marketing approach. The new tools allowed the vendor to deal with additional customers—buyers that would not purchase enough to justify calls by an expensive field salesperson but that became economically attractive to the vendor if they were served with the lower-cost catalog-telephone approach. The new tools also allowed the vendor to fill small orders from its larger, established customers quickly and efficiently. Customers did not have to wait for the sales representative to call; instead they could call in their own routine orders by telephone.

The use of different tools has the advantage of tailoring the tool to the specific marketing task. It has the potential disadvantage of presenting the customer with a variety of different representatives who, if not properly coordinated, may convey confusion more than commitment. Another potential disadvantage is that the particular vendor representative most likely to act on some type of information is not always the representative most likely to learn the desired information from the customer.

True, even if a vendor does not enjoy long-term relationships with customers, it can face challenges that are similar in kind when it uses a variety of marketing tools to market elements of a cascade. In relationship marketing, however, the challenges are substantially worse in degree. Poor deployment of marketing tools can easily sour important, valuable, long-term commitments. In relationship marketing, the newer tools and combination approaches can be attractive, but only if used with proper regard for their potential effects on longer-term commitment and exposure and in sensible coordination with the vendor's other resources.

The Cascade for Offset Platemakers

A vendor that offered a cascade related to offset platemakers provides a more detailed example of the challenges and concerns of a vendor with a single sales force and its different challenges and concerns after it had changed its approach. The vendor was the subject of a 1971 case study in which it was called by a disguised name. This discussion uses the same disguise to describe the vendor in 1982, after it had changed its field forces.

Copier Systems manufactured and sold platemakers, equipment for making the plates used in offset reproduction. Customers included commercial printers, quick-copy shops, and larger firms that had in-house (or captive) reproduction departments. The plates were used on offset duplicators to provide plain paper copies of printed and some graphic material.

Platemakers required what were called materials, the silver-based supply item used in the plates. They also required chemical supply items and service. Copier Systems sold materials, chemicals, and service. It manufactured the chemicals but purchased the materials for resale.

In 1971, Copier Systems's best-selling platemaker model sold for $6,250. A typical user might use half that dollar amount per year in plate materials. Chemicals might cost the user 7.5 percent and service 10 percent of the original sale price per year. Thus, taken together, the follow-ons might cost two-thirds of the original equipment price each year.

The plate materials were important economically to Copier Systems and to the manufacturers of those supplies. Typically one of the few makers of the plate materials would develop a new supply and would then approach Copier Systems, asking it to develop equipment to use the new material. The material-manufacturer's objective would be to increase its share by having Copier Systems sell its exclusive new supply along with hardware for that supply.

Over time, the other major manufacturers of plate materials would bring out competitive supplies, and the margins on supplies would drop. At that point it would be especially attractive for a materials manufacturer to give Copier Systems another new material to start a new cycle. Copier Systems and the materials manufacturer apparently both earned considerable margin on those supplies.

By 1982, managers at Copier Systems felt that the typical supply cycle had shortened; competitive supplies appeared more quickly than in the past, and margins on supplies dropped more quickly. A weak economy, increased customer attention to costs (and thus increased price sensitivity), and pressures on the materials manufacturers for sales and profits all seemed to be factors in this change. (Such factors seemed to be important in many industries in 1982.)

Contrasting Marketing Approaches

In 1971 Copier Systems used one sales force for equipment and supplies. Service was provided by a different group of people, but that service force reported to the individual sales regions. The 1971 organization raised issues typical in a combined sales approach for different products: how to induce the salespeople to pay appropriate attention to each part of the cascade and how to compensate them. The vendor's challenge was to motivate the single sales force to work for the best overall value to the vendor from the commitments of its customers.

Copier Systems compensated its salespeople with salary plus commission: 10 percent for sales of equipment and 1 percent for sales of supplies (plate materials and chemicals). The case study raises the question of whether separate forces would have been preferable; one manager noted that field representatives had to sell large amounts of supplies to earn as much as they did on one equipment placement. The compensation scheme (and a common desire by salespeople for larger and more visible successes) biased the sales effort strongly toward equipment. Yet the case notes that Copier Systems's philosophy was to place the equipment so that it would use supplies. Moreover, the firm faced competition for many of the supply items, so that follow-on supply sales were not automatic.

The challenges that Copier Systems faced in 1971 were typical of those of vendors with combined sales forces selling a range of products. Naturally enough, salespeople tend to emphasize strongly the products that they are better at selling and the ones for which they are best compensated. Managers in such organizations frequently devote considerable time, energy, and worry to designing sales-compensation schemes that will motivate the salespeople to behave in the best long-term interests of the company.

Interestingly, those managers usually report that some individual salespeople seem almost instinctively to know that they will benefit from taking a longer-term perspective in their relationships with customers; others, generally the weaker performers, do not. In other words, some of the salespeople intuitively understand and work to implement ideas of relationship marketing. Where such a marketing approach is appropriate, the vendor's challenge is to impart such understanding and motivation to other salespeople too.

By 1982 Copier Systems had changed its organization. The service people had been separated organizationally from the salespeople. An inside sales force had been established to sell supplies. The field sales force concentrated on equipment sales. The new organization was apparently motivated in part by the high and still rising costs of the field sales force. It was motivated by the vendor's awareness of telemarketing. And it was motivated by the speed-up in the cycle of competition for supplies, which put increased pressure for efficiency on the supplies part of the business. The 1982 organization raised questions typical of a field organization of specialists: how to coordinate the different representatives dealing with a single account to provide good service overall to the customer and to provide good sales and profits for the vendor.

The field salespeople in the new organization received commissions, but the inside salespeople and the service people did not. The field salesperson received the commission for all supply sales made by the inside (telephone) salesperson responsible for the same geographic territory. The field sales force should therefore have supported the inside sales force (and did in fact appear to do so).

Effective coordination would also require the inside salesperson and the service person to provide information to the field salesperson handling the same account. The telephone salesperson had most frequent contact with the account and was most likely to know the customer's status, the likelihood of additional equipment sales, and other useful information. The service person was especially familiar with problems with the customer's equipment and might therefore have an especially good idea of when the salesperson should call.

Copier Systems's managers reported that good salespeople were highly aware of the importance of the other vendor employees dealing with their customers. Such salespeople reportedly treated those internal sources of information very well (almost like additional customers), cultivating them and developing relationships to maintain the flows of information about the accounts.

This pattern is typical of coordinated marketing approaches. The best field representatives understand the importance of coordination of the vendor's team, and they work hard to achieve that coordination. The vendor's challenge is to extend the understanding and effective implementation more widely in its sales organization.

Summary

In cascaded demand, a vendor offers customers both equipment and follow-on parts, supplies and/or service for that equipment. Cascaded demand provides both additional challenge and additional opportunity in relationship marketing. In offering a cascade of products, a seller has available a variety of levers to affect the customer and the relationship—in general, more levers than would be available to a vendor that offered a more limited line. On the other hand, the vendor offering a cascade of products faces additional challenges of coordinating its approaches for those products.

The challenges that cascaded demand presents to the relationship marketer are not different in kind from the challenges it raises in transaction marketing. They are, however, substantially more serious in degree in relationship marketing because long-term customers frequently feel strongly about consistency from their vendors and because the long-term relationships are so individually valuable (and damaging them so individually painful) to the vendor.

Most discussions of cascaded demand emphasize the question of how much profit the vendor should try to earn from the different elements of the cascade. It is true that the elements usually serve different roles in providing the vendor with immediate economic value. What the more transaction-oriented discussions do not stress is that the elements also usually serve different roles in winning or maintaining commitments from customers.

Marketers will benefit from understanding those different longer-term roles and from making policy decisions and deploying marketing tactics in the light of the differences. In particular, it is important to distinguish between follow-ons with strong impacts on the performance of the vendor's equipment and follow-ons without such impacts. A vendor should be especially motivated to counter or head off competition for follow-ons with important performance implications, particularly if competitive offerings are likely to be inferior in quality.

The vendor's policy about follow-ons helps determine its position on the product-policy spectrum between modularity and a systems orientation. A competitive vendor can sometimes use an initial modular sale of a follow-on such as parts or supplies to gain a toehold in an account. If the initial experience with that competitor builds the customer's confidence enough, the competitor may proceed to win additional more substantial business from the buyer. An established vendor may therefore (in some cases) find it worth while to offer whatever short-term concessions are needed to keep its valuable long-term customers from having the immediate incentive to buy specific follow-ons from alternative vendors.

The different elements of a cascade frequently require substantially different types of selling and marketing. Equipment sales tend to be infrequent, carefully made purchases. Supply sales are usually more frequent, smaller purchases (that may, however, add up to substantial dollar amounts over time).

Vendors sometimes choose different marketing tools, such as different sales forces, for different elements of the cascade. Such an approach has the attraction of fitting the marketing tool to the marketing task. It has become increasingly popular recently as the costs of field salespeople have escalated and as marketers have had an increasing variety of available marketing tools.

The choice of specialized marketing tools also presents challenges of co-ordination. Especially in long-term relationship marketing, the vendor must coordinate the different tools so as to provide a consistent and committed approach to the customer. In addition, the specialization creates challenges in obtaining and using the information obtained from the account. Frequently the person in the vendor's organization most likely to obtain a particular type of information is not the person best placed to act on that information.

References

Corey, E. Raymond. *Industrial Marketing: Cases and Concepts.* 2d ed. Englewood Cliffs, N.J.: Prentice-Hall, 1976.

Shapiro, Benson P. *Deere & Company: Industrial Equipment Operations.* Case 9-577-12. Boston: Harvard Business School, 1977.

8
Relationship Marketing: Making the Concepts Work

*M*arketing to win, build, and maintain strong, lasting relationships with industrial customers. Certainly the outcome of successful relationship marketing sounds extremely attractive. But this book has argued that relationship marketing is also a complex and difficult task and that it is not the best choice for all vendors or for all product-marketplaces. Even when relationship marketing is the best choice for a vendor, there are many important factors, and much can go wrong.

There is no simple way to cut through those challenges, but that does not mean that the challenges can safely be ignored. Often confronting the issues explicitly is a major part of the job. Once the marketer faces the challenges of relationship marketing, the concepts presented in this book can help in analyzing the vendor's possible choices and in making sensible decisions.

There cannot be any cookbook or even any relatively complete set of rules for relationship marketing. Applying the ideas of this book will require careful, detailed consideration of the specific vendor, its product-marketplace, and its particular customers and potential customers. At the same time, however, marketers can use the principles and concepts discussed in the preceding chapters to guide the effort. They can also use other examples of relationship marketing to suggest ideas and approaches.

As an aid in making the concepts of relationship marketing work, this chapter briefly summarizes major ideas discussed in this book. It then offers a few additional general suggestions for making the concepts work in practice. Finally, because the successful application of the ideas will depend strongly on the specifics of a particular situation, the chapter presents analyses of two particular situations using the concepts of this book.

Both examples extend illustrations that have been used in previous discussions. The first uses concepts of accounts' commitments to analyze the question of why customers use multiple sources. It considers the product-marketplace for proprietary additives for electroplating. That discussion reaches two different explanations for multiple sourcing, with extremely different implications for marketers. The second example uses this book's concepts to analyze key aspects of a product-marketplace over an extended period of time. It considers the computer-mainframe marketplace from the 1960s to the 1980s.

The Individual Account, the Full Marketing Mix, and Time

Marketers will frequently benefit importantly from focusing on the individual account and considering that account's behavior over extended time periods. The individual account and time should be a key for analyzing and deploying the full range of marketing tools: product policy as well as communication or the sales force, for example.

It is, after all, the individual account that buys. Individual account relationships can be extremely valuable to the industrial marketer. Vendors can influence those relationships, so they should be conscious (and clever) in their actions to influence the behavior of customers.

Not all industrial marketing relationships last. Some customers have short time horizons in their commitments to vendors; others make long-term commitments. Insufficient understanding of accounts' behavior can lead marketers into trouble, as, for example, in attempting relationship marketing when transaction marketing would be more appropriate. Consideration of the individual account, the full marketing mix, and time can help marketers avoid such problems and can also lead them to successful profitable marketing actions.

Lost-for-Good and Always-a-Share

The lost-for-good and always-a-share models of customers' behavior over time highlight the differences between short-term and long-term buyers. They are the end points of a spectrum of accounts' behavior.

The lost-for-good customer faces high switching costs and is not likely to change vendors. Commitments from such a customer tend to last (to be won for a long time). The customer will generally use a long time horizon in its commitments. In a lost-for-good world, accounts with high retention probabilities are extremely attractive to the vendor; the vendor will often benefit from concentrating its sales and marketing efforts on such accounts.

By contrast, the always-a-share buyer can relatively easily switch some or all of its patronage from one vendor to another. It can take a short time horizon in its commitments to sellers. It can make purchase decisions on the basis of immediate inducements to buy.

High-share accounts are attractive in always-a-share, to be sure, but they are not nearly as overwhelmingly attractive as are high-loyalty customers in lost-for-good. In addition, high shares for any one vendor are less likely in an always-a-share world, where many customers will want to take advantage of their abilities to use multiple vendors. Further, the presence of more than one vendor in the always-a-share account (either over time or at one time) will usually create pressure on each of the vendors for lower prices or other competitive concessions.

For these reasons, vendors will frequently prefer long-term commitments, suggestive of the lost-for-good model. Relationship marketing will not always be feasible, however. And even if it is feasible, it will require considerable skill to pull off successfully.

The first step for the would-be relationship marketer is to decide whether the approach makes sense. To that end, the marketer can consider approximate positions of customers in relation to the behavior spectrum between lost-for-good and always-a-share. Of interest are both the customer's current behavior and the future behavior that actions by the vendor (or its competitors) might help create.

The behavior spectrum is not a precise tool, and marketers will not be able to locate the positions of real accounts with precision along that spectrum. Nevertheless, the spectrum can help importantly in making relationship marketing work. The determinants of position and additional characteristics of the models can help marketers identify approximate positions. They can also help suggest how possible marketing actions would change accounts' behavior. Although it would be nice to be able to identify a clear position for a customer with precision, in the absence of the ability to do so, it is far preferable to obtain more general insights into the customer's current and future position and behavior than it is to ignore the issue.

Determinants of Accounts' Behavior

Switching costs are the basic determinant of the account's position along the spectrum between lost-for-good and always-a-share. The product category itself is one determinant of switching costs. Another is the customer's usage system or the way it uses the products. The role of the product in the customer's own business strategy is a factor; so is the extent of modularity in the usage system. The attitudes and characteristics of individuals within the buyer's organization are also important in determining how willing or reluctant the account will be to change.

As an aid in analyzing and identifying switching costs, we can consider investment actions and exposure, or more and less tangible costs. The major categories of investment actions are money, people, lasting assets, and procedures. (These categories are not mutually exclusive.) Exposure is risk—financial and performance exposure faced by organizations and personal exposure faced by individual buyers.

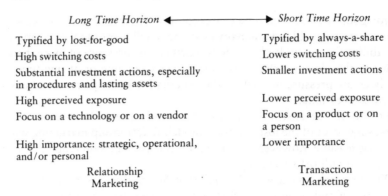

Figure 8–1. Time, Accounts' Behavior, and Marketing Approach

Figure 8–1 summarizes the typical characteristics of accounts at the two ends of the behavior spectrum. It includes switching costs (both investment actions and exposure), time horizon, and level of importance to the buyer. That figure also includes the focus of the account's commitment, showing that longer-term commitments tend to focus more on a vendor or on technology while shorter-term commitments focus on a product or on a person.

In analyzing the approximate positions of real customers, the marketer can use any of the characteristics in figure 8–1. In some cases, the clue to behavior toward the lost-for-good end may be substantial investments in procedures. In another case, the marketer may feel that high perceived exposure is key. In still other cases, a combination of the characteristics may provide the relevant clues.

Benefits of Analyzing Accounts' Behavior

Matching Marketing Approaches to Customers' Commitments

The first benefit of the analysis of customers' behavior in relation to time is that it allows the marketer to select marketing tools most appropriate to the nature of the customer's commitment. Several principles, which use the concept of the time dimension of marketing tools, can help the marketer in that job.

Long-term marketing tools take long times to deploy; once deployed, they give lasting effects. Short-term tools take considerably less time to bring effects, but those effects are short-lived.

To some extent, the time characteristics of tools depend on specifics of products, buyers, and vendors. Nevertheless, many product-marketplaces share a common time ordering of tools. Price is generally the shortest-term tool. Advertising is generally a short- to medium-term tool. The vendor's general product policy, technological stance, and technical capabilities are especially long-term tools.

The basic deployment principle is to use and emphasize marketing tools with time characteristics that correspond to the time horizons of the customer. Short- and medium-term tools are best suited for transaction marketing. Relationship marketing requires long-term tools; customers with long time horizons will not buy on the basis of short- and medium-term tools alone.

Short- and medium-term tools do have roles in relationship marketing, however. They can support longer-term tools, often by tailoring general long-term tools to the needs of specific customers. Although the shorter-term tools cannot win long-term commitments alone, those tools can lose such commitments alone. Therefore the relationship marketer faces the challenge of coordinating a variety of tools consistently well over time.

Two additional principles can help the relationship marketer in deploying the variety of tools typically needed for success. The longer-term tools are selected first; the medium- and short-term tools can then be added in support of the longer-term ones. In addition, more general tools are also deployed first; account-specific tools fill in the gaps to make the less specific tools fit the needs of individual accounts.

Changing Customers' Commitments

The second major benefit of analyzing customers' behavior in relation to time is that vendors can sometimes use the insights from that analysis to change customers' positions along the behavior spectrum and the natures of their commitments to their vendors. A variety of other factors (such as the nature of the product category, actions by competitors, and the legal and regulatory environment) constrain the vendor's ability to change customers' behavior. Within the relevant constraints, however, vendors' actions to influence buyers' behavior can bring important competitive advantage.

Not surprisingly, since switching costs are the key determinants of position along the behavior spectrum, analysis of changes in switching costs is key to understanding actions to change position. Actions that build switching costs move the customer closer to lost-for-good; actions that reduce switching costs move the account closer to always-a-share.

A variety of marketing tools can influence customers' switching costs. Not surprisingly given the importance of long-term tools in long-term relationships, however, long-term tools such as product policy are often especially important. Modularity in product policy and modularity in usage allow a customer to make a relatively low-risk initial trial of a vendor. Modularity can be extremely effective for winning new commitments.

By the same token, however, modularity can also allow another vendor to gain a toehold in an account. Once it has won a commitment from a customer, the vendor will prefer a systems orientation. It will want the customer to obtain valuable systems benefits from buying more of its individual products and using them together. Systems benefits can be extremely effective for maintaining commitments.

The vendor can sometimes effect a product policy that changes (on the clock of the individual account) from modularity to systems. The vendor may be able to use modularity to win commitments but also to offer substantial but optional systems benefits to induce customers to buy and use more of its products. The modularity allows the customer to move closer to the always-a-share end of the behavior spectrum; the systems benefits move the buyer back toward lost-for-good again.

Formal industry standards provide one possible tool for such a product policy. A vendor may be able to use standardization to allow customers to focus on the common technology and to try a new vendor with relatively low risk. At the same time, the vendor may build systems benefits into its own products, using higher levels at which the formal standards do not apply.

Information technology (computers and communications) has become an important marketing tool for building switching costs and strengthening the commitments of customers. Frequently that technology is able to induce substantial investment actions by customers in procedures.

The now-classic examples of the uses of information technology to build relationships and induce investments in procedures highlight both an opportunity and a challenge of relationship marketing. Suppose that to date no vendor has enjoyed strong relationships with customers in some product-marketplace. The first vendor to build strong relationships will generally gain a substantial competitive advantage; getting there second is likely not to be worth much by comparison. Thus, timing can be critical in changing the natures of customers' commitments. Effective actions to build strong customer relationships may be preemptive competitive moves. The opportunity—and the threat—of such moves make it especially important to manage with regard to the individual account, the full marketing mix and time.

Additional Principles for Relationship Marketing

Several additional suggestions can help the marketer in the challenging but potentially highly rewarding practice of relationship marketing.

Emphasize the individual account. For too long the individual account has been the focus of the sales force but not of the marketer. Vendors will benefit substantially if marketers also monitor and understand individual customers over time. (In some cases, they will also profit if salespeople adopt wider, longer-term marketing perspectives.) This principle suggests that a vendor view its markets as collections or portfolios of individual customers; that individual customer is the basic unit for analysis and for marketing action.

Be explicit. Managers regularly implicitly make judgments about issues addressed explicitly in this book. For example, in deploying a sales force, they implicitly make judgments about the attractiveness of individual customers. Or product-policy decisions generally involve some discussion of customers, although they do not often involve detailed consideration of individual account histories over extended periods. (When vendors do consider individual accounts, they are likely to use only a few unusually important customers and not also to use more typical examples.) Even if marketers cannot make precise determinations of retention probabilities or accounts' behavior, they will generally do better to make judgments explicitly than to make them implicitly or by default.

Involve the full vendor organization. Relationship marketing uses a range of marketing tools, with the term *marketing* widely defined. Many parts of the vendor's organization control or affect those tools: sales, marketing, product development, R&D, and other departments. Coordinating the appropriate range of tools to address individual customers will require the involvement of most of the vendor organization. Top management will generally be needed to ensure the needed coordination and to establish measurement systems that motivate a sound balance between short-term and longer-term goals.

Coordinate sources of information. It is valuable in relationship marketing to consider the individual customer as part of the vendor's basic strategic process; the individual account would also be the basis of more tactical marketing actions. Many parts of the vendor's organization will have information and insights useful for understanding and monitoring customers' behavior and likely influences on that behavior. The sales force can provide detailed information about accounts' usage systems, plans, and reactions; technologists and product developers can provide information about changes in technology, especially as they relate to future products and to existing products; more senior managers in the vendor's organization who help with major sales can provide insights into the attitudes and interests of senior managers in the customer's organization.

Sound marketing requires using and coordinating all of these sources of information. To be sure, in current practice the sales force often tries to obtain information from senior managers and others who have contact with their customers. The needs of relationship marketing suggest a considerable widening of this practice. They suggest the regular and conscious use of all available sources of account information, not just to support sales efforts but to influence the full range of marketing decisions as well.

Manage marketing strategy as an ongoing process. Desires of long-term customers for consistency limit the agility of the relationship marketer. It is therefore especially important in relationship marketing to make management of strategy along the time dimension an ongoing process—monitoring, adjusting to, and, whenever possible, anticipating changes in customers, technology, and competitors so as to act effectively but smoothly. In general, a product-marketplace as a whole will change over time, modifying the typical customer patterns of behavior, perhaps in different ways for different buyers. Customers' commitments will change in terms of focus, importance, investment actions, and time horizon. Customers' actual and perceived feelings of exposure will also change. Hence, sound analyses of marketing strategy along the time dimension would consider time within the individual account and would also consider how more general changes in the product-marketplace affect buyers over time.

Why Customers Insist on Multiple Sources

*The Marketplace for Proprietary Additives
for Electroplating*

In discussing focus on the personal representative of the vendor, chapter 4 briefly described the marketplace for proprietary chemical additives for electroplating. This chapter returns to that example to illustrate the use of some of the concepts of this book to analyze a frequent question in industrial marketing: Why do customers insist on multiple sources? How strongly will customers be willing to link to a single vendor for some product?

Electroplating is a process to transfer a thin layer of metal onto the surface of plastic or metal parts. The process consists of a series of steps. First, solutions of special cleaners clean the parts. Then another bath removes the surface film left by the cleaners. Next the parts are plated in the actual plating bath. Finally, they are dried.

The entire plating process is difficult to control. Vendors of the specialized chemicals used in that process provide customers with substantial technical help, regularly testing the customers' plating baths (to help keep those baths in a proper chemical balance) and also assisting in troubleshooting when problems occur. The importance of such technical help creates considerable customer focus on the personal representative of the vendor, who provides most of the assistance.

Harshaw Chemical Company was one of the sellers of the specialized proprietary additives, chemicals used in the plating bath to provide desirable properties, such as a smooth, level finish. Harshaw also sold relative commodities (metals and metal salts) used in plating. The firm used a single sales and service force to sell the proprietaries, metals, and metal salts and to provide technical service. Managers explained that they wanted to make the person who made promises to a customer the one responsible for handling any subsequent problems the customer encountered.

By strong industry tradition, Harshaw did not charge for analytical service (in which it tested bath solutions) or other forms of technical assistance, although service was a substantial expense. Harshaw's managers were especially motivated to control that expense because they were facing new small competitors that offered less technical expertise and charged lower prices; those competitors held perhaps 10 percent of the market in 1981.

Harshaw's managers felt that they could not begin to charge for service; the largest seller in the industry had once reportedly tried to do so and had lost business. Harshaw's managers tried controlling service problems by analyzing why problems arose and then by making other marketing changes (in product policy, as it turned out) to address the issue. The changes had not been entirely successful, however.

At one time, Harshaw had sold proprietary additives but not the cleaners used in the first bath in the plating process. Many of the problems in plating arose from improper cleaning rather than from the later plating bath, which used Harshaw proprietaries. Yet the customers did not (in many cases, could not) distinguish between problems from the cleaning step and problems from the plating bath. They called Harshaw for service whenever problems arose.

The vendor began to make cleaners as well as proprietaries. Its managers reasoned that they could then control the quality of the cleaners and earn contribution on their sale. Harshaw also began to push a concept it called total responsibility: the idea that the customer would be better off if it committed to a single vendor for all of its plating supplies. That vendor would then have total responsibility for the account.

Harshaw managers reported, however, that most of their customers would not accept the concept of total responsibility. They insisted on using more than one vendor. Harshaw's managers were perplexed as to why. Price sensitivity could not be the major explanation, despite the presence of price-oriented smaller vendors; those vendors did not have enough of the market to provide the full explanation. Instead, there had to be other reasons that the buyers insisted on using more than one source.

The Usual Explanation

The most common explanation for using multiple vendors brings to mind the purchasing motivations and procedures of the major Detroit buyers. This book calls that motivation *vendor redundancy*: the customer wants alternative sources for each input to its operation (dual sources for each required grade of steel, dual sources for each integrated circuit, and so on).

Customers believe that vendor-redundancy purchasing gives them benefits of safety in dealing with their vendors. The policy would reduce the customer's exposure to problems encountered by the vendor. If a vendor's labor force went on strike or if a vendor's plant were shut down because of fire, the customer would continue to operate, receiving the required inputs from other sources. (The exception would be a problem that extended to the vendor's competitors, such as an industry-wide strike in the vendor's industry.)

In addition, vendor redundancy is considered to give the buyer leverage in negotiating lower prices or other favorable conditions (such as special delivery schedules or inventory arrangements) from the vendor. The buyer can play off one vendor against another, thus obtaining better terms from either or both. For such leverage in negotiation to have most effect, the buyer must have two or more fully credible vendors whose resources and commitments to the account are sufficient for them to provide most or all of the buyer's needs. A vendor-redundancy buyer has flexibility in the actions it can threaten or use in negotiating with vendors; in particular, it can usually rather easily change a specific vendor's share of its business by a small amount (5 or 10 percent, perhaps).

In some instances of vendor-redundancy buying, the customer would buy from multiple vendors in the same time period; for example, an account might obtain 60 percent of its needs for carbon steel in a year from one producer and 40 percent from another. In other cases, an account might by policy award individual orders to give two or more vendors business in successive time periods; for example, an account might buy reactor vessels through bidding and negotiation and might by policy award at least one-third of the orders to each of two vendors so as to maintain interest and commitment of each vendor.

A vendor-redundancy policy therefore creates an always-a-share buyer. By its definition, vendor redundancy precludes lost-for-good commitments.

In serving vendor-redundancy buyers, the vendor can sensibly try to win shares of customers' patronage for all products it can market credibly and profitably. The vendor will not try to win sole-source commitments. Indeed, a vendor trying to sell a specific new product to vendor-redundancy buyers might find it advantageous to help a competitor enter the business so that potential buyers would have a second source for carrying out their vendor-redundancy policies.

An Alternative Reason for Multisourcing

The vendor-redundancy model does not seem to fit the customers of Harshaw Chemical who refused the concept of total responsibility. Nor does another explanation for using multiple sources, one rather frequently advanced by industrial marketers frustrated by their customers' refusals to award them more sales. Such marketers suggest that individual buyers value access to multiple suppliers because of the entertainment benefits (such as lunches) afforded by such access.

The concepts of this book suggest another, more professional, reason for Harshaw's customers to insist on having access to more than one vendor for their plating supplies. That analysis in turn suggests another general motivation for multiple sourcing.

Harshaw's customers relied strongly on the vendor's sales-service person to keep their operations working smoothly. Technical service and trouble-shooting help were extremely important to customers. Customers' commitments included strong focus on the personal representative of the vendor.

A customer that accepted the total-responsibility concept and committed to Harshaw for all of its plating supplies would have only one representative to call in time of trouble. But even a highly competent field representative would not always be available; for example, the customer might have a problem when the representative was on vacation. Further, the black-art flavor of the plating operation and the difficulty of finding the causes of some problems suggest that a customer would want access to more than one good problem solver. If, for example, a customer bought cleaners for nickel plating from one vendor and proprietary additives for the separate plating bath on the same line from another, it would have access to two vendors' problem solvers for help with its nickel-plating operation.

Thus, Harshaw's customers encountered account-specific performance problems. To deal with the resulting exposure, customers valued the actions of the vendor's representatives in solving problems. With commitments that had important elements of personal focus on the vendor's representative, customers felt less exposure if they had multiple commitments (with personal foci on representatives of more than one vendor). The customers' failure to accept the idea of total responsibility seems reasonable.

This example suggests a second basic model for buyers' motivation in insisting on multiple vendors: vendor diversity. Its basic concept is that a customer wants multiple suppliers for some operation taken as a whole (an entire nickel-plating line, for example) in order to obtain access to unpriced aspects of the offerings of more than one vendor. The explanation advanced here to explain the behavior of Harshaw Chemical's customers is that they wanted access to technical assistance, a part of the vendor's offering that was unpriced but that was especially valuable to the buyer.

A buyer interested primarily in the benefits of vendor diversity would not need dual sources for a particular item—a chemical in the Harshaw example. In fact, it would be unlikely for one of Harshaw's customers to use proprietary additives from more than one vendor for the same task; a customer might not even want to mix vendors for different items in the same bath on a line. The customer might fear that using multiple sources for the same bath or even the same line would create added risk of performance problems. Under vendor diversity, the benefits of multiple commitments come from having relationships with different vendors, not from dealing with different vendors for the same product.

Under vendor diversity, the seller could not win commitments for all products used in a specific operation, but it might receive 100 percent of the orders for those particular products that it did sell successfully to a customer.

When customers use a vendor-diversity policy, the vendor may find it sensible to limit its product line, concentrating its efforts on the items it finds most attractive. At least, the vendor would want to have its own organization try to determine which specific products a customer buys from that vendor rather than having the customer choose on its own or, worse, having a competitor determine the choice. The vendor will want to select products in the light of both short-run and, very important, long-run attractiveness.

It can be possible within vendor-diversity behavior for the vendor to induce a strong, long-term, lost-for-good commitment from a customer for a specific product if the product's characteristics and the customer's usage system allow such commitments. The vendor-diversity policy implies that the customer will not form such commitments to the same vendor for all needs. The policy does not preclude such commitments to a vendor for one or more individual product types.

The concepts of this book about commitments and exposure can help the vendor determine which specific products it wants to sell to a particular customer. The customer's usages of different products are likely to differ in terms of key factors of importance, accompanying investment actions, exposure, and modularity. The customer will face higher costs of switching vendors for some products than for others. Its commitments for some products will be closer to the lost-for-good end of the spectrum than will its commitments for other products. Some vendors will profit from targeting products for which the customer will make strong, lasting commitments; others may prefer approaches closer to transaction marketing.

Thus, using the concepts of this book in a careful consideration of buyers' reasons for insisting on multiple sources suggests two very different motivations: vendor diversity and vendor redundancy. Those motivations have markedly different implications for sound marketing decisions by the vendor. The same concepts about the behavior of individual customer accounts over time can help marketers to understand other issues in industrial account relationships and also to select and implement effective marketing actions.

The Computer Marketplace

1960s Marketplace

As a second example of analysis with the concepts of this book, the discussion now considers the computer market, starting in the 1960s. At that time, most customers were just learning to use and manage computers. Initial users depended strongly on their vendors for advice, help, and support. Many commitments made by such customers were medium-term ones that focused on the vendor. Customers were uncomfortable with and often afraid of computers and wanted help from vendors in reducing their immediate exposure in learning to use machines. (The buyers were generally not yet aware of the substantial longer-term exposure they would later face if they had to undergo conversions, especially from one vendor to another.)

Vendors sold bundled products—hardware and systems software together. Hardware was expensive, and in developing applications software, users put considerable emphasis on using the equipment efficiently. There was little modularity in computer systems. Programmers were not plentiful, managers were not experienced in supervising programmers, and programming efforts were often difficult. Vendors provided training, help with software design, and other support.

IBM was the market leader, but in the 1950s and 1960s it did not lead technically. In fact, it was not considered especially strong technically. Instead the industry leader's strength lay in sales and support—more medium-range tools for handling more immediate customer exposure. IBM had an unusually strong reputation for understanding customer businesses and for helping users to learn to work with computers. It had a strong reputation with senior managers and was considered the safe choice, the way to limit exposure.

IBM was willing to invest substantial resources in beginning users and users that were substantially increasing their applications of data processing. Once an account began doing business with IBM, it generally remained committed to the vendor for an extended period. Hence, IBM's strategy seems sensible; it was quite reasonable to invest resources to win new, smaller users that could be expected to grow with IBM.

While IBM was considered the safe choice for new users in the 1960s, it had become fashionable for many heavily technical users to look down on IBM; they considered the vendor as almost a nursemaid for unsophisticated users. IBM's strategy at the time did not seem to cater to more technical users. The choice seems sensible since such accounts were not likely to make vendor-focused commitments to IBM that would last, while IBM's typical customers did make such commitments.

The other general-purpose mainframe vendors in the 1960s seemed to fit in the cracks left by IBM's extensive coverage. They might serve technically advanced or confident users or provide special expertise in some business area. Often customers viewed these vendors primarily as alternatives to dealing with big, powerful, perhaps insensitive IBM. Such customers seemed to feel that they would be more important to alternative vendors, that the vendors would therefore commit more strongly to serve customers' specific needs. With slogans like "The Liberator" and "The Other Computer Company," the other vendors emphasized that market role.

Control Data (CDC) was especially strong in large computation-oriented machines. The scientific users of such machines did not require IBM's extensive support, and they valued CDC's product features. They focused on technology. At the time, that focus made them favor CDC. In the 1970s some would follow specific computer designers who moved to new firms. (Thus they would focus on a person whom they expected to provide a stream of technology.)

Burroughs was strong in banking, a market segment to which it was particularly committed. Burroughs was also favored by some users who valued the fact that its machines had been especially designed to run the Algol programming language. (Algol was popular and fashionable in academic computer-science departments at the time. IBM equipment did not run Algol.)

Although DEC has generally been described as a minicomputer company, the vendor's original (1960s) positioning is better described as that of a supplier to highly technically sophisticated users. It happened that such users needed small machines, and DEC built small machines. The vendor emphasized product features and price, not support and marketing. Its sophisticated users, in settings such as laboratories, needed to link a variety of peripherals to their main computers. DEC's hardware architecture (based on a "bus") facilitated linking to the main processor a wide variety of peripherals that DEC did not make but that its customers demanded. At the time such interfaces were not automatic and might require users to adjust or modify the equipment. DEC's users had both the technical confidence and the required equipment (such as testers and oscilloscopes) to perform the adjustments. Thus, DEC targeted sophisticated customers that would not commit strongly on the vendor focus. DEC's stripped-down marketing program was appropriate to that approach. Over time, DEC began to serve a somewhat broader market segment but remained primarily a supplier to technically knowledgeable users.

The general impression in the 1960s was that unless there were very specific product features that led a buyer to select a non-IBM product, non-IBM buyers needed more self-confidence than did IBM customers. Early users for vendors such as DEC needed high levels of specifically technical skills. Customers for the other vendors did not need as much technical expertise but needed general confidence in their abilities to manage vendor relations and computer operations. Often, though certainly not always, such confidence was found in more experienced users. Thus, alternative vendors could sensibly target some experienced IBM accounts, in addition to any first-time users whose needs those vendors fit well.

Changes in the Computer Marketplace

Substantial and important changes occurred in the computer marketplace between the 1960s and the early 1980s. Customers became considerably more experienced in using computers and needed less initial training from vendors. At the same time, however, the growing complexity and importance of many customers' usage systems made buyers more interested in longer-term types of support, such as help with designing systems architectures that would last or with running a substantial data-processing organization smoothly. Vendors unbundled, selling hardware and software separately. As hardware costs plummeted but software costs did not, buyers became increasingly concerned with the transferability of their past investment actions in software.

Customers' experiences with computers also made them considerably more aware of the exposure involved in their commitments, especially exposure to traumatic conversions. The combination of customer experience, growing importance, and greatly increased feelings of exposure created long-term orientations among many more advanced users. After slowing in the early 1970s, technological pace increased again. Customers grew more concerned with remaining adequately up-to-date for the long term.

Several types of vendors entered the marketplace between the 1960s and the 1980s. New vendors offered small (mini) computers. It was increasingly possible for users to join alternatively sourced peripherals such as disks or tape drives to the mainframes from the major manufacturers, and peripheral manufacturers entered the market. In addition, vendors of plug-compatible machines (PCMs) entered the market for IBM mainframes (at lower prices).

Regulatory and legal considerations had long been important in this marketplace. Those pressures had eased by the 1980s.

Within many user organizations, relations between the data-processing departments and the end users followed a typical pattern. End users increasingly felt that the data-processing department had not been adequately responsive to their needs; in part as a result, small computers proliferated outside data-processing departments.

Changes in Vendors' Strategies

The established vendors became increasingly receptive to and concerned with customers' long-term orientations and the users' concerns with graceful upgrades.

IBM made several important changes. It built its technical capabilities substantially and in the process made more advanced users much more confident in committing to IBM and less confident in dealing with competitors. With help from its customers in understanding the importance of the issue, IBM emphasized increased upward compatibility of hardware and software systems—the ability to build on past investment actions. IBM's support seemed to grow in sophistication with its users' experience levels and emphasized longer-term issues; examples are advanced classes on network systems and on planning for data processing. Facing reduced regulatory pressures, IBM also became more aggressive in pricing and in wooing other vendors' customers.

As IBM increased its technical abilities, buyers had increasing doubts about the technical capabilities of its large mainframe competitors, which were not building customer confidence for the long term. The more advanced buyers in the 1980s, especially those setting up network architectures, felt they were establishing systems whose basic outlines would remain in place for considerably longer periods than had past choices. Their commitments to their lead vendors were growing in importance and in time horizon.

These factors appeared to create a strong movement to IBM among advanced users. Such moves seemed to be initiated very little, if at all, by any specific attention from IBM sales representatives. Instead the buyers approached IBM; they were most influenced by IBM's technical and product strengths, overall size, and financial strength. In other words, the advanced buyers were most influenced by long-term marketing tools as they made important long-term commitments focused on a vendor.

The alternative large-mainframe vendors had increasing difficulty attracting new customers. Both Sperry (Univac) and Burroughs made major new introductions during 1982 of products compatible with their existing offerings. The introductions might give the vendors' existing customers both the specific options for growth and also more general confidence in the vendors' capabilities and commitments. Although the vendors said that the products were also intended to attract new users, industry watchers considered it unlikely that they would succeed in doing so to any appreciable extent. In other words, existing customers might remain with those vendors in order to amortize past investment actions. New customers, however, were not likely to commit to such vendors for the long term.

Some of the other mainframe manufacturers seemed to be seriously considering IBM compatibility. Burroughs was rumored in the industry to be considering an acquisition to achieve IBM compatibility. (Burroughs's own hardware had in the past been quite unlike IBM's.)

IBM compatibility was not a new idea. RCA had marketed 360 emulators in the 1960s, for example. The basic concept of the PCM vendors of the 1970s and 1980s was to produce hardware that performed the same functions as did their IBM counterparts and to sell those PCM machines at substantially lower prices than the IBM models. The PCMs could use the substantial software available for IBM mainframes and did not require their purchasers to convert existing programs.

Despite these examples of IBM compatibility, however, it does not seem that the idea will be a successful choice for the other full-service mainframe vendors in the 1980s. Those firms have considerably more sales, marketing, and support structure than do the PCM vendors and are not likely to be able to offer the cost savings of the stripped-down PCM organizations. At the same time, most IBM customers are likely to want their IBM-oriented support to come from IBM itself. While customers in the 1980s may make specific routine decisions to save money, watershed decisions are long-term commitments focused on the vendor.

Discussions with computer customers suggest challenges for the PCM vendors and a limited role for their products. Most buyers would not consider PCM vendors as their sole-source mainframe supplier. They would, however, consider mixing and matching PCM equipment with IBM equipment in a multiple-mainframe environment. The managers expressed concern about the PCM vendors' abilities to compete successfully against a more aggressive IBM, however. They reported that their worries about the PCM vendors were greater than they had been in the past.

The most common specific concern was that IBM would change its uses of hardware versus software versus firmware (microcode) and make it harder for the PCMs to provide comparable power. The increasing use of field hardware upgrades was relevant to this concern. Vendors could accomplish major hardware upgrades by changing a few parts, especially the logic cards, of a computer. A physical card change could change the microcode of an IBM machine. PCM vendors could not easily produce corresponding cards; microcode was not easy to copy.

The PCM vendors made some changes in the early 1980s, moving a bit toward selling systems and away from selling only hardware. The press interpreted these moves as the vendors' attempts to make themselves somewhat less vulnerable to IBM's moves. Although the analysis does suggest the need for such concern by the vendors, these moves were likely to require more expensive fixed marketing investments. Hence, they would require careful cost management if they were not to ruin the PCM vendors' basic strategies of satisfying customers' desires for specific, shorter-term, more price-based purchases.

Challenges for the 1980s

This analysis shows that IBM's position with larger users seemed strong and growing stronger. IBM's strategic responses to and anticipation of changes in commitment and exposure between the 1960s and the 1980s had been extremely impressive. At the same time, however, the vendor faced considerable additional marketing challenges in the 1980s, particularly in regard to winning new commitments economically and maintaining the commitments of advnced users profitably.

The first challenge, of winning new commitments economically, was related to personal computers (PCs). PCs were proliferating rapidly in the early 1980s. Smaller organizations might purchase such machines as their first computers. PCs were also being used by new users in larger organizations, generally individual managers outside the data-processing departments who were obtaining their own computing power.

The PCs were of strategic importance for two reasons. They were the first steps on usage escalators for new users in some small organizations. In large organizations they increasingly served as numerous end points in large computer networks.

Because of their strategic importance, IBM could not sensibly deemphasize the PC market (as it could deemphasize markets for relatively unimportant peripherals). The lead vendor could economically sell PCs in quantity to large organizations through its existing sales force, thus serving one strategic purpose. The second role—as first computers in small organizations—created a more difficult challenge. A first-time user organization generally bought only one PC; it usually required substantial support but lacked the in-house data-processing expertise generally present in large organizations. Consequently selling PCs profitably to small organizations was a considerable challenge.

Success for IBM in the PC market would require marketing with substantially lower investments of resources than the vendor had devoted to initial users in the past. IBM had to control the use of its competent but expensive sales force in selling PCs and helping new PC users. The vendor also had to control the resources it devoted to software development for PCs. At the same time, however, the vendor needed to develop links to the few PC purchasers in small organizations that would join the main escalator of IBM usage.

Several moves by IBM can be interpreted as attempts to achieve these objectives. The vendor was experimenting with a variety of channels of distribution for the PCs, including Sears Roebuck, as well as some computer retailers like ComputerLand. In addition, IBM treated the PCs differently from other products in regard to its sales organizations.

A customer's IBM salesperson (or team) could serve essentially all of the account's needs. The exception was PCs. A salesperson could not sell his or her customers PCs in quantities of fewer than twenty. By contrast, a salesperson could sell a customer even a single IBM typewriter.

One possible explanation offered for this policy is that IBM did not want to compete with its new channel partners such as Sears and ComputerLand. I reject this explanation, feeling that the IBM brand name was so strong that the retailers would have been glad to handle and actively support that IBM product regardless of whether IBM was also selling its PC direct. Instead the IBM policy can be viewed as an attempt to prevent the expensive IBM field sales force from spending time handholding new PC users. (By contrast, a new IBM typewriter would not require much help and support, so it would be reasonable to allow customers to buy typewriters through their normal IBM representatives.)

Other IBM policies with regard to PCs also fit this analysis. The vendor's original policy for PC software encouraged outside developers to submit programs to IBM. If the vendor approved a program, it would help distribute it and pay royalties to the originator. IBM was also encouraging users' groups for its PCs; the groups were likely to share software developed by members. These moves seemed designed to give IBM users quick access to a rich variety of software while controlling the vendor's own costs of software development.

Thus, IBM seemed to be making sensible choices in regard to winning new commitments. Other moves could be expected, such as actions to identify higher potential PC users and to get them efficiently onto the escalator of mainstream IBM usage and commitment.

IBM faced another set of challenges in marketing profitably to advanced users. Increasingly in the 1980s, advanced users were adopting network architectures; those designs greatly increased the extent of modularity in customers' usage systems. Some such users were already mixing and matching hardware boxes from different vendors on their networks. Other buyers were still too concerned with potential performance problems to mix and match components from different suppliers. But the large majority of customers expected modularity to continue to increase; they expected to be able to mix and match in the near future.

Much of the behavior of the computer industry had been predicated on the lack of full intervendor compatibility. Changes in the degree of such compatibility would require adjustments in vendors' strategies. Many advanced users made extremely strong lost-for-good-type commitments (with high retention probabilities) to IBM for the vendor's general capabilities and technological stance. At the same time, however, in purchasing specific pieces of hardware or software, the account could act increasingly like an always-a-share customer, and this tendency could be expected to continue.

What it meant for a customer to have a strong lost-for-good commitment was changing. The account could commit strongly for some but not all parts of the vendor's offerings. This change will, I believe, require changes in IBM's policies in pricing and in providing support to customers. To make such changes wisely, the vendor will need a sound understanding of the economics of individual account relationships.

The basic problem for IBM is that it has offered its customers a rich, augmented product with many parts like general support that are not priced separately. Customers have come to value the nonpriced parts increasingly, but at the same time they have become increasingly able to obtain the priced parts elsewhere. To adjust its strategy sensibly, IBM will need to understand well the role of different aspects of its augmented product in maintaining accounts' commitments, in generating cash inflows to the vendor, and in requiring cash outflows.

Conclusions

Long-term relationships with industrial customers are frequently hard to win, hard to maintain, and hard to understand. They can also be extremely attractive to the vendor. Relationship marketing is difficult to execute well, but, if well executed, it can bring profits and market share to the vendor. The concepts of this book can help in understanding and in affecting the behavior of individual industrial customers. These concepts cannot be applied mechanically, however. Their successful use requires in-depth analysis of the specifics of a particular product-marketplace, individual customers, and specific vendors.

References

Fisher, Franklin M.; McGowan, J.; and Greenwood, Joen E. *Folded, Spindled and Mutilated: Economic Analysis and U.S. v. IBM*. Cambridge: MIT Press, 1983.

Gibson, Cyrus F., and Nolan, Richard L. "Managing the Four Stages of EDP Growth." *Harvard Business Review* (January–February 1974):76–88.

Jackson, Barbara Bund. *Harshaw Chemical Company: Metal Finishing Department*. Case 9-582-037. Boston: Harvard Business School, 1982.

McFarlan, F. Warren, and McKenney, James L. *Corporate Information Systems Management: The Issues Facing Senior Executives*. Homewood, Ill.: Richard D. Irwin, 1983.

Sobel, Robert. *IBM: Colossus in Transition*. New York: Times Books, 1981.

References

Numerous books and papers in a variety of disciplines have contributed insights and important background to this book, even though *Winning and Keeping Industrial Customers* does not follow closely in any of the literature traditions cited here. The following list gives key references in the major relevant areas of literature: marketing and industrial marketing, product policy, perceived risk, industrial buyer behavior, purchasing, market segmentation, models of consumer behavior, sales management, channels of distribution, business policy, portfolio analysis, diversification, relational governance, other microeconomics, organization for marketing, behavioral theory of the firm, organizational development and learning, diffusion of innovations, game theory and negotiation, and the management and history of computers. The end of the references also lists important business case studies.

Abell, Derek F., and John S. Hammond. *Strategic Market Planning: Problems and Analytical Approaches.* Englewood Cliffs, N.J.: Prentice-Hall, 1979.

Adams, William James, and Janet L. Yellen. "Commodity Bundling and the Burden of Monopoly." *Quarterly Journal of Economics* 90 (1976):475–498.

Ames, B. Charles. "Dilemma of Product/Market Management." *Harvard Business Review* (March–April 1971):66–74.

———. "Trappings vs. Substance in Industrial Marketing." *Harvard Business Review* (July–August 1970):93–102.

Argyris, Chris. "Double Loop Learning in Organizations." *Harvard Business Review* (September–October 1977):115–125.

———. "Single-Loop and Double-Loop Models in Research on Decision Making." *Administrative Science Quarterly* 21 (1976):363–375.

———, and Donald A. Schön. *Organizational Learning: A Theory of Action Perspective.* Reading, Mass.: Addison-Wesley, 1978.

Arndt, Johan. "Toward a Concept of Domesticated Markets." *Journal of Marketing* (Fall 1979):69–75.

Bailey, Earl L. *Product-Line Strategies.* Report 816. New York, The Conference Board, 1982.

Bass, Frank M. "A New Product Growth Model for Consumer Durables." *Management Science* 15 (1969):215–227.

Bass, Frank M. "The Relationship between Diffusion Rates, Experience Curves and Demand Elasticities for Consumer Durable Technological Innovations." *Journal of Business* 53 (1980):551–567.

Biggadike, E. Ralph. *Corporate Diversification: Entry, Strategy and Performance.* Cambridge: Harvard University Press, 1979.

Bonoma, Thomas V., Gerald Zaltman, and Wesley J. Johnston. *Industrial Buyer Behavior.* Cambridge, Mass., Marketing Science Institute Report 77-117. December 1977.

Borden, Neil H. "The Concept of the Marketing Mix." *Journal of Advertising Research* (June 1964):2–7.

Bower, Joseph L. "Solving the Problems of Business Planning." *Journal of Business Strategy* (Winter 1982):32–44.

Brock, G.W. *The U.S. Computer Industry: A Study of Market Power.* Cambridge, Mass.: Ballinger, 1975.

Bucklin, Louis P. "A Theory of Channel Control." *Journal of Marketing* (January 1973):39–47.

———. *A Theory of Channel Structure.* Berkeley: Institute of Business and Economic Research, University of California, 1966.

Burnett, Gerald J., and Richard L. Nolan. "At Last, Major Roles for Minicomputers." *Harvard Business Review* (May–June 1975):148–156.

Bursk, Edward, C. "View Your Customers as Investments." *Harvard Business Review* (May–June 1966):91–94.

Cardozo, Richard N. *Product Policy: Cases and Concepts.* Reading, Mass.: Addison-Wesley, 1979.

Chandler, Alfred D., Jr. *Strategy and Structure: Chapters in the History of the Industrial Enterprise.* Cambridge: MIT Press, 1962.

Choffray, Jean-Marie, and Gary L. Lilien. "Assessing Response to Industrial Marketing Strategy." *Journal of Marketing* (April 1978):20–31.

———. "A New Approach to Industrial Market Segmentation." *Sloan Management Review* (Spring 1978):17–29.

Corey, E. Raymond. *Industrial Marketing: Cases and Concepts.* 2d ed. Englewood Cliffs, N.J.: Prentice-Hall, 1976.

———. "Key Options in Market Selection and Planning." *Harvard Business Review* (September–October 1975):119–128.

———. *Procurement Management: Strategy, Organization and Decision-Making.* Boston: CBI Publishing, 1978.

———. "Should Companies Centralize Procurement?" *Harvard Business Review* (November–December 1978):102–110.

———, and Steven H. Star. *Organizational Strategy: A Marketing Approach.* Boston: Division of Research, Graduate School of Business Administration, Harvard University, 1971.

Cox, Donald F., ed. *Risk Taking and Information Handling in Consumer Behavior.* Boston: Division of Research, Graduate School of Business Administration, Harvard University, 1967.

Cyert, Richard M., and James G. March. *A Behavioral Theory of the Firm.* Englewood Cliffs, N.J.: Prentice-Hall, 1963.

Cyert, Richard M., Herbert A. Simon, and Donald B. Trow. "Observation of a Business Decision." *Journal of Business* 29 (1956):237–248.

Davis, Stanley M., and Paul R. Lawrence. "Problems of Matrix Organizations." *Harvard Business Review* (May–June 1978):131–142.

Day, George S. "Diagnosing the Product Portfolio." *Journal of Marketing* (April 1977):29–38.

——— . "Incorporating the Customer Dimension into the Business Definition." In A.D. Shocker, ed., *Analytic Approaches to Product and Market Planning.* Cambridge, Mass., Marketing Science Institute Report 79-104. April 1979.

Day, George S., Allan D. Shocker, and Rajendra K. Srivastava. "Customer-Oriented Approaches to Identifying Product Markets." *Journal of Marketing* (Fall 1979): 8–19.

Duncan, Robert, and Andrew Weiss. "Organizational Learning: Implications for Organizational Design." *Research in Organizational Behavior* (1979):75–123.

Eccles, Robert G. "The Quasifirm in the Construction Industry." *Journal of Economic Behavior and Organization* 2 (1981):335–357.

Fisher, Franklin M., John J. McGowan, and Joen E. Greenwood. *Folded, Spindled and Mutilated: Economic Analysis and U.S. v. IBM.* Cambridge, Mass.: MIT Press, 1983.

Frank, Ronald E., William F. Massy, and Yoram Wind. *Market Segmentation.* Englewood Cliffs, N.J.: Prentice-Hall, 1972.

Geiss, Charles G., and John M. Kuhlman. " 'Buying In' and the Sealed Market Bid." *Applied Economics* 10 (1978):219–231.

Gibson, Cyrus F., and Richard L. Nolan. "Managing the Four Stages of EDP Growth." *Harvard Business Review* (January–February 1974):76–88.

Goldberg, Victor P. "The Law and Economics of Vertical Restrictions: A Relational Perspective." *Texas Law Review* 58 (1979):91–129.

——— . "Toward an Expanded Economic Theory of Contract." *Journal of Economic Issues* 10 (1976):45–61.

Greiner, Larry E. "Evolution and Revolution as Organizations Grow." *Harvard Business Review* (July–August 1972):37–46.

Haley, Russell I. "Benefit Segmentation: A Decision-oriented Research Tool." *Journal of Marketing* (July 1968):30–35.

Hanan, Mack. "Reorganize Your Company around Its Markets." *Harvard Business Review* (November–December 1974):63–74.

Harding, Murray. "Who Really Makes the Purchasing Decision." *Industrial Marketing* (September 1966):76–81.

Haspeslagh, Philippe. "Portfolio Planning: Uses and Limits." *Harvard Business Review* (January–February 1982):58–73.

Howard, W.C. *Selling Industrial Products.* Worcester, Mass.: Norton Company, 1973.

Johnston, Wesley J., and Thomas V. Bonoma. "Reconceptualizing Industrial Buying Behavior: Toward Improved Research Approaches." In Barnett A. Greenberg and Danny N. Bellenger, eds., *Contemporary Marketing Thought*, pp. 247–251. Chicago: American Marketing Association, 1977.

Kidder, Tracy. *The Soul of a New Machine.* Boston: Little, Brown, 1981.

Kotler, Philip. *Marketing Management: Analysis, Planning, and Control.* 4th ed. Englewood Cliffs, N.J.: Prentice-Hall, 1980.

Learned, Edmund P., C. Roland Christensen, Kenneth P. Andrews, and William D. Guth. *Business Policy: Text and Cases.* Rev. ed. Homewood, Ill.: Richard D. Irwin, 1969.

Lehmann, Donald R., and John O'Shaughnessy. "Difference in Attribute Importance for Different Industrial Products." *Journal of Marketing* (April 1974):36–42.

Levitt, Theodore. *Industrial Purchasing Behavior.* Boston: Division of Research, Graduate School of Business Administration, Harvard University, 1965.

——— . *Innovation in Marketing.* New York: McGraw-Hill, 1962.

——— . *The Marketing Mode.* New York: McGraw-Hill, 1969.

Lochridge, Richard K. "Strategy in the Eighties." In *The Boston Consulting Group: Annual Perspective 1981.* Boston: Boston Consulting Group, 1981.

Luce, R. Duncan, and Howard Raiffa. *Games and Decisions.* New York: John Wiley & Sons, 1957.

Macaulay, Stewart. "Non-Contractual Relations in Business: A Preliminary Study." *American Sociological Review* 28 (1963):55–69.

McFadden, Daniel. "The Revealed Preferences of a Government Bureaucracy: Empirical Evidence." *Bell Journal of Economics* 7 (1976):55–72.

——— . "The Revealed Preferences of a Government Bureaucracy: Theory." *Bell Journal of Economics* 6 (1975):401–416.

McFarlan, F. Warren, and James L. McKenney. *Corporate Information Systems Management: The Issues Facing Senior Executives.* Homewood, Ill.: Richard D. Irwin, 1983.

McNicol, David L. "The Two Price Systems in the Copper Industry." *Bell Journal of Economics* 6 (1975):50–73.

Mansfield, Edwin. *The Economics of Technological Change.* New York: W.W. Norton, 1968.

Mansfield, Edwin, John Rapoport, Jerome Schnee, Samuel Wagner, and Michael Hamburger. *Research and Innovation in the Modern Corporation.* New York: W.W. Norton, 1971.

March, James G., and Herbert A. Simon. *Organizations.* New York: John Wiley & Sons, 1958.

Menge, John A. "Style Change as a Market Weapon." *Quarterly Journal of Economics* 76 (1962):632–647.

Monteverde, Kirk, and David J. Teece. "Supplier Switching Costs and Vertical Integration in the Automobile Industry." *Bell Journal of Economics* 13 (1982):206–213.

Morein, Joseph A. "Shift from Brand to Product Line Marketing." *Harvard Business Review* (September–October 1975):56–64.

Moriarty, Rowland T. *Industrial Buying Behavior: Concepts, Issues and Applications.* Lexington, Mass.: Lexington Books, 1983.

Moriarty, Rowland T., and Morton Galper. *Organizational Buying Behavior: A State-of-the-Art Review and Conceptualization.* Cambridge, Mass.: Marketing Science Institute Report 78-101. March 1978.

Morrison, Donald G., Richard D.H. Chen, Sandra L. Karpis, and Kathryn E.A. Britney. "Modeling Retail Customer Behavior at Merrill Lynch." *Marketing Science* 1 (1982):123–141.

Murray, George R., Jr., and Harry B. Wolfe. "Length of Product Line." *California Management Review* (Summer 1970):79–85.

Oi, Walter Y. "A Disneyland Dilemma: Two-part Tariffs for a Mickey Mouse Monopoly." *Quarterly Journal of Economics* 85 (1971):77–96.

Oxenfeldt, Alfred. R. "Product Line Pricing." *Harvard Business Review* (July–August 1966):137–144.

Peters, Thomas J., and Robert H. Waterman, Jr. *In Search of Excellence*. New York: Harper & Row, 1982.

Porter, Michael E. *Competitive Strategy: Techniques for Analyzing Industries and Competitors*. New York: Free Press, 1980.

Porter, Michael E., and Michael Spence. "Vertical Integration and Differentiated Products." Working Paper. September 1978.

Raiffa, Howard. *The Art and Science of Negotiation*. Cambridge: Belknap Press of Harvard University Press, 1982.

Ratchford, Brian T., and Gary T. Ford. "A Study of Prices and Market Shares in the Computer Mainframe Industry." *Journal of Business* 49 (1976):194–218.

Robinson, Patrick J., Charles Faris, and Yoram Wind. *Industrial Buying and Creative Marketing*. Boston: Allyn and Bacon, 1967.

Rogers, Everett M. *Diffusion of Innovations*. New York: Free Press of Glencoe, 1962.

Rumelt, Richard P. *Strategy, Structure, and Economic Performance*. Boston: Division of Research, Graduate School of Business Administration, Harvard University, 1974.

Salter, Malcolm S., and Wolf A. Weinhold. *Diversification through Acquisition: Strategies for Creating Economic Value*. New York: Free Press, 1979.

Schelling, Thomas C. *The Strategy of Conflict*. New York: Oxford University Press, 1963.

Schendel, Dan E., and Charles W. Hofer, eds. *Strategic Management: A New View of Business Policy and Planning*. Boston: Little, Brown, 1979.

Schmalensee, Richard. "Product Differentiation Advantages of Pioneering Brands." *American Economic Review* 72 (1982):349–365.

Schön, Donald A. "Deutero-Learning in Organizations: Learning for Increased Effectiveness." *Organizational Dynamics* (Summer 1975):2–16.

Shapiro, Benson P. *Industrial Product Policy: Managing the Existing Product Line*. Cambridge, Mass., Marketing Science Institute Report 77-110. September 1977.

———. "Manage the Customer, Not Just the Sales Force." *Harvard Business Review* (September–October 1974):127–136.

———. *Sales Program Management: Formulation and Implementation*. New York: McGraw-Hill, 1977.

Shapiro, Benson P., and Rowland T. Moriarty. *National Account Management: Emerging Insights*. Cambridge, Mass., Marketing Science Institute Report 82-100. March 1982.

Shapiro, Benson P., and Ronald S. Posner. "Making the Major Sale." *Harvard Business Review* (March–April 1976):68–78.

Sheth, Jagdish N. "A Model of Industrial Buyer Behavior." *Journal of Marketing* (October 1973):50–56.

Simon, Herbert A. "Rational Decision Making in Business Organizations." *American Economic Review* 69 (1979):493–513.

Skinner, Wickham. "The Focused Factory." *Harvard Business Review* (May–June 1974):113–121.

Sobel, Robert. *IBM: Colossus in Transition*. New York: Times Books, 1981.

Stern, Louis W., and Adel I. El-Ansary. *Marketing Channels*. 2d ed. Englewood Cliffs, N.J.: Prentice-Hall, 1982.

Strauss, George. "Tactics of Lateral Relationship: The Purchasing Agent." *Administrative Science Quarterly* 7 (1962):161–186.

von Hippel, Eric. "Get New Products from Customers." *Harvard Business Review* (March–April 1982):117–122.

———. "Successful Industrial Products from Customer Ideas." *Journal of Marketing* (January 1978):39–49.

Webster, Frederick E., Jr. "Communication and Diffusion Processes in Industrial Markets." *European Journal of Marketing* 5 (1971):178–188.

———. *Industrial Marketing Strategy*. New York: John Wiley & Sons, 1979.

———. "Informal Communication in Industrial Markets." *Journal of Marketing Research* 7 (1970):186–189.

———. "Modeling the Industrial Buying Process." *Journal of Marketing Research* 2 (1965):370–376.

———. "New Product Adoption in Industrial Markets: A Framework for Analysis." *Journal of Marketing Research* 33 (1969):35–39.

Webster, Frederick E., Jr., and Yoram Wind. "A General Model for Understanding Organizational Buying Behavior." *Journal of Marketing* (April 1972):12–19.

———. *Organizational Buying Behavior*. Englewood Cliffs, N.J.: Prentice-Hall, 1972.

White, Harrison C. "Production Markets as Induced Role Structures." In S.L. Leinhardt, ed., *Sociological Methodology 1981*, pp. 1–57. San Francisco: Jossey-Bass, 1981.

———. "Where Do Markets Come From?" *American Journal of Sociology* 87 (1981): 517–547.

Williamson, Oliver E. *Markets and Hierarchies: Analysis and Antitrust Implications*. New York: Free Press, 1975.

———. "Transaction-cost Economics: The Governance of Contractual Relations." *Journal of Law and Economics* 23 (1979):233–261.

Wind, Yoram. "Product Portfolio Analysis: A New Approach to the Product Mix Decision." In Ronald C. Curhan, ed., *Combined Proceedings*. American Marketing Association, 1975.

Wind, Yoram, and Richard Cardozo. "Industrial Market Segmentation." *Industrial Marketing Management* 3 (1974):153–166.

Case References

Copier Systems by William E. Matthews under the direction of E. Raymond Corey, in Corey's *Industrial Marketing: Cases and Concepts*, 2nd edition, Englewood Cliffs, N.J.: Prentice-Hall, 1976.

Deere & Company: Industrial Equipment Operations by Benson P. Shapiro, (Harvard Business School, 9-577-112).

Harshaw Chemical Company: Metal Finishing Department by Barbara Bund Jackson (Harvard Business School, 9-582-037).

Xerox Corporation—the 9200 in Barbara Bund Jackson's *Computer Models in Management*, Homewood, Ill.: Richard D. Irwin, 1979.

Index

About the Author

Barbara Bund Jackson is a specialist in marketing, particularly industrial marketing. She is currently vice president of Index Systems, a consulting firm headquartered in Cambridge, Massachusetts, that helps its clients use information and information technology for competitive advantage. Previously Dr. Jackson spent eleven years on the faculty of Harvard Business School, where she taught industrial marketing, general marketing, and the use of computers and quantitative methods in business. She holds the A.B. in applied mathematics from Radcliffe College and the Ph.D. in applied mathematics from Harvard University.

Dr. Jackson conducted much of the field research for *Winning and Keeping Industrial Customers* while she was at Harvard Business School. After joining Index Systems, she continued the work, particularly that related to using information and information technology to establish and to strengthen relationships with customers.